AI Management Framework

Practical Solutions for Ethical AI Deployment and Continuous Improvement

John Kyriazoglou

AI Management Framework: Practical Solutions for Ethical AI Deployment and Continuous Improvement

John Kyriazoglou
Toronto, ON, Canada

ISBN-13 (pbk): 979-8-8688-1535-5
https://doi.org/10.1007/979-8-8688-1536-2

ISBN-13 (electronic): 979-8-8688-1536-2

Copyright © 2025 by John Kyriazoglou

This work is subject to copyright. All rights are reserved by the Publisher, whether the whole or part of the material is concerned, specifically the rights of translation, reprinting, reuse of illustrations, recitation, broadcasting, reproduction on microfilms or in any other physical way, and transmission or information storage and retrieval, electronic adaptation, computer software, or by similar or dissimilar methodology now known or hereafter developed.

Trademarked names, logos, and images may appear in this book. Rather than use a trademark symbol with every occurrence of a trademarked name, logo, or image we use the names, logos, and images only in an editorial fashion and to the benefit of the trademark owner, with no intention of infringement of the trademark.

The use in this publication of trade names, trademarks, service marks, and similar terms, even if they are not identified as such, is not to be taken as an expression of opinion as to whether or not they are subject to proprietary rights.

While the advice and information in this book are believed to be true and accurate at the date of publication, neither the authors nor the editors nor the publisher can accept any legal responsibility for any errors or omissions that may be made. The publisher makes no warranty, express or implied, with respect to the material contained herein.

Managing Director, Apress Media LLC: Welmoed Spahr
Acquisitions Editor: Susan McDermott
Development Editor: Laura Berendson
Project Manager: Jessica Vakili

Distributed to the book trade worldwide by Springer Science+Business Media New York, 1 New York Plaza, New York, NY 10004. Phone 1-800-SPRINGER, fax (201) 348-4505, e-mail orders-ny@springer-sbm.com, or visit www.springeronline.com. Apress Media, LLC is a Delaware LLC and the sole member (owner) is Springer Science + Business Media Finance Inc (SSBM Finance Inc). SSBM Finance Inc is a **Delaware** corporation.

For information on translations, please e-mail booktranslations@springernature.com; for reprint, paperback, or audio rights, please e-mail bookpermissions@springernature.com.

Apress titles may be purchased in bulk for academic, corporate, or promotional use. eBook versions and licenses are also available for most titles. For more information, reference our Print and eBook Bulk Sales web page at http://www.apress.com/bulk-sales.

This book also contains 41 Appendices. All appendices and other supplementary material referenced by the author in this book is available to readers on the Github repository: https://github.com/Apress/AI-Management-Framework or by scanning the QR code below:

If disposing of this product, please recycle the paper

Table of Contents

About the Author

John Kyriazoglou is currently Editor-in-Chief of *TheIIC e-Magazine* and represents Western Europe on the Advisory Board of the Institute for Internal Controls. He is also consulting on data privacy and IT security issues (GDPR, e-Privacy, etc.) to a large number of private and public clients and has published several books on these issues.

John is a business thinker, consultant, and an author. He is a graduate of the University of Toronto, a Certified Internal Controls Auditor (CICA), and a management consultant with more than 40 years of global experience on data management, IT auditing, IT security, IT project management, and data privacy issues. He has written many books (more than 60) on data privacy protection, business management controls, IT, corporate wellness, duty of care, etc.

John has worked in Canada, England, Switzerland, Luxembourg, Greece, Saudi Arabia, and other countries for over 40 years as a senior IT manager, managing director, IT auditor, and consultant for a variety of clients and projects, in both the private and the public sector.

Book Review by Dr. Martha Beck

John Kyriazoglou's book is a valuable contribution to the emerging literature on AI. The level of particularity in his description of all the types of decisions leaders will have to make, what they should aim for, and what they should watch out to avoid will be an important handbook as leaders move forward into the AI world. At the 2024 Davos conference, the world's business leaders could not stop talking about AI, the latest shiny new product. Sam Altman, the CEO of OpenAI, made clear that AI could be used for good or evil purposes, like all other technologies. As Socrates would say: Is anyone taking seriously our continual need for self-examination and the examination of others as we transition into an AI world?

Writing as a professor who has focused on teaching rather than leadership, I cannot identify personally with the particular situations he often describes. However, as a Professor of Philosophy with a specialization in Ancient Greek philosophy and culture, I can recognize the value of his approach. He and I agree that professionals today in all areas of leadership need to integrate what Aristotle called the moral virtues and the intellectual virtues into a complete, flourishing way of life, both personal and professional. As the teacher of future leaders, I have been applying the insights of many aspects of Ancient Greek civilization into my own classes and publications.

Today, after the reelection of Donald Trump and the fusion of extreme wealth with politics, it is clearer than ever that brilliance in intellectual skills, such as engineering, can easily lead to a society's self-destruction and the destruction of the ecosphere from which we evolved. Three professional engineers, Charles Koch, Bill Gates, and Elon Musk, are extremely different in their approaches to how to move toward the integration of nature and culture and a sustainable global civilization. Mark Zuckerberg and Jeff Bezos seem more focused on getting people distracted by social media or saturation advertisements. Our collective need to completely change our way of life to move to a sustainable future is the last thing on people's minds. Rupert Murdoch has made billions by playing on fear, polarizing public opinion and ignoring climate change. American culture needs to change.

My own work has explained how the worldview of the Ancient Greeks and the culture they developed is one way to create a sustainable culture and way of life. Most importantly, current trends in the physical sciences (biology, chemistry, and physics), the social sciences, and the humanities are showing that we have to make a radical change from the materialistic and mechanistic worldviews of the Western Enlightenment that still have a powerful influence over the way we think and the way our society is organized.

The new view, systems thinking, is compatible with the foundations of Greek culture, but not only Greek culture. Systems thinking is compatible with the basic foundations of all of the ancient wisdom traditions, including Islam, Buddhism, Hinduism, Confucianism, indigenous cultures, Christianity (especially Catholicism), and certain types of secular humanism. This review focuses on the Greeks because that is what Mr. Kyriazoglou and I know best.

Aristotle's ethical and political work is founded on a model of the completely flourishing human being and their role in creating a flourishing society. There are over a dozen virtues, personal, social, and political. However, the one vice that is most destructive of social and political life is greed, the desire for more than one's share. When parents seek wealth and raise their children to become wealthy, they will organize the entire cultural system – political, social, economic, etc. – to give their children an advantage. The rich will get richer and the poor poorer. The concentration of wealth and power can occur in a free society, where parents freely choose to separate their children from the vast majority, or it can happen in an authoritarian society where those in power use it to further concentrate their power for their children to inherit. Eventually, without a middle class, the society becomes unstable. The poor rise up; everyone suffers, and the rich usually end up even farther ahead.

Clearly, Americans have not taken Aristotle's wisdom to heart. Many don't believe it or even consider it anti-American. Aristotle wanted a huge inheritance tax, so parents could not pass down their wealth. A flourishing society has to use the legal system and cultural norms to prevent the formation of an entrenched wealthy class. Such societies might devolve into civil war, and they will become more vulnerable to outside attacks. Even if they avoid the worst possibilities, they will always prevent the vast majority of citizens from being able to flourish when they could be flourishing. Today, the cost of greed is much higher: greed is destroying the ecosystem from which we evolved. We do not know to what extent we will destroy life on earth or how nature will change. We do know that without a radical change, human life will degenerate into a more primitive way of life, at best.

Jeffrey Sachs points out in his book, *The Ages of Globalization*, that we are now in the Seventh Age of Globalization, the Fourth Industrial Revolution: the switch from an industrial economy to a digital one. This will involve (at least) four great disruptions:

technological, ecological, digital, and demographic (the percent of people living in cities globally will change from 50% to 80%). In the past, these radical changes have brought on wars. This time, however, military conflicts could escalate to nuclear war, leading, again, to a permanent alteration of life on earth. AI is and will continue to be a major factor in this change. It is hard for us at the moment to imagine the types and extent of the changes in civilization that AI will bring about, but we do know that we must continually reflect on how we are using AI.

Although readers of the book and this review are certainly aware of all of this, they might not understand how Ancient Greek wisdom could serve as a foundation for their vision of how to live in the face of this new age. Sachs himself uses Aristotle as the foundation for his own vision of a flourishing society in a digital age. As an economist, I am sure that Sachs would agree with most, if not all, of Kyriazoglou's advice. This review will give another, broader, perspective, from which to reflect on what the Greeks can teach us about our current moment, fraught with a potential for good or evil greater than ever before.

Kyriazoglou begins his book with a list of "Greek principles": temperance (sophrosyne, or soundness of mind), faith (seeing human life in the context of the universe, as a microcosm in the macrocosm, leading to hubris, or overstepping the bounds, as the worst evil), justice (rule for the benefit of the ruled, in every social role), harmony (integrity, the integration of emotions, thoughts, and a way of life), friendships (relationships: every friendship is a virtue because it consists of acting virtuously in your relationship to that person), *kalokagathia* (the union of beauty and truth in a way of life), and courage (reacting to situations involving fear appropriately, not running away or avoiding and not taking unnecessary risks).

In what follows, I will give a broader view of the way Greek culture was structured over time to motivate citizens to embrace this model of virtue, enabling them to preserve a free society and avoid the kind of instability that enables an authoritarian leader to take over power. I hope you will indulge me, because the punch line will bring us right back to AI and what the Greeks educated us and warned us about long ago. My extended description of Greek culture and its importance today is also an affirmation of Mr. Kyriazoglou's book.

Mr. Kyriazoglou includes me in his book: "Based on my varied consulting and management experience and on the experience of noted philosophy professor Martha Beck,[1] there is a need for a common set of categories that gives a theoretical description of universal and cross-cultural principles for humans and organizations.

The ancient Greeks have such principles.

The ancient Greeks showed that the most important criterion for wisdom is the recognition of higher powers in the universe than human beings – powers humans cannot control. Human beings must create cultures within the context of those greater powers; they must integrate culture with nature, etc.

The principles I am presenting are one way of articulating a universal and cross-cultural set of standards, based on the wisdom of the past, wisdom that gets passed down from one generation to the next in theory but also applied in practice in ways that differ, based on historical contexts.

There are many, many principles and other ways of articulating virtue and vice in classical Ancient Greek philosophers. I have chosen seven that I think are most important based on my experience in the business world."

Since Mr. Kyriazoglou has arrived at this list after years of experience in the business world, as a manager and a consultant, I would prefer to describe this list as recurring patterns in human affairs. These are the patterns Mr. Kyriazoglou has discovered while being a manager and consultant. These are patterns I have observed in my own experience as a teacher and scholar, but most of all as a human being with pleasures and fears and families and friends. Wisdom literature, in this case Aristotle's ethics and politics, has been able to define these patterns because we are the species that is capable of recognizing patterns in a natural and cultural world where such patterns exist.

The most important patterns are those we experience in relation to our most primitive drives, pleasure and fear, which we share with the animals because we are a kind of animal. We have a biological origin, but we have evolved into creatures of culture because the societies we live in all include many norms and laws related to appropriate behavior when we are driven by pleasure (food, drink, sex) or fear. Even though there are cultural differences in exactly how those drives are trained, every society expects its children to learn how to respond to those drives by listening to and imitating adults. In relation to pleasure, they have to learn self-control. In relation to fear, they have to learn courage: how to avoid overreacting or underreacting.

The emergence of Greek civilization in 800 BCE occurred because the society in that area had become complex enough for people to recognize that they are the creature with a capacity to understand patterns. In his *De Anima*, Aristotle gives a very systematic description of the natural powers or capacities (dunamai) of the human soul, beginning with immediate sensations and ending with the power of the mind (nous). The powers of the soul (psyche) are natural: they emerge in our responses to the world around us.

We move from sensation to perceptions (sensations in space and time), to memory, to cognition, to gaining knowledge based on sensations and cognitions about many objects of thought, natural and cultural. At a certain point, says Aristotle, after learning all the sciences, the "mind thinks itself." Cognition gives way to the insight, the intuition, that we are the creature that accumulates all of this knowledge in a world that is ordered and capable of being understood. "All human beings, by nature, seek understanding." Grasping patterns and using them to educate each other about how to live well is how we actively live out our unique place in the world, our telos, our way of flourishing.

At around that time, Hesiod, Homer, the Pre-Socratics, the Olympics, and the Oracle at Delphi all were created or reformed based on this new insight. Mr. Kyriazoglou quotes from some of the Pre-Socratics. Although they disagreed, sometimes profoundly, with each other, the fundamental insight or intuition that drove all of them was the recognition that the universe was ordered. We are capable of understanding the basic foundations of order beneath the constant change we experience through our sensations. Further, we need to understand that order in order to know how to live. Each school of thought had a community of disciples. Their way of life was structured so that they would act based on their basic intuition of the foundation of reality. They wanted their way of life to be a microcosm in the macrocosm.

In his *Theogony*, Hesiod describes the evolution from nature to culture. My work focuses on the 12 Olympian deities and how Hesiod's work tried to create a systematic account of their place in the evolution of human culture. Each deity represents some aspect of a uniquely human culture, one based on the cultivation of our natural capacity and desire to understand.

Aristotle describes this transition from nature to culture in human society. The extended family is the most basic type of human interaction, all focused on *zen*, mere life, survival, and the nurturing and integration of children into social life. The second level is *suzen*, living together, the kind of society that evolves when people come together to survive more efficiently (a division of labor in the provision of material needs) and to provide protection from external threats. At some point, says Aristotle, a political genius understood that there is another level of human interaction, the polis, or political community, based on activating and providing for everyone to activate our natural desire to understand. The goal of this level is *euzen*, the good life, the flourishing life. To create a political community, people have to be educated to think like citizens. They have to be able to identify with the emotions, thoughts, and choices of other people, both good and bad, so they understand our common humanity.

At the very beginning of the *Theogony*, Hesiod describes being inspired by the Nine Muses: music, dance, epic poetry, religious poetry, erotic poetry, tragedy, comedy, history, and astronomy. All of them dance to Apollo playing his lyre. The Muses are on Mt. Olympus, inspiring Zeus, who is on his throne, making judgments "straight" or exercising practical wisdom as he governs gods and men. Hesiod, by analogy, is inspired by the divine Muses and speaking to human rulers, telling stories that will enable them to exercise practical wisdom in their judgments about human affairs. We have a natural desire to move our bodies, but "a dance" has a beginning, middle, and end and is designed to teach us something about our emotions and about how to live. A dance can be passed down to posterity and should communicate some aspects of our psyches that is close enough to the brain stem, to our deepest drives, so the main message can be recognized by people living in very different cultural contexts. The same is true of all the Muses.

Again, for the purposes of this review (bear with me please), all 12 deities represent sacred passions - passions we have as part of wanting to live flourishing lives. A flourishing society must recognize the powers of each god and be structured so that citizens live their lives in ways that acknowledge and respect those powers. Readers should recognize that every flourishing human life requires harmonizing all of these "deities" or forces in human culture. The deities themselves are obsessed with their own particular passion. When human beings get similarly obsessed, they do great damage to those who have a different sacred passion. Unlike the gods, humans have to compromise and have to continually reexamine the particular balance between them in their lives. At any point, people using AI could undermine or balance all of these cultural forces, leading to cultural evolution or devolution.

Demeter, the goddess of the fertility of humans and the earth, and Poseidon, god of the sea and the winds, represent natural forces beyond human control that a well-structured society must respect. Culture must be integrated with nature, or it will eventually self-destruct. The worst evil is hubris, to overstep the bounds, which happens in our relation to nature as well as human relationships. Hades and Persephone are the god and goddess of the underworld. Hades reminds humans about what legacy they want to leave behind, how they want to live so that others will be inspired to imitate them and preserve a flourishing society. Persephone punishes those who have used others for their own irrational ends: pleasure, wealth, power, or glory.

Within the context of culture, Zeus and Athena are the god and goddess of justice, those who focus on the well ordering of societies, through institutions of all sorts, the application of the laws, rules, and policies to particular cases and the nature of punishments for violating the norms. Athena is also the goddess of wisdom, who even counsels her father on occasion. Hera and Ares are the goddess and god of honor. Hera supports her husband by weaving people together in informal ways, creating a robust system of social networks that create trust and good will between people. Ares is the god of war. Those willing to give their lives to protect their societies are honored for doing so, but Ares is criticized when he goes too far and expects to be honored for taking unnecessary risks, causing unnecessary death and suffering. This can happen in economic wars as well as military ones.

Aphrodite is the goddess of beauty, which is not about activating male lust. Rather, this power is about our natural love of style, design, and the way our five senses can be activated to become passionate about color, smell, taste, touch, and sound in ways that lead us from the merely sensual to the spiritual, wanting to create beautiful lives and a beautiful physical context within which to live. Dionysus is the god of wine and the theater, the only god who dies and is reborn. The stories told at the theater, including recitations of Homer, are stories about people going to extremes and causing unnecessary suffering. The stories are intended to activate our awareness of our capacity to do harm and the kind of desperate situations any of us could experience that might cause us to make such mistakes. Once we are aware of this capacity, if we find ourselves in similar situations, we are supposed to remember these stories and avoid overreacting. Or, we can get into situations that we can imagine creating a new story about, with the goal of avoiding making a mistake in judgment. This is why Dionysus dies: we have to flush out those desires, thoughts, and choices and be even more motivated to create lives and societies that will prevent people from getting into such desperate situations.

Hermes and Hestia represent the "light of the mind," the light that is kindled at the hearth of the home, where people begin thinking about life, telling stories, reflecting on how they feel and think so they have the wisdom necessary to go out and live. Hermes is the god who lights his torch with Hestia's flame and brings the messages from the gods to human beings. The last pair are Apollo and Artemis, the god of reason and the goddess of the wilderness. Artemis does not want anything to do with Apollo's cities that are built with the powers of reasoning that lead to creating technology, human-creating births. She protects the wilderness from the intrusions of those motivated by her brother's powers.

This is where Greek mythology's description of Apollo is so relevant today. Apollo is emotionally immature. He chases after nymphs, females he is attracted to strictly for their physical appearance. He is driven by lust. When those women reject him, for various reasons, he takes revenge. His relationship to one of his sons also follows a pattern. He feels guilty about being an absent father, so he lets his son have whatever he wants. His son wants to drive Apollo's chariot, holding the sun, across the sky. Apollo knows he cannot do this because he is not a god; his mother is a mortal. When he relents, the result is exactly what Apollo knew would happen. Apollo is also indifferent to justice. In the Trojan War, Apollo begins on the side of the Achaeans, who clearly have the just cause. However, when they begin to fight between themselves, especially when Agamemnon and Achilles have a power struggle, he changes side. He prefers the man who follows him, Hector, who unified the Trojans, even though Hector knows his father is wrong to allow Helen into the city. He knows his little brother is spoiled, but he wants to protect his people and his city.

How is this analogous to what we are experiencing today? It should be clear by now that at least since 800 BCE the powers of Apollo have made societies more complicated, but have not made them more virtuous. Instead, our primitive drives keep emerging. Children need to be taught from a very young age to be self-controlled and to be able to face fearful situations appropriately. When children are allowed to be self-indulgent, greedy, power-hungry, or obsessed with becoming famous, they undermine the social fabric, and a society becomes unstable and might fall apart. Instability leads to the rise of a power-hungry citizen who takes advantage to convince citizens he will fix their problems. The political community is lost; authoritarianism prevails.

Even a relatively limited knowledge of the backgrounds and family stories of the lives of Musk, Zuckerberg, and Jeff Bezos shows that they see no connection between their personal lives, their behavior as CEOs, and their capacity to be good citizens. They just do not understand our collective need to form political communities as Aristotle describes them. Mr. K does understand this connection. His advice about governing well within a business applies to every social network and institution. A good leader of any sort creates a community that is a microcosm in the macrocosm and that enables every member of the community to flourish to the highest degree possible.

A flourishing society needs to give citizens the ability to create beautiful spaces, homes, furniture, and in general a material context that leads to the spiritual love of beauty for its own sake, as an expression of living well, over and above meeting material needs. It needs to give citizens the freedom to create social networks that cultivate friendships based on exercising as many virtues as possible, weaving together a strong social fabric that can withstand outside threats, natural disasters, or other types of disruption. It needs to respect the natural wilderness as part of a healthy culture. It needs to include opportunities for people to tell their stories and listen to the poets, so they develop a complex and true idea of the human condition, always adding complexity, reexamining previous assumptions, and adjusting to external and internal changes. It needs to avoid resorting to war as a way to solve problems and value diplomacy instead. When unavoidable, it needs to constantly monitor wars, so soldiers do not overreact and do unnecessary damage. It needs to value justice, rule for the benefit of the ruled, in every institution, law, policy, judicial decision, and treatment of transgressors. It needs to make people cognizant of the fact that what they do is remembered by those whose lives they affect and motivate people to want their life stories to be inspirational rather than leaving behind trauma. For those whose desires are corrupt, there has to be a story of divine punishment for eternity, in the hope that a wicked character will control itself out of fear. It has to motivate people to engage in dialogue about the patterns that are emerging in their time and how what we know from the wisdom of the past can inform us about what decisions to make today.

The goal is practical wisdom, to "hit the mark," to do what is, in fact, best in any given situation. This tradition is a dialectical tradition, because hitting the mark is extremely difficult and requires a lot of dialogue: considering all points of view, bringing in all relevant experts, considering the context, etc. The person with practical wisdom possesses all the virtues, moral and intellectual, but can also bring them to bear in each situation, in various contexts, in relation to different people, etc. Also, they are able to speak persuasively, to convince those involved to do what they have decided is best. Practical wisdom, clearly, is rare, but something we should all aspire to achieving or getting better at over time.

The way the Oracle at Delphi changed around 800 BCE is another aspect of the social evolution in Greece at this time. Before then, the location, at the foot of Mount Parnassus, was where the Great Goddess was worshipped. She was protected by the Python. Apollo arrived, killed the Python, and replaced her. At first glance, this looks like a violent overthrow of matriarchy by patriarchy. If you study the underlying mythology, the history of the site, and the activities that went on there, I think the message is much more subtle and very important for us today. Mythologically, according to one story (there are many), Apollo arrived at the site after another of his failed romances had ended, reminding people of Apollo's emotional immaturity. The presence of the Python reminds people of the nature of goddess-centered cultures. The snake is a symbol of goddess cultures because it sheds its skin each year, but goes through the same process every year, without any substantial changes. Goddess culture was based on the cycles of nature, without much historical progress or change. In 800 BCE, the leap in consciousness, when the mind becomes conscious of itself, led to the realization that from now on the powers of Apollo, reasoning in its many forms, was going to dominate culture and drive it toward higher and higher levels of complexity. The mythology, history, and activities of the site all are sending the message: this kind of development is not necessarily progress. It will not necessarily make human life better. The powers of Apollo have to be limited and guided by Athena and Zeus, the love of justice and wisdom. Most importantly, Apollo's protection of the goddess must be based on a deep respect for her and her powers. Culture must be integrated with nature, not forced upon it in ways that harm Mother Nature.

After killing the Python, Apollo has to spend seven years of penance as a shepherd. He has to reflect upon the position he will take up while living as a shepherd who tends to the flock to provide for human food, but he would presumably have some sensitivity to the animal world and a healthy relationship between nature and culture. When he does return, Apollo brings with him his sister Artemis and his mother, Leto. He is integrating them into the new paradigm for culture. Artemis was worshipped in fields outside of the Oracle, reminding visitors of the need to balance the wilderness with Apollo's cities.

Next, in the historical story of the origin of the site, the first priests who delivered the Oracle's messages came from Crete, which had a female-centered culture, the Minoans. Further, the people chosen were not military leaders; they were businessmen. The Minoans were not a military society; rather, they engaged in international trade and created economic ties with other city-states to prevent war. These businessmen, when, would have traveled extensively and would understand our common humanity beneath the external differences between city-states.

The purpose of the site was for leaders throughout the region to come to get advice. The site made clear that there are universal, natural standards of justice and ways of behaving justly that every city-state must conform to. Rulers did not decide justice and injustice, and in the relation between city-states, might does not make right. The site had laws inscribed on the stones that the suppliants saw before they got to the temple. The priests gave Lycurgus the laws of Sparta; the site represented the leap of social evolution from the rule by the rulers to the sanctity of international law. When convicted criminals came there, the Oracle asked them to determine their punishment. The message was that people should internalize the rule of law; when they violate it, they offend the gods. They don't just suffer at the hands of other, more powerful, men.

xxviii

As suppliants are traveling to Delphi, when they go around a bend in the mountain and see the site on the hill, they also walk beside a temple to Athena. This reminds them that this Apollo is both inspired by the goddess of wisdom and justice and is protected by her. Athena's father, Zeus, also has a powerful presence here. The Oracle is located at the foot of Mt. Parnassus, which was considered the center of the world. Supposedly, Zeus released two eagles (animals that symbolized Zeus) who flew in opposite directions and ended up meeting each other here. Also, as the suppliants begin walking toward the temple, they pass by the stone that Chronos swallowed in the place of Zeus, thereby saving his life. Zeus was taken to a cave in Crete to be raised, another indication of the link between female and male culture.

Another reason this site was considered sacred was because it was located above a fissure in the earth. For nine months, fumes were emitted by the earth. Inhaling these fumes lead to a trance. This was interpreted to be a place where the messages from the underworld, from Hades, were being sent to earth. The temple was built so that the suppliants were first greeted by a woman sitting on a tripod, inhaling the fumes. The priests then interpreted her trances. The symbolism must have reminded suppliants of the presence of Hestia at the hearth on Mt. Olympus and the hearth in every home and the role of Hermes who brought the message from the gods to men and the priests who brought the message from Hades to men.

On the outside of the temple are two injunctions: know thyself and nothing in excess. If suppliants seek excesses of any sort – pleasure, wealth, power, or glory – they will misinterpret the oracle to achieve their ulterior goal. They must know themselves as having minds, the capacity to recognize what is just and best, grasped by an intuition that emerges from a strong and stable moral character. Within the temple, the two ends have engraving that send another important message. On one end is Apollo with his sister and mother, dressed in a short toga and holding his favorite lyre. On the other end is Dionysus, wearing the same toga and surrounded by the Maenads, the women who engaged in wild, orgiastic dances during his rituals. He is holding the same lyre. As it turns out, the fumes only arise for nine months each year. During the three dormant months, Dionysus is worshipped at the site. Apollo gives his favorite lyre to Dionysus. The message is that the rise of Apollonian culture splits emotion from intellect in a way that had not occurred before. A constant effort has to be made to avoid repressing emotions and to give our emotions, even powerful emotions, to be expressed in the context of honoring the sacred passions.

Before going to hear the oracle, suppliants took a ritual bath, purifying their bodies as well as their souls. Finally, when they go to hear the priests, they are not given an answer to their questions. Instead, they are given a riddle. They have to solve the riddle. They have to use their own power of choice to decide what it means. Their interpretation is a reflection of their character. If they use the riddle to justify their irrational motives, their corruption will be exposed. The priests also sent out spies to find out if a military campaign they are being questioned about is likely to be successful or not. They would deliver a riddle most likely to promote the best outcome, even if a just war had to be averted because it would become a massacre.

The Oracle also promoted international culture and religious pluralism. It rejected any kind of prejudice between city-states, regions, or nations. This was a universal standard of justice: ruling by law and ruling for the sake of the well-being of the ruled. The site cultivated practical wisdom in the creation, application, and enforcement of laws.

This brings me back to Mr. Kyriazoglou's book and why it can stand out among the many texts with a similar content: giving advice to managers in every kind of situation. Combining Aristotle's virtues with the Greek vision of the integration of nature and culture provides a universal foundation that is grounded in nature, not in some type of explicitly social construction with no natural foundation. Applying Aristotle's virtues and vices with a focus on the power of our instinctual drives.

A good manager should know that the cultural context within which any organization exists is important. Employees who live in communities that are designed to trigger the desire to live moderately and to build bonds of trust are much more likely to be productive and to contribute positively to the company culture than employees that live in communities based on greed, impulsivity, and lack of trust. Managers should find ways to contribute to broader cultural events, to contribute to meaningful debates about what legislation is most likely to lead to cultural flourishing, and to give employees opportunities to do volunteer work or community service and/or to change their hours to attend their children's school events. A theoretical framework that considers such policies to be only socially constructed will not understand the deep interconnections between all the virtues.

Contemporary neuroscience has discovered the intricate networks in our brains and the way they need to be integrated to have a flourishing life. The most basic networks are those connected to our automatic drives (growth, breathing, etc.). We need to be very conscientious about how those networks are being formed in children, so that the networks that emerge from them, going from simpler to more complex social and political networks and local, national, and international, can be integrated and enable adults to have the practical wisdom they need in our technologically complex and internationally connected world. In his highly acclaimed book, *Looking for Spinoza: Joy, Sorrow, and the Feeling Brain*, Antonio Damasio explains how neuroscience today rejects the models of the psyche during the Enlightenment, both the "blank slate" of the empiricists and the mechanistic, dualistic, reason-as-detached from body view of the rationalists. Instead, our brains are a complex set of neural networks. When they get complex enough, our minds emerge: ideas form, ideas cause more ideas, and new neural networks are created. The more recent neural maps are created by ideas, not by any physical cause. The new maps are physical, but they were formed by an idea. The goal of life is homeostasis, when all the neural maps, from most basic and automatic, are integrated with the most recent, formed by ideas. Body, emotions, thoughts, and a way of life are integrated. Damasio even refers to Aristotle's idea of flourishing as a closer model than the Enlightenment models that still influence Western culture today.

At this point, I want to quote from Mr. Kyriazoglou, because his list of Aristotle's virtues should make clear that he has the Greek worldview in the back of his mind. His model of a good manager is someone who has these virtues and is influenced by them as he is constantly making decisions and judgment calls about what is best in the many situations managers encounter each day.

Principle 1. Temperance: Self-control in relation to the basic drive for survival and pleasure – food, drink, sex, material acquisition. Clearly, these drives are based on the human condition. Every cultural tradition has moral lessons and moral archetypes that encourage self-control and condemn excesses.

Principle 2. Faith, the Microcosm in the Macrocosm: Every cultural tradition has some view of the limits of human powers and condemns human beings when they "overstep the bounds," the Greek hubris.

Principle 3. Justice: Rule for the well-being of the ruled. Every society is a complex network of relationships based on authority. Every society has taught its citizens to rule for the well-being of those over whom they rule (even when the rulers are abusing their power and hiding behind the rhetoric of justice).

Principle 4. Harmony: Personal integrity, the integration of emotions, thoughts, and actions, so one can live one's life in a way that is beautiful and good, always finding the middle group between extremes and doing what is best for the right reason, in the right way, and motivated by the desire to do what is noble because it is noble and for no other reason.

Principle 5. Friendship: This refers to all sorts of relationships – family, friends, employers, teachers, political leaders, doctors, lawyers, people in the business sector who provide all sorts of goods and services.

The quality of one's life is developed and sustained (or undermined and corrupted) by the quality of one's relationships.

Principle 6. *Kalokagathia*: In Greek, the union of the word for beautiful and the word for goodness or human excellence. A well-functioning adult is exercising all the virtues to the highest level possible: personal, social, political, intellectual, artistic, etc. Such a person is both beautiful and good because they have the qualities that make a natural or cultural artifact beautiful and good: proportionality, adaptability to the surrounding environment, the full flourishing of a natural specimen or an artifact that expresses the wisdom and insight of its creator. This is the real meaning of Aphrodite as the goddess of beauty.

Principle 7. Courage: Knowing how to react in situations involving fear. Human beings are by nature extremely vulnerable, which is why they are so dependent upon each other to meet their needs and to enable each other to survive. A courageous person recognizes vulnerability but does not overreact. They know how to act bravely in a situation of vulnerability and does so because it is the noble thing to do, not to get the approval of others or to avoid social condemnation.

The US Founders and cultural leaders since the founding honored Greek culture. They structured a society based on the rule of law, with a balance of powers. Aristotle said that the best legal systems have a combination of positions that are appointed and elected, as the United States does. US citizens are asked to serve on juries. The Founders also understood the importance of childhood habituation, so children would develop and maintain the virtues. Many of the Founders liked Confucius' *Analects* and wanted to use them as a foundation for the creation of "Virtue Clubs." They wanted citizens to recognize that the ancient virtues they needed to develop in order to be good citizens are not exclusively Christian, nor are they taught only in a certain Christian denomination. Rather, they are universal and based on the human condition. Along with this, the Founders wanted a broad-based system of public education, so citizens would be informed about public affairs and learn to think like citizens. They were very aware of the way powerful and power-hungry leaders in Europe used "God" and other purely manipulative rhetorical techniques to centralize power and destroy the young democracy. Today, for the first time, American democracy has been listed among the nations whose democracies are floundering. Historians are telling us about the average lifetime of free societies, suggesting that the US experiment in democracy might have run its course. This outrages me because the function of academics is to continually motivate students to do everything they can to preserve a free society. They will be the next generation of leaders; they can turn the society around, back to the love of justice and wisdom. They should never be complacent. They should realize how miserable we would be under an authoritarian leader and speak and live in a way that prevents any degree of cultural decline. This book contributes to our responsibility to avoid authoritarianism, specifically by using AI in ways that prevent it and that promote flourishing.

This brings me to one more important lesson from the Greeks. In spite of the many ways Athens was structured to cultivate practical wisdom in the citizens, the Athenians abused their freedom. Instead of using freedom to discuss public affairs, without censorship, and engage in critical thinking about how their leaders were using their power, they used their freedom to get rich, powerful, popular, or to indulge themselves in every possible distraction. When the Oracle told Socrates' friend that "there was no one wiser than Socrates," Socrates decided to test this riddle. He went about Athens, questioning those with power and asking them what they knew or what they have done that shows they are using their power for the well-being of those over whom they have it. When they could not answer Socrates' questions, they were humiliated in public. Instead of reexamining themselves, they blamed Socrates for "not believing in the city's gods" and "corrupting the youth." The rampant corruption eventually led to internal strife and the unraveling of the social fabric. Critias ran for President by claiming that he would "make Athens great again" by returning to the "traditional values" of loyalty to family, patriotism, and belief in the traditional gods. This was exactly the kind of anti-democratic, authoritarian culture that Athenians prided themselves on rejecting and replacing with the stories that demanded critical thinking. After getting elected, Critias instantly initiated an authoritarian purging of his enemies and confiscated the wealth of foreigners.

As we move forward, it is important to keep in mind that AI is being incorporated into the cultures of many nations right at a time of decline in democracies and the rise of authoritarian regimes. Managers should also keep this in mind and try to use AI to promote critical thinking rather than to stifle it. Any technological tool can be used for good or evil, to promote justice or injustice. The job of managers will become more difficult in this time of disruption, but they should be even more motivated to carefully examine how AI is used in their institutions. The manager class must be mindful, but leaders should also be aware of how employees are using or abusing AI. Since they tend to be younger, recent employees might be able to give managers good advice on what to do and what to avoid when using AI.

As Mr. Kyriazoglou wisely says, it will take a lot of courage to take on the risk of incorporating AI. There should be a working group that meets regularly to collaborate on all of the particular issues involved. Reflections of what went wrong and why and what worked and why are the way we learn. As the Greeks described it: what "hit the mark" and what "missed the mark," with the underlying assumption that there is one best choice to make and other choices are closer or farther from it. Given the complexity of the human condition in general, but this issue in particular, there might be a range of possible good choices, but having the standard against which to discuss each choice is important. I would suggest inviting younger employees to join the working group or to come in an advisory role at various points as this would improve employee morale and lead to better outcomes. Older employees bring wisdom that comes from experience, which might mean not acting impulsively and not expecting immediate results or results that are clearly better or worse. Experience makes us comfortable with gray areas while we are also cognizant of how important making good choices now is because of the consequences long into the future of some of our choices now. Younger employees bring skills and speed. The generations need each other to get to what is best. Studying the different regulations in nations around the world, how they are being implemented, what is working or not, and to what extent are the outcomes related to the overall culture would also be beneficial. As the history of AI use grows, books and articles will emerge that can be used as reference materials.

In my own field, figuring out how to use AI or how to prevent students from cheating by using AI is currently under debate. This will continue long after I am gone. I just hope that the next generation of students does not grow up believing that reading and reflecting are not important and are "dated" now that we have all the information we need on a machine. Once again, ancient wisdom is important because it distinguishes between what the students have access to, knowledge and facts, and wisdom. Students are very aware of the way people are being brainwashed and all the misinformation they are bombarded with. Educators can help them navigate through the maze. I am always enraged when a colleague is resigned to reading "machine-generated papers." We should find a way to prevent students from cheating for the students' sake. We owe them an education that awakens their minds and convinces them on how important it is for them to continually reflect on what is going on around them. We live and teach in a society that gives us freedom: freedom of speech, freedom of association, free intellectual inquiry, free artistic expression, and all the other freedoms we have that enable us to be fully human. We inherited this great legacy, and we owe it to our students to do what we can to pass it down and to give them the intellectual motivation and tools to pass it to their children, families, and friends. As a professor whose entire career, as a student, graduate student, and teacher, has been spent at small liberal arts colleges, I know why our cultural leaders went out into the wilderness and established so many of them. I hope they can survive this next technological revolution. They educate students for reflective thought: for continually examining themselves and others. The US Founders understood the importance of this kind of education.

As a Plato scholar, I am more motivated than many colleagues because Plato's Academy is considered the original or one of the early examples of this kind of education. Plato's students were the future leaders in the city-states or regions where they lived. They would go back home and lead in every social sector and in monarchies, aristocracies, and more self-governing societies. The dialogues show them why they should use their authority for the benefit of those over whom they have it, if they want their societies to stay stable and their people to flourish. Plato tries to motivate them by showing what was happening before the fall of their free society.

I am very worried that I do not know of any professional philosopher who teaches either Plato or Aristotle this way. My favorite Aristotelian is Jeffrey Sachs, an economist who is focused on practical wisdom. Professional conferences are focused on the minutiae of dissertations or even more specialized dialogues related to some subgroup of scholars with similar dissertations. I have no idea how my colleagues teach Plato or Aristotle, and no one seems to want to talk about teaching, even though Socrates is supposedly a great teacher. He was an educator, not a professor. He educes from students' minds what they think about serious questions and asks them to reexamine the worldviews they were not very aware that they were creating in the back of their minds. He does not profess to others what only he knows and what he is giving students the honor of hearing.

So, this is the punch line: I think Mr. Kyriazoglou's book is important because it brings in the Greeks. I have asked readers to indulge me because I want to provide the best argument I can for why we should keep the Ancient Greek cultural tradition alive. I think Mr. Kyriazoglou would agree with me, or with most of what I said, as he did that last time I wrote an extensive book review for him. If he does like what I have said, both of us will have the opportunity to pass down the insights we so desperately need at this most precarious moment. AI, Elon Musk, and the Apollonian "geniuses" are on the rise, as is authoritarianism. Greek wisdom, especially the insights about the difference between knowledge and cognition (Apollo) and wisdom and mind (Athena, a woman by the way), is critical for our time, for developing a sustainable civilization and for preserving a free society. We need creative insights about how to become sustainable, not the dictates of an authoritarian leader.

Overview

This book describes the *Artificial Intelligence (AI) Management System*. It includes (a) how to prepare your organization for AI, (b) how to develop and operate (deploy) AI systems/solutions, and (c) how to assess and improve your whole AI ecosystem.

The AI Management System is made up of four **Components** that contain

Component 1. A philosophical framework

Component 2. Relevant to AI laws and regulations

Component 3. A five-phase AI (64 steps) implementation approach (AI Preparation, AI Management Framework, AI Systems Development, AI Systems Operation, and AI Infrastructure and Systems Assessment)

Component 4. Numerous support tools (policies, procedures, etc.)

The actions of the steps and various tasks of **the AI Management System** result in the establishment, development, crafting, and use of numerous products classified in **seven types** (see the full list in Annex 3 of Chapter 1 and details in each chapter of the book). These are designed to enable, facilitate, manage, operate, assess, and improve your whole AI environment (infrastructure and systems).

They include

- Type 1. Organizational functions/HR resources

- Type 2. Assessment Reports

- Type 3. Reference Documentation

- Type 4. AI/ICT Infrastructure

- Type 5. Administrative support controls

- Type 6. AI governance, development, and operations support controls

- Type 7. Live AI systems/solutions/tools

Objective

The objective of this book is to facilitate and enable the management of an AI Ecosystem for private-sector companies and public-sector organizations. This includes the establishment of an effective AI Infrastructure and the development, operation, and assessment of AI Systems and Solutions for better decision-making, customer support, and other beneficial consequences.

Prologue: Can Computers Think?

The medium is the message. This is merely to say that the personal and social consequences of any medium – that is, of any extension of ourselves – result from the new scale that is introduced into our affairs by each extension of ourselves, or by any new technology.[1]

—Marshall McLuhan

Introduction to Artificial Intelligence

The technology of Electronic or Digital Information and the fast and reliable processing and transmission of information, production of knowledge, and learning is an event of the technological revolution of the last decades. The *three main axes* of this technology are the Electronic or Digital Computer, IT and Telecommunications, and Artificial Intelligence (AI). We will concentrate more on AI which is the scope of this book.

An English Dictionary definition of Artificial Intelligence is "The theory and development of computer systems able to perform tasks normally requiring human intelligence, such as visual perception, speech recognition, decision-making, and translation between languages."

According to IBM, Artificial Intelligence, or AI, is a technology that enables computers and machines to simulate human intelligence and problem-solving capabilities.[2]

On its own or combined with other technologies (e.g., sensors, geolocation, robotics), AI can perform tasks that would otherwise require human intelligence or intervention. Digital assistants, GPS guidance, autonomous vehicles, and generative AI tools (like OpenAI's ChatGPT) are just a few examples of AI in the daily news and our daily lives. As a field of computer science, artificial intelligence encompasses (and is often mentioned together with) machine learning and deep learning. These disciplines involve the development of AI algorithms, modeled after the decision-making processes of the human brain, that can "learn" from available data and make increasingly more accurate classifications or predictions over time.

Artificial intelligence also refers to the ability of a computing machine to reproduce or even simulate with software and special algorithms written in a computer language, in many cases, the cognitive functions of humans (HSS: *Homo sapiens sapiens*[3]), such as thinking, learning, planning, creativity, etc. For more definitions of AI concepts and terms, see Appendix 1.

The new technology of AI with the rapid development and advancement of artificial intelligence systems (e.g., ChatGPT, Instagram, Facebook, Twitter, Viso Suite Platform, Jupyter Notebooks Software, Cloud AI Platform Software, Azure Machine Learning Studio, etc.[4]) has raised questions about whether they can actually think and understand.

While it can produce text that appears to display thought, understanding, and creativity, this question cannot be answered through technological progress alone. A careful philosophical analysis is thus necessary to understand both the benefits and the risks of the AI revolution. Without addressing these philosophical issues, we will never fully understand the potential of artificial intelligence.

Whether humans dominate this technology (Computers, IT, AI, Telecommunications) or it (this technology) dominates humans and what philosophical, psychological, social, and economic implications the use of this technology brings to our lives in the 21st century is a serious matter. This has been analyzed and is continuously reviewed by many notable scholars and scientists.

Several researchers (McCulloch, Pfeiffer, Asimov, and J. Von Neumann[5]) have analyzed and compared the behavioral repertoire of humans as an analogue to the behavioral repertoire of computers (in terms of a program of instructions).

Newell and Simon[6] have hypothesized that the human brain's symbol processing is analogous to computer symbol processing.

Carl Sagan predicted[7] (in 1975) that in the wider future, the human brain will be wired with microcircuits containing special knowledge and experiences. This was already announced recently.[8]

Thus, the human brain will be able to be enriched with artificial intelligence just like the Personal Computer (PC).

The assumption that the brain of humans is analogous to the PC, but there is no PC analogous to humans, is probably wrong. As P. Armer has said,[9] the demonstration of computer intelligence does not presuppose a functional similarity of the computer to humans, just as the fact that airplane flying does not presuppose a functional similarity of airplanes and birds.

But before we try to offer an answer to this question, we must examine what is meant by the term "thought."

Analysis of the Terms and Concepts of "Thought"

Thales: "Nothing is more active than thought, because it travels over the universe."[10]

Thinking is an important part of our human experience and one that has captivated people for centuries. Imagine all your thoughts as if they were physical entities, swirling rapidly through your mind. How is it possible that the brain can move from one thought to another in an organized, orderly way?

The modern human brain is endlessly perceiving, processing, planning, organizing, and remembering – it is always active. However, you don't notice most of your brain activity as you go about your daily routine.

This is only one aspect of the complex processes involved in cognition. Simply put, cognition is thinking and includes the processes associated with perception, knowledge, problem-solving, judgment, language, and memory.

The term "**thought**" may refer to the ideas or arrangement of ideas (sequence) produced by the intellect, to the art of producing thoughts, or to the process of producing thoughts. Despite the fact that thinking is a fundamental human activity common to all, there is no generally accepted agreement on what it is or how it is created.

Because thought underlies many human actions and interactions, understanding the physical and metaphysical origins, processes, and effects of thought has been a long-standing goal of many disciplines, including artificial intelligence, biology, philosophy, psychology, and sociology.

Thinking allows people to interpret, visualize, and understand the world they experience, as well as make predictions about it.

What is meant by "thinking" and how do we distinguish who is thinking (a human, a computer, or a robotic or other machine)? This is very difficult as Taube[11] also asks.

The Oxford Dictionary definition of "think" is[12] "to have a particular idea or opinion about something/somebody; to believe something." Its synonyms include believe, feel, reckon, be under the impression.

Socrates set the agenda for the tradition of critical thinking, that is, to thoughtfully question commonly held beliefs and explanations, carefully distinguishing those beliefs that are reasonable and explainable from those that – however appealing to our egocentricity, however much they serve our own interests, or however convenient or comforting they may be – lack sufficient evidence or the rational basis to justify our belief.

The practice of Socrates[13] was followed by the critical thinking of Plato (who recorded Socrates' thought), Aristotle, and the Greek skeptics.

All of them emphasized that things are often very different from what they appear to be and that only the trained mind is prepared to see through the way things appear on the surface (illusory appearances) to how they really are beneath the surface (the deeper realities of life).

From this ancient Greek tradition arose the need, for anyone who aspired to understand the deeper realities, to think systematically and to trace the implications in breadth and depth, for only thinking that is comprehensive, reasoned, and responsive to objections can lead us beyond the surface.

Aristotle[14] defines practical wisdom (practical thinking is part of practical wisdom) as the successful finding, reasoning, and examination, which, by the method of sorting, begins with the individual goals and aims at the final solution of the issue.

According to Drever's *Dictionary of Psychology*,[15] "thinking" is "a set of ideas and more specifically a set of ideas for solving a particular problem."

"I think" means "I intend for the truth" according to philosopher A. Blanchard.[16] E. Dimnet[17] considers the term "think" to be synonymous with the term "meditate."

"Thinking" is defined as a sequence of two or more symbolic acts with graphic messages and symbols according to A. J. Caron.[18]

B. H. Bode defines "thinking" as finding and testing semantic relations.[19]

Sir F. Bartlett[20] defines "thinking" as a set of high-level behavioral repertoires, with the necessary graphic messages and symbols as its means of expression and with the characteristics that they are controlled by humans, in terms of the properties of time, direction, and result.

Dewey[21] defines "thinking" (a) as a set of uncontrollable ideas, such as fantasies, dreams, and other uncontrollable mind-wandering scenarios or reveries of negative or positive outcome ("journeys"), (b) as a set of ideas with goals and objectives for solving a specific problem, and (c) as a synonym of "believe."

R. Thompson[22] defines "thinking" as (a) fantasies, dreams, etc., (b) synonym of "I remember," (c) ponder, (d) pay attention to the execution of an act, (e) synonym of "believe," and (g) test of values, such as comparing logical arguments, translation, creating music, mathematical analysis, literature, solving a practical problem in many ways, etc.

Turing and P. Armer[23] do not define "thinking" in specific terms, but as a set of behavioral repertoires of modern man.

There are six levels of thinking according to the revised version of Bloom's Taxonomy.[24] Each level is conceptually different. The six levels are remembering, understanding, applying, analyzing, evaluating, and creating.

Critical thinking, according to Michael Scriven and Richard Paul,[25] is the intellectually disciplined process[5] of actively and skillfully apprehending, applying, analyzing, synthesizing, and/or evaluating information gathered from, or generated from, observation, experience, reflection, reasoning, or communication, as a guide to belief and action.

According to Kahneman,[26] there are two thinking systems in modern man. The first is fast, intuitive, and emotional, and it works automatically. The second is slow, judicious, and rational and operates with low effort.

In summary and for analysis purposes, the above definitions of "thinking" can be summarized in two sets, namely:

a) The set of reasoning concepts, such as judge, reason, study, intend, expect, meditate, test values, examine, produce a unique product of thought, etc.

b) The set of metaphysical concepts, such as believe, imagine, dream, feel, recall, expect, aim at the truth, etc.

At the level of psychological function, "thinking" is understood as the behavioral repertoire of high intelligence that processes symbols and messages with three main characteristics – time, direction, and result.

Characteristic examples of the function of "thinking" in the daily life of modern man are

- "The thought of failure scares me."
- "I am very tired of thinking too much how to solve this problem."
- "I thought about how happy I was in my childhood."
- "My first thought was to refuse the offer."
- "Learning a foreign language requires a lot of thinking."
- "I use all my thinking in writing this book."
- "The thought of her weighs heavily on my soul," etc.

Do Computers Think?

Aristotle:[27] "Thought is different from perception and is considered to be partly imagination, partly judgment."

At this point in the analysis, **the question arises**: "Is it possible for computers (Electronic or Digital Computers with hardware and software and through artificial intelligence technology) to think?"

The answer will be **negative** if thought is defined as the exclusive property of modern man, somewhat mysterious, supernatural, or metaphysical as life itself is. Thus, thought is beyond machines and computers, as machines and computers are not equivalent to HSS (modern human) and, therefore, cannot think.

The answer will be **positive** if we compare the behavior of modern man in terms of thinking properties with the behavior of computers in terms of the same properties.

This way, the behavior of computers is clearly analyzed and compared to the behavior of the modern human. If the behavior is similar, then computers can think.

Defining the thought and by extension the behavior of high intelligence, as the property of modern man, leads to a wrong analysis. For example, presenting the functions of the human heart with a mechanical heart is wrong, because the mechanical heart is not a living organ.[28]

But it is not the physical properties of humans or computers that matter, only the results produced.

Another logical argument about the ability of computers to think is this: computers are capable of processing data and information, acting with some predetermined logic and producing results, just because they are programmed.

Therefore, there are limits to logical operations and generally to the behavior of computers.

On the contrary, modern man has the ability to demonstrate intelligence abilities to solve problems, beyond the third level of intelligence (simple, complex, wicked problems[29]).

At this time, this (i.e., solving third-level problems) is not possible or efficient for computers, although there is ongoing research with various models (e.g., Machine Learning Models) to solve this issue, etc.

And since it is not known how modern man acts at this level of intelligence, it is not possible to program computers to act at this high level of intelligence.

This argument is not logical and correct since the fact that there are currently no ways, methods, or techniques that allow computers to behave (think) at the third level of problem-solving does not mean that this possibility will not exist in the future (e.g., deep learning).

Completing the analysis, summarizing the arguments, and bearing in mind that the definition of "thinking" is multidimensional, the answer to the question "Is it possible for computers to think?" is in the affirmative.

Because computers exhibit a repertoire of behavior that includes or presupposes a relevant level of intelligence.

Computers learn, teach, solve problems, operate simple and complex machines and devices, ask multidimensional questions in intelligence tests, compose music, replace test animals in scientific laboratories, etc.

In this behavioral repertoire, the difference between modern human and computers is very small and perhaps insignificant.

Of course, computers are not metaphysical beings, because they do not have life, nor do they create life. But they enable modern humans to change their way of life and become more creative by having the computers take over all the time-consuming, monotonous, laborious, and difficult tasks in the various phases of life for humans so that people devote more time in the quality improvement of their life.

Impact of Artificial Intelligence

Epictetus: "The wise do not confuse information or data, however miraculous or cleverly developed, with comprehensive knowledge or transcendent wisdom."[30]

We live, without a doubt, in the electronic or digital age. The characteristics of the electronic age[31] include the following:

- The information revolution that creates a knowledge-based society.

- The most effective use of information during this time.

- Better efficiency of production and service provision.

- Greater productivity through the use of advanced technology.

- Better resource management through the use of data science.

- Machines begin, little by little, to replace humans in production, leading to a gradual loss of jobs, etc.

These were made possible by advancements in computer microprocessors, the invention of personal computers, the Internet and the World Wide Web, Artificial Intelligence, etc.

As stated in a recent Stanford University report,[32] "Artificial intelligence beats humans in some tasks, but not all. Artificial intelligence has surpassed human performance in many benchmarks, including some in image classification, visual reasoning, and English comprehension. However, it lags behind in more complex tasks such as competitive math, visual commonsense reasoning and planning."

All these bring dystopia[33] to people and their souls as well as to human societies. The electronic or digital age began around the 1970s, as the information age, and continues to this day.

This is a period of transition from the traditional society and economy to an economy based on the full integration of all services in digital technologies, computing systems, and artificial intelligence applications and the increasing digitization[34] of information and data for all purposes.

We will increasingly depend on robots and machines to perform functions previously performed by humans. Through the development of artificial intelligence and machine learning, machines can learn human emotions. With this, they are able to make decisions that should have been made by humans, thus helping and improving production, decision-making, services, etc.

As digital technology and devices connect us with unimaginable fury, many of us feel empowered mentally, physically, and emotionally. But virtual reality surrounds our subconscious and fills it with our baseless virtuous materialistic vanity, making our soul enter a dystopian state. Thus, our own endless holiday of consciousness fills our restless soul and spirit with great existential boredom.

Because as digital devices rule our homes, connecting everything, they add a lot of stress and anxiety. Our level of concern is now reaching surreal levels, the brainchild of a world full of online fantasy and moral turpitude.

This anxiety is the greatest danger in the life of modern man.

There are also, epigrammatically, other risks related to Artificial Intelligence and a number of issues, such as

1) The protection of personal data[35] of customers, employees in businesses and public organizations, patients in hospitals, citizens in their dealings with public organizations, passengers, etc.

2) The violation of the confidentiality of trade secrets

3) Management of intellectual property issues

4) Issues of unfair competition

5) Theft or falsification of the algorithms, processing model, and data used by the specific artificial intelligence technology

6) Development and management of artificial intelligence solutions

7) Analysis and uncontrolled use of big data,[36] etc.

All these risks must be effectively addressed at the level of society (for society as a whole, such as the new Artificial Intelligence Act of the European Union[37]) and at the level of businesses and public organizations.

Measures to mitigate these risks for businesses and organizations include (but not limited to) the following:

1) The application of ethical rules for the use of artificial intelligence may be based on the principles of ancient Greek philosophy of Socrates, Aristotle, Epicurus, and Plato (e.g., Temperance, Faith, Justice, Harmony, Friendship, Kindness, and Courage)

2) Informing and training all those involved (management, technical staff, users, etc.) in the proper application of this technology

3) Informing and protecting all members of society from the possible malicious use of the results of the exploitation of artificial intelligence, etc.

Recommendation

For private companies and public organizations, I recommend a set of interrelated measures and controls embodied in an **Artificial Intelligence (AI) Management System** (as described in the summary below).

AI Management System: Contents

This system contains four components:

> **Component 1: Philosophical Framework** (vision, mission, and values statements, the Seven Ancient Greek Wisdom Principles, AI Ethical Standards Policy, Corporate Ethics Policy, etc.)

> **Component 2: Legal and Regulatory Environment** (external legal and regulatory frameworks and controls, such as EU's GDPR, EU's AI Act, Digital Nations' Charter, etc. related to AI)

> **Component 3: AI Implementation Approach** (five phases: AI Preparation, AI Management Framework, AI Systems Development, AI Systems Operation, and AI Infrastructure and Systems Assessment)

> **Component 4: AI Support Tools** (AI glossary, policies, and procedures)

AI Ecosystem Journey

The AI Management System will be implemented on the conceptual basis of seven distinct milestones:

> Milestone 1: Develop AI Management System. See Chapter 1.

> Milestone 2: Define a robust AI ethics framework. See Chapters 2 and 3.

> Milestone 3: Consider the impact of AI regulations and standards. See Chapters 4-6.

> Milestone 4: Establish an AI infrastructure management framework. See Chapters 7-10.

> Milestone 5: Develop and operate AI systems. See Chapters 11 and 12.

Milestone 6: Improve AI infrastructure and systems.
See Chapters 13–18.

Milestone 7: Develop Support Tools. See Appendixes 1–41.

More details of the AI Management System are presented in the next chapter. Full details of all steps, actions, and tools are included in other chapters of this book.

In closing, the book is a sequel to my other Data Protection and IT books. I am totally responsible for any potential errors, omissions, and faults found in this book. Your comments are welcome and will be acknowledged. Also, contact me if you need any support or advice on any issue contained in this book.

John Kyriazoglou

Disclaimer

The material, concepts, ideas, plans, policies, procedures, forms, methods, tools, etc. presented, described and analyzed in all chapters and appendices, are for educational and training purposes only. These may be used only, possibly, as an indicative base set, and should be customized by each organization, after careful and considerable thought as to the needs and requirements of each organization, taking into effect the implications and aspects of the legal, national, religious, philosophical, cultural and social environments, and expectations, within which each organization operates and exists.

Every possible effort has been made to ensure that the information contained in this book is accurate at the time of going to press, and the publishers and the author cannot accept responsibility for any errors or omissions, however caused. No responsibility for loss or damage occasioned to any person acting, or refraining from action, as a result of the material in this publication can be accepted by the publisher or the author.

PART I

Foundation

The development of the AI Management System enables and facilitates the establishing of an ethical, effective, and innovative AI Ecosystem to improve your business operations by the deployment and use of AI Systems/Solutions. This also supports you to achieve the **first** milestone (***Develop AI Management System***) of your AI Ecosystem Journey.

Extensive details are included in Chapter 1 and the three annexes that follow it.

CHAPTER 1

AI Management System

Peter Drucker:[1] "Management is about human beings. Its task is to make people capable of joint performance, to make their strengths effective and their weaknesses irrelevant."

Overview: This chapter describes, in summary terms, the *Artificial Intelligence (AI) Management System*. This is made up of four **Components** that include a philosophical framework, relevant to AI laws and regulations, a five-phase (with 64 steps) AI implementation approach, and numerous support tools. All these are designed to facilitate and enable the management of an AI ecosystem for private-sector companies and public-sector organizations.

This includes, for better decision-making, customer support and other beneficial consequences:

(1) The establishment of an effective AI Infrastructure on the basis of an AI Risk Assessment and the identification of AI risks (see example in Annex 1) and the implementation of relevant AI controls (see example in Annex 2)

(2) The development and operation of AI systems and solutions

(3) The assessment of the AI ecosystem (infrastructure and AI systems and solutions)

AI Management System

The Artificial Intelligence (AI) Management System is composed of four interrelated components (see Figure 1-1).

© John Kyriazoglou 2025
J. Kyriazoglou, *AI Management Framework*, https://doi.org/10.1007/979-8-8688-1536-2_1

Component 1: Corporate Philosophical Framework

Component 2: Legal and Regulatory Environment

Component 3: AI Implementation Approach

Component 4: AI Support Tools

Figure 1-1. *AI Management System*

The goal of this system (AI Management System) is to establish and operate an effective AI environment so that AI systems and solutions could be developed and run to enable the specific company or organization to reap the best benefits accrued by using the Artificial Intelligence (AI) technology.

The products of the AI Management System are listed in Annex 3.

Component 1: Corporate Philosophical Framework

The first component includes a set of ethical and cultural elements within which AI operates effectively and beneficially within the specific company or organization. These include

- Vision, mission, and values statements

- The Seven Ancient Greek Wisdom Principles

- AI Ethical Standards Policy

- Corporate Ethics Policy

- Corporate Social Responsibility Policy, etc.

These are contained in Chapters 2 and 3.

Other corporate policies and procedures that also support AI are included in Component 4 (Part VII, Support Tools) of the AI System.

Component 2: Legal and Regulatory Environment

The second component includes a set of external legal and regulatory frameworks and controls which influence and impact the specific corporation and its AI aspects. These include

- The EU AI Act

- The EU GDPR (General Data Protection Regulation)

- Other Data Privacy Regulations

- ISO Standards (Information Security, Management, Environment Protection, etc.)

- Various National Health, Employment Protection, Labor and other laws, etc.

The EU AI Guidelines and other AI relevant standards are summarized in Chapters 4–6. GDPR and ISO Information Security Measures are included in the books listed in the "Additional Resources" section of this book.

Component 3: AI Implementation Approach

The third component includes an implementation approach with a set of five phases (and 64 steps) which facilitate and enable the effective establishment, development, and operation of AI infrastructure and systems for a specific company or organization. These phases are shown in Figure 1-2.

Phase A	AI Preparation
Phase B	AI Management Framework
Phase C	AI Systems Development
Phase D	AI Systems Operation
Phase E	AI Infrastructure and Systems Assessment

Figure 1-2. *AI Implementation Approach*

Each of the five phases with their goals, objectives, and steps are outlined below.

Phase A (AI Preparation)
Goal and Objectives of Phase A

The **goal of Phase A** is to "Prepare the company better for AI."

The objectives that support the achievement of this goal are

Objective 1: Evaluate AI corporate readiness

Objective 2: Engage top management in AI

Steps of Phase A (AI Preparation)

The seven steps to support the achievement of the goal and objectives of Phase A are

Step A1: Conduct AI Needs and Gap Analysis

Step A2: Carry Out AI Regulations and Standards Analysis

Step A3: Perform AI Readiness and Awareness Assessment

Step A4: Establish AI Steering Committee

Step A5: Appoint AI Project Manager

Step A6: Draft AI Budget

Step A7: Educate Board and Senior Management

These steps and their actions are fully described in Chapter 7.

Phase B: AI Management Framework

Phase B is composed of three parts:

Part B-1: Establish AI Governance Controls

Part B-2: Establish Data Governance Controls

Part B-3: Establish IT Governance Controls

Goal and Objectives of Phase B (AI Management Framework)

The **goal of Phase B** is to "Establish an efficient framework for managing AI."
    This goal is achieved by the eight objectives of the three parts of Phase B listed next.

Phase B-Part 1 (AI Governance) Objectives

Objective 1: Establish AI Governance Controls

Objective 2: Establish AI Strategy and Ethics

Phase B-Part 2 (Data Governance) Objectives

Objective 1: Establish Data Management Controls

Objective 2: Organize and manage corporate data

Objective 3: Prepare data for AI projects

Phase B-Part 3 (IT Governance) Objectives

Objective 1: Establish AI computer infrastructure

Objective 2: Ensure effective information security and privacy controls

Objective 3: Ensure critical IT controls include AI aspects

The 27 steps to support the achievement of the overall goal of Phase B ("Establish an efficient framework for managing AI") and the specific objectives of each part of Phase B are presented below.

Steps of Phase B (Part B-1: Establish AI Governance Controls)

The seven steps to support the achievement of the overall goal of Phase B and the specific objectives of Phase B (Part B-1) are

Step B1-1: Ensure Corporate Governance Controls Operation

Step B1-2: Establish AI Governance Roles and Responsibilities

Step B1-3: Establish AI Governance Framework

Step B1-4: Develop and Issue AI Strategy

Step B1-5: Establish AI Third-Party Controls

Step B1-6: Determine AI Ethical Principles and Values

Step B1-7: Educate and Train Employees on AI

These steps and their actions are fully described in Chapter 8.

Steps of Phase B (Part B-2: Establish Data Governance Controls)

The six steps to support the achievement of the overall goal of Phase B and the specific objectives of Phase B (Part B-2) are

Step B2-1: Establish Data Governance Function

Step B2-2: Establish Data Governance Policies and Procedures

Step B2-3: Manage Corporate Data Storage

Step B2-4: Locate and Organize AI Data

Step B2-5: Manage Business Records and Intelligence

Step B2-6: Protect Intellectual Property (IP) Assets

These steps and their actions are fully described in Chapter 9.

Steps of Phase B (Part B-3: Establish IT Governance Controls)

The 15 steps to support the achievement of the overall goal of Phase B and the specific objectives of Phase B (Part B-3) are

Step B3-1: Manage AI Computer Infrastructure

Step B3-2: Manage Information Security and Privacy Policies and Procedures

Step B3-3: Manage Vulnerabilities and Malware

Step B3-4: Manage Robotic Accounts

Step B3-5: Manage Human Accounts

Step B3-6: Manage Account Provisioning and Revocation

Step B3-7: Manage Password Controls

Step B3-8: Manage Segregation of IT Duties

Step B3-9: Manage Third-Party Access Controls

Step B3-10: Manage IT Changes

Step B3-11: Manage AI Solutions Inventory

Step B3-12: Manage IT Resources

Step B3-13: Manage IT Knowledge Retention

Step B3-14: Manage IT Configuration

Step B3-15: Manage Backup and Recovery Process

These steps and their actions are fully described in Chapter 10.

Phase C: AI Systems Development
Goal and Objectives of Phase C

The **goal of Phase C** is to "Develop AI Systems."

The objectives that support the achievement of this goal are

Objective 1: Analyze and document AI System requirements and needs

Objective 2: Organize and manage hypotheses, algorithms, and the learning model of the AI System

Objective 3: Test the AI System and Learning Model

Steps of Phase C (AI Systems Development)

The 12 steps to support the achievement of the goal and the specific objectives of Phase C are

Step C1: Establish AI Development Team

Step C2: Select AI Project to Be Developed and Run

Step C3: Establish AI System Owner

Step C4: Perform AI System Regulatory Risk Analysis

Step C5: Develop AI System

Step C6: Check AI System's Hypotheses, Algorithms, and Model

Step C7: Document Business Case for AI System

Step C8: Document Business Processes for AI System

Step C9: Include Internal Application Controls in AI System

Step C10: Include "Explainability by Design" in AI System

Step C11: Include Security and Privacy Controls in AI System

Step C12: Test AI System

These steps and their actions are fully described in Chapter 11.

Phase D: AI Systems Operation
Goal and Objectives of Phase D (AI Systems Operation)

The **goal of Phase D** is to "Operate (deploy) AI Systems effectively."
The objectives that support the achievement of this goal are

Objective 1: Run and monitor the activities and results of AI Systems

Objective 2: Manage AI Incidents

Objective 3: Assess AI Systems after initial implementation

Steps of Phase D (AI Systems Operation)

The ten steps to support the achievement of the goal and the specific objectives of Phase D are

Step D1: Review the IT Operational Aspects of AI Systems

Step D2: Review the Quality of AI Systems

Step D3: Review the Auditability of AI Systems

Step D4: Review Application Controls and Logging of AI Systems

Step D5: Operate (Deploy) the AI System

Step D6: Monitor Performance of AI Systems

Step D7: Manage Results and Errors of AI Systems

Step D8: Manage User Requests of AI Systems

Step D9: Manage AI Incidents

Step D10: Carry Out Post-Implementation Review of AI Systems

These steps and their actions are fully described in Chapter 12.

Phase E: AI Infrastructure and Systems Assessment

Goal and Objectives of Phase E (AI Infrastructure and Systems Assessment)

The **goal of Phase E** is to "Improve AI Infrastructure and Systems."
The objectives that support the achievement of this goal are

Objective 1: Audit, review, and assess governance issues

Objective 2: Audit, review, and assess development and operation of AI systems

Steps of Phase E (AI Infrastructure and Systems Assessment)

The eight steps to support the achievement of the goal and the specific objectives of Phase E are

Step E1: Assess Corporate Governance

Step E2: Assess HR Management

Step E3: Assess AI Governance

Step E4: Assess AI Data Management

Step E5: Assess AI Model and Hypotheses Management

Step E6: Assess AI System Development

Step E7: Assess AI System Operation

Step E8: Assess IT Governance

The AI Audit Process and these steps are fully described in Chapters 13–18.

Component 4: AI Support Tools

The fourth component includes numerous tools (e.g., glossary, checklists, policies, procedures, guidelines, etc.) that support the other three components (Corporate Philosophical Framework, Laws and Regulations, and AI Implementation Approach) as well as the effective establishment, development, and operation of AI infrastructure and systems for a specific company or organization.

These are contained in the Appendix (Part VII).

AI Management System Implementation Approach

The AI Management System will be implemented on the conceptual basis of seven distinct milestones:

Milestone 1: Develop AI Management System (this chapter).

Milestone 2: Define a robust AI ethics framework. See Chapters 2 and 3.

Milestone 3: Consider impact of AI regulations and standards. See Chapters 4–6.

Milestone 4: Establish AI infrastructure management framework. See Chapters 7–10.

Milestone 5: Develop and operate AI systems. See Chapters 11 and 12.

Milestone 6: Improve AI infrastructure and systems. See Chapters 13–18.

Milestone 7: Develop Support Tools. See Appendixes 1–39.

Recommendations

As regards the better development and implementation of the above-described **AI Management System** and use for your AI purposes, the following recommendations (REC) are proposed:

> REC 1. Review all aspects of this proposed ***Artificial Intelligence (AI) Management System*** (components, phases, steps, risks, controls, products, etc.) and consider how they impact your operating landscape and how you may utilize them to improve your AI operations.

> REC 2. Prepare documentation of your own AI Management System (**Product: AI Management System Handbook**) and your implementation specifics, get board approval, and craft a presentation of its major elements.

> REC 3. Ensure all your corporate staff (IT, AI, HR, Compliance, etc.) and relevant stakeholders as well as board members are fully aware of what this AI Management System and AI journey entails for all functions of your organization and how they may best support it to reach its full potential.

> REC 4. Ensure you keep current the documentation of your own AI Management System (**Product: AI Management System Handbook**) by reviewing it and updating every two to three years or as needs, expectations, and operating conditions and circumstances warrant.

Conclusion

The development of the AI Management System marks the achievement of the **first** milestone (***Develop AI Management System***) of your AI Ecosystem Journey. Other notable approaches to implement AI include Microsoft's,[2] IBM's,[3] etc.[4] You may wish to consider these as well as the proposed AI Management System of this book before you craft your own AI implementation approach. Note, however, that the proposed AI Management System (described in this book) enables and facilitates the establishing of an ethical, effective, and innovative AI ecosystem to improve your business operations by the deployment and use of beneficial AI Systems/Solutions.

The next chapter continues this exciting journey by describing the Seven Ancient Greek Wisdom Principles and how they may be used in implementing ethical AI systems/solutions.

Annex 1: AI Risk Catalogue

AI Governance Risks

Lack of AI strategy

Lack of strategic alignment

Poor AI program management framework

Non-compliance with internal or external requirements, standards, and rules

Misalignment to the organization's cultural and ethical values

Misunderstanding of AI concepts and terms

Unclear AI expectations

Weak organization governance mechanisms

Unclear ownership and management roles and responsibilities of AI solutions

Lack of software license compliance

People Risks

Unclear AI data governance roles and responsibilities

Unclear resourcing requirements

Untrained staff

Insufficient IT knowledge

Insufficient capability and human capacity

Incomplete corporate knowledge retention

Insufficient IT knowledge retention

Insufficient AI third-party controls

AI Systems Development Risks

Lack of AI architecture

Explainability principles not embedded in the AI design

"Security by design" not implemented

"Privacy by design and by default" not implemented

Inefficient IT architecture

Insufficient capacity and availability of AI solution

Data poisoning

Data corruption

Poor data quality

Inaccurate data used

Inadequate AI hypotheses governance

Poor quality of AI algorithms

Poor quality of AI model

Incorrect results produced

Poor AI benefits management

No business case for AI

Ineffective AI design and development methodology

Lack of understanding of "As-Is" and "To-Be" processes

AI Systems Operation Risks

AI Solution risks and controls not completely defined

Incomplete AI Application controls

Inability to trace activities performed by the AI solution

Insufficient testing of the AI Application

Lack of monitoring of AI solution results produced

Undetected AI solution operational errors

Inability to recover after an AI incident

AI vendor solution not fully understood

Lack of exit capability of AI solution

No AI Solution auditability

IT Governance and Data Protection Risks

Incomplete IT security management policies and procedures

Ineffective Data Protection (e.g., GDPR) Controls (e.g., lack of consent mechanisms, lack of procedure for managing data breaches, etc.)

Poor vulnerability and malware management

Ineffective access controls

Poor Bot account access controls

Lack of human account access controls

Incomplete procedures (e.g., account provisioning procedure, access revocation procedure, password controls policy, segregation of IT duties, third-party access controls, IT change management, etc.)

Improper inventory of AI solutions

Annex 2: AI Controls

AI Strategy

 AI application review procedure

 Compliance with internal or external requirements, standards, and rules

 Corporate ethical rules and values

 AI language and definitions awareness plan

 AI expectation management

 AI governance framework

 AI policy

 Ownership and management roles and responsibilities of AI solutions

 AI solution exit strategy

 Human resource requirements management

 AI awareness and training policy

 IT knowledge management and documentation

 AI third-party controls

 AI architecture and development methodology

 "Explainability by design" in AI solution

 "Security by design" in AI solution

 "Privacy by design and by default" in AI solution

 AI software license management

 IT architecture controls

 IT capacity and availability controls

 AI data governance roles and responsibilities

 Data corruption controls

 Data governance policies and procedures

 AI hypotheses governance controls

 AI Algorithms governance

 AI Model governance

 AI results review/verification procedure

 Completeness of data

 AI program management methodology

 AI benefits management

 Business case documentation for AI Solution

 AI design and development methodology

 "As-Is" and "To-Be" business process documentation

17

AI risks and controls framework

AI Application controls implementation plan

AI solution activity logging

AI testing methodology

AI solution results monitoring

Information security management policies and procedures

AI Solution Auditability Strategy

Vulnerability and malware management

Bot account access controls

Human account access controls

Account provisioning procedure

Access revocation procedure

Segregation of IT duties

Password controls policy

Third-party access controls

IT change management

Inventory of AI solutions

IT resource management

AI incident management

IP protection policy

IT assets and configuration management policy

Backup and recovery policy and procedures

AI vendor support controls

Human resource management

AI rollback process

Corporate knowledge retention management

IT knowledge retention management

Large volume data management plan

AI training data validation and verification procedure

Secure AI data storage procedure

AI encryption policy

AI training data separation procedure

Access controls

AI monitoring and auditing plan

AI model validation procedure

Annex 3: AI Management System Products

The products (outcomes, results, and outputs) define (a) what's required (i.e., organizational functions, HR resources, ICT hardware and software, policies, etc.) to establish, develop, operate, implement, and assess AI infrastructure and systems/solutions and (b) what outputs and results (i.e., reference documentation, assessment reports, decisions of live AI systems, AI data, etc.) are produced, managed, used, and maintained by AI systems/solutions and their developmental, implementation, operational, and assessment aspects.

Products (Outcomes, Results, and Outputs) of the AI Management System

The main outcomes, results, and outputs of the AI Management System include the following seven types of products (examples only, full details, in each part and chapter):

> **Type 1. Organizational Functions/HR Resources**: These include (a) establishing an AI Steering Committee, an AI Ethics Committee, a Data Governance Committee, an AI Project Team and staffing it accordingly, a Data Management Office, a Corporate Data Steering Committee, an AI Incident Management Team and staffing with relevant staff, an AI Development Team with relevant staff, an AI Operations Support Team with staff, and an AI Auditing Team with audit staff and (b) appointing an AI Project Manager, an AI System Owner, a Chief Data Officer, Data Management Staff, an IT person to manage the AI inventory, and an AI System Human Supervisor for each AI System.

> **Type 2. Assessment Reports**: These include carrying out the necessary assessment and review actions and issuing the following analyses and reports (over 23 items): AI Needs Analysis Report, AI Gap Analysis Report, AI Risk Assessment Report, AI Readiness Report, Privacy Readiness Report, etc.

> **Type 3. Reference Documentation**: This includes crafting and issuing reference documentation (over 43 items), such as "The Seven Ancient Greek Wisdom Principles handbook," "The AI Global Standards and Guidelines handbook," "The Major Data Protection Laws and Privacy by Design handbook," "The Digital and Secure AI System Development Guidelines

handbook," Updated (with AI) Corporate Governance Controls Documentation, AI Program (with list of approved projects), AI Operating Model Documentation, AI Glossary (printed), AI Training Presentation (printed), etc.

Type 4. AI/ICT Infrastructure: This includes the installation and operation of specialized computer servers, storage units, and other AI equipment and software to enable the effective development and operation of AI systems/solutions and other tools.

Type 5. Administrative Support Controls: These include issuing, sharing, and retaining on file (over 30 items): AI Steering Committee Announcement and Minutes of Meetings, AI Project Manager's updated (with AI duties) employment agreement, AI Budget, Procurement order for AI Infrastructure components, Board and Senior Managers' AI presentation (printed), etc.

Type 6. AI Governance, Development, and Operations Support Controls: These include issuing, sharing, using, implementing, and keeping current policies and procedures (over 55 items), such as Conflict of Interest Policy, AI Ethical Standards Policy, Corporate Ethics Policy, Corporate Social Responsibility Policy, Corporate Diversity Policy, Environment Protection Policy, Data Ethics Policy, etc.

Type 7. Live AI Systems/Solutions/Tools: This includes issuing, managing, using, sharing, and retaining on file: Board and Senior Managers' AI presentation (digital), Repository of AI-related IT Assets (digital), Live Enterprise Data Repository, Live Big Data Repository, Live Corporate Data Storage, Live Corporate Data Dictionary, Live AI Test Data for each AI Project, Live AI "Learning Data" for each AI Project, Test data for each AI system, Tested AI Systems, Production AI Systems, etc.

PART II

AI Ethics Framework

Part II contains

Chapter 2: The Seven Ancient Greek Wisdom Principles

Chapter 3: Corporate Philosophy Statements and Policies

Establishing an effective AI Ethics Framework supports you to achieve the **second** milestone (***Define a robust AI ethics framework***) of your AI Ecosystem Journey.

The extensive details included in Chapters 2 and 3 define several philosophical aspects related to AI ethics, such as vision, mission, and values statements, the Seven Ancient Greek Wisdom Principles, AI Ethical Standards Policy, Corporate Ethics Policy, etc.

All these (contents of Chapters 2 and 3) compose the **first** component (**Philosophical Framework**) of your **AI Management System**.

CHAPTER 2

The Seven Ancient Greek Wisdom Principles

Overview: This chapter describes the Seven Ancient Greek Wisdom Principles (Temperance, Faith, Justice, Harmony, Friendship, Kalokagathia (Goodness and Kindness), and Courage), what various noted Greek thinkers have quoted about them, and how these may be applied in an Artificial Intelligence (AI) environment (with specific examples of measures). These principles are the first part of *Component 1: Corporate Philosophical Framework (of the AI Management System)*.

Why the Ancient Greeks?

Based on my varied consulting and management experience and on the experience of noted philosophy professor Martha Beck,[1] there is a need for a common set of categories that gives a theoretical description of universal and cross-cultural principles for humans and organizations.

The ancient Greeks have such principles.

The ancient Greeks showed that the most important criterion for wisdom is the recognition of higher powers in the universe than human beings – powers humans cannot control. Human beings must create cultures within the context of those greater powers; they must integrate culture with nature, etc.

The principles I am presenting are one way of articulating a universal and cross-cultural set of standards, based on the wisdom of the past, wisdom that gets passed down from one generation to the next in theory but also applied in practice in ways that differ, based on historical contexts.

There are many, many principles and other ways of articulating virtue and vice in classical Ancient Greek philosophers. I have chosen seven that I think are most important based on my experience in the business world.

© John Kyriazoglou 2025
J. Kyriazoglou, *AI Management Framework*, https://doi.org/10.1007/979-8-8688-1536-2_2

Principle 1. Temperance: Self-control in relation to the basic drive for survival and pleasure – food, drink, sex, material acquisition. Clearly, these drives are based on the human condition. Every cultural tradition has moral lessons and moral archetypes that encourage self-control and condemn excesses.

Principle 2. Faith, the Microcosm in the Macrocosm: Every cultural tradition has some view of the limits of human powers and condemns human beings when they "overstep the bounds," the Greek hubris.

Principle 3. Justice: Rule for the well-being of the ruled. Every society is a complex network of relationships based on authority. Every society has taught its citizens to rule for the well-being of those over whom they rule (even when the rulers are abusing their power and hiding behind the rhetoric of justice).

Principle 4. Harmony: Personal integrity, the integration of emotions, thoughts, and actions, so one can live one's life in a way that is beautiful and good, always finding the middle group between extremes and doing what is best for the right reason, in the right way, and motivated by the desire to do what is noble because it is noble and for no other reason.

Principle 5. Friendship: This refers to all sorts of relationships – family, friends, employers, teachers, political leaders, doctors, lawyers, people in the business sector who provide all sorts of goods and services.

The quality of one's life is developed and sustained (or undermined and corrupted) by the quality of one's relationships.

Principle 6. Kalokagathia: In Greek, the union of the word for beautiful and the word for goodness or human excellence. A well-functioning adult is exercising all the virtues to the highest level possible: personal, social, political, intellectual, artistic, etc. Such a person is both beautiful and good because they have the qualities that make a natural or cultural artifact beautiful and good: proportionality, adaptability to the surrounding environment, the full flourishing of a natural specimen or an artifact that expresses the wisdom and insight of its creator.

Principle 7. Courage: Knowing how to react in situations involving fear. Human beings are by nature extremely vulnerable, which is why they are so dependent upon each other to meet their needs and to enable each other to survive. A courageous person recognizes vulnerability but does not overreact. They know how to act bravely in a situation of vulnerability and do so because it is the noble thing to do, not to get the approval of others or to avoid social condemnation.

More detailed aspects of each principle and their potential impact and use in AI deployments for organizations are outlined below.

Principle 1: Temperance

Description of Temperance

Temperance, as a principle, in everyday personal life and business operations has to do with the management of emotions, self-control, patience, prudence, humility, civic duties, wealth, mercy, errors, forgiveness, happiness, hate, anger, personal character, trust, truth, listening, speaking, managing time and work, effectiveness, hope, fortune, punishing, association with others, marriage, family, women, children, parents, and living.

Temperance is what the ancient Greeks called "*sophrosyne*": the quality of wise moderation; Greek, "prudence, moderation in desires, discretion, temperance," from "*sophron*" of sound mind, prudent, temperate. Also, it is the practice of always controlling your actions, thoughts, or feelings so that you do not eat or drink too much, become too angry, etc. It denotes self-restraint and self-control. Prudence was considered by the ancient Greeks as the cause, measure, and form of all virtues.

Temperance Quotations

An example of Temperance quotations by noted ancient Greek thinkers is as follows:

The Seven Sages: "Control yourself." "Restrain your anger." "Hold your tongue."

> **Aristotle**: "Good temper is a mean with respect to anger; the middle state being unnamed, and the extremes almost without a name as well, we place good temper in the middle position, though it inclines towards the deficiency, which is without a name. The excess might be called a sort of 'irascibility'. For the passion is anger, while its causes are many and diverse."

The guidance of **Socrates** to his students was "To keep interested in the truth; to make sure that your soul is as good as possible; and to get a good soul, maintain the four virtues of prudence, temperance, courage and justice."

Temperance and AI

In the context of AI, the **Temperance Principle** focuses on the moderation of AI's abilities, particularly in terms of data usage, data security, data quality, data protection, and user privacy. An AI system/solution designed with temperance would respect user privacy, avoid data misuse, and operate within ethical boundaries, not simply exploiting all available technological capabilities for gain. An AI system/solution imbued with temperance would not pursue objectives blindly but would consider the ethical boundaries and potential consequences of its actions. It would also make it paramount that a continuous mechanism is in place to enable humans to review all decisions, outcomes, and results of AI systems/solutions.

The principle of temperance encourages organizations to maintain a balanced and reasoned approach in decisions and actions. It suggests caution against extreme or hasty decisions, excessive risk-taking, and unsustainable growth plans.

Temperance Measures (Example)

An example of measures related to *temperance* that may be implemented by companies to bolster AI deployments includes Management Duty of Care Policies,[2] Business Conduct Handbook, Employee Disciplinary Policy, Data Quality, Data Protection, Managing AI Expectations, etc.

Principle 2: Faith

Description of Faith

Faith, as a principle, in its broadest sense in today's socioeconomic environment, is also a comprehensive sociological term used to refer to the numerous aspects of religiosity, such as religious activity or behavior, devoutness, dedication, and belief in God or Supreme Being and Nature.

Faith in everyday personal life and business operations has to do with the quality of commitment, being ethical and religious, worship, religious and moral behavior, devoutness, beliefs, believing in the existence of God, praying, meditation, living in agreement with nature, Divine Providence, hope, and Divine Punishment.

Faith: Trust in others, belief in a higher power, being persuaded of something. "*Pistis*," the Greek word for faith, denotes intellectual and emotional acceptance of a proposition. *Pistis*, in Greek mythology, was the personification of good faith, trust, and reliability. She is mentioned together with such other personifications as *Elpis* (Hope), *Sophrosyne* (Prudence), and the *Charites*, who were all associated with honesty and harmony among people.

Faith Quotations

An example of Faith quotations by noted ancient Greek thinkers is as follows:

> **The Seven Sages**: "Follow God." "Worship God." "Pray for happiness." "Pray to fortune."

> **Pindar**: "What is God? It is everything."

> **Plato**: "Goods are of two kinds, Divine and human. And the human goods depend upon the Divine," and "Divinity is beauty, wisdom, goodness and everything that is the same with these."

> **Heraclitus**: "Human laws are the creation of Divine Law, as it (the Divine Law) is superior to all other laws and it is applicable to all people the same way."

Faith and AI

In the context of AI, the **Faith Principle** focuses on aligning AI's abilities, outcomes, and results with the users' and social community's religious virtues and values. Faith influences our attitudes and expectations toward AI. Depending on our faith background and beliefs, we may view AI as a threat or an opportunity, a rival or a partner, a servant or a master. We have to ensure that the AI systems/solutions we deploy are designed with faith aspects and the universal religious values of the major world religions and would respect individual or specific ethnic group religious and moral values, while it would operate within religious boundaries and the UN principles of 2030 agenda[3] ("Human Rights–Based Approach," "Leave No One Behind," and "Gender Equality and Women's Empowerment").

Faith Measures (Example)

Examples of measures related to *faith* that may be implemented by companies to bolster AI deployments include Vision, Mission, and Values Statements, Corporate Ethics Policy, AI Ethics Policy, Environment Protection Policy, etc. See examples in Chapter 3.

Principle 3: Justice

Description of Justice

Justice, as a principle, in everyday personal life and business operations has to do with the law, wealth, application of justice, public office, governance, political system of governing, and protection of homeland, family, and business.

Justice, in its broadest context, includes both the attainment of that which is just and the philosophical discussion of that which is just. It denotes ethical correctness and fairness. In his dialogue in *Republic*, Plato uses Socrates to argue for justice that covers both the just person and the just City-State. Justice, according to Socrates, is a proper, harmonious relationship between the warring parts of the person or city. In ancient Greek culture, "*Dike*" ("justice") was the goddess of justice and the spirit of moral order and fair judgment based on immemorial custom, in the sense of socially enforced rules, standards, and norms.

Justice Quotations

An example of Justice quotations by noted ancient Greek thinkers is as follows:

> **The Seven Sages**: "Obey the law." "Your laws should be old, your dinners fresh."

> **Aristotle**: "Laws govern and should be above all other rules." "There is a law which is superior to all written laws and this is the law of morality."

> **Dimosthenis**: "The soul of every state is its laws. And as every human body dies when its soul is lost, so the state dies when its citizens do not comply with nor respect its laws." "No government can maintain itself if it is based on injustice, betrayal and perjury."

> **Epicurus**: "Among the things held to be just by law, whatever is proved to be of advantage in men's dealings has the stamp of justice, whether or not it be the same for all; but if a man makes a

law and it does not prove to be mutually advantageous, then this
is no longer just. And if what is mutually advantageous varies and
only for a time corresponds to our concept of justice, nevertheless
for that time it is just for those who do not trouble themselves
about empty words, but look simply at the facts."

Justice and AI

In the context of AI, the **Justice Principle** means developing and deploying fair algorithms with no bias, with query capabilities for users, and that do not discriminate on anyone based on biased data or prejudiced software programming techniques. This principle is crucial in applications like hiring or loan approval processes, where the AI must evaluate all applicants on a level playing field, ensuring everyone is given what they rightfully deserve without any kind of favoritism or prejudice. It would also make it paramount that a query mechanism is in place to enable humans (managers, developers, users, etc.) to review and understand better all decisions, outcomes, and results of AI systems/solutions.

Justice, according to the Stoics, isn't simply a legal term but a comprehensive ethical principle that encompasses fairness, equity, respect for others, and commitment to the common good. For Stoics, justice represented living in harmony with others by treating them fairly and respectfully.

This perspective aligns with modern notions of corporate social responsibility, which stresses the importance of businesses behaving in ways that benefit not just shareholders but all stakeholders, including colleagues, customers, and the wider community.

A justice-centered AI strategy is not only about avoiding harm or adhering to rules and regulations. It prioritizes ethical considerations, including fairness, privacy, and transparency. It involves actively ensuring AI models are fair, unbiased, and transparent. It respects data privacy and abides by ethical data collection and usage practices.

Justice Measures (Example)

An example of measures related to *justice* that may be implemented by companies to bolster AI deployments includes Employee Punishment Policy, Workplace Procedural Justice Policy, Anti-Discrimination Policy, Diversity and Inclusion Policy, Corporate Social Responsibility Policy, Data Protection Policy, etc.

Principle 4: Harmony

Description of Harmony

Harmony, as a principle, in everyday personal life and business operations defines how to live in harmony. To live in harmony requires that we be conscious of the hopes and needs that surround us and flexible in our own course of action. In a harmonious relationship, each party at times sets aside their own desires to nurture the relationship itself. We can be in harmony with others only when we are in harmony with ourselves – living true to our deepest sense of what is real and what matters.

Harmony is defined as the agreement in action, opinion, feeling, or sounds in a social setting. The term harmony derives from the Greek word "*harmonía*," meaning "joint, agreement, concord," from the verb "*harmozo*," meaning "to fit together, to join."

To the ancient Greek mentality, harmony was an attribute of beauty. The ancient Greeks believed there to be three "ingredients" to beauty: symmetry, proportion, and harmony. This triad of principles infused their life. They were very much attuned to beauty as an object of love and something that was to be imitated and reproduced in their lives, architecture, education, and politics. They judged life by this mentality. Aristotle believed that the soul is a kind of harmony, for "harmony is a blend or composition of contraries," etc. He says that developing good habits can make a good human being and that practicing the use of The Golden Mean (the desirable middle between two extremes, one of excess and the other of deficiency) when applicable to virtues will allow a human being to live a healthy, happy life. Harmonia (harmony) was the goddess of harmony and concord.

Harmony Quotations

An example of Harmony quotations by noted ancient Greek thinkers is as follows:

> **Aristotle**: "Harmony is a blend or composition of contraries." "And happiness is thought to depend on leisure; for we are busy that we may have leisure, and make war that we may live in peace." "Hate has no place in polite hearts." "The logical man thinks, the wise man doubts and the man who does not know anything is always certain."

Heraclitus: "Opposition brings concord. Out of discord comes the fairest harmony." "Everything flows and nothing abides." "Everything gives way and nothing stays fixed." "Opposition brings concord. Out of discord comes the fairest harmony."

The Seven Sages: "Pursue harmony."

Harmony and AI

In the context of AI, the **Harmony Principle** is about applying ethical knowledge and rules in practical scenarios and models, ensuring that AI actions contribute positively to human welfare and overall harmony. This involves designing AI models that can learn from past interactions and improve their reasoning over time, aligning more closely with manifestations of human harmony. In a world where technology continues to advance at a rapid pace, the harmony between AI and human reasoning remains the key to success in the digital age. It would also make it paramount that a documentation mechanism is in place to explain in simple language with clear examples to humans all logic used in the decisions, outcomes, and results of AI systems/solutions.

Harmony Measures (Example)

An example of measures related to *harmony* that may be implemented by companies to bolster AI deployments includes Wellness Policy,[4] Stress Reduction Policy, Health and Safety Policy, Data Quality Policy, etc.

Principle 5: Friendship

Description of Friendship

Friendship, as a principle, in everyday personal life and business operations has to do with the aspects of living in relation to social interactions, practicing friendship, supporting friends, handling enemies, love, mercy, errors, forgiveness, happiness, education, knowledge, and learning.

Friendship defines how people relate to each other, feel equal to them in most standards, but still respect each other irrespective of their attributes or shortcomings.

Friendship was pivotal in the life of ancient Greeks, and no one could attain happiness and tranquility without it. According to the ancient Greeks, "friendship" ("*filotis*") was more important than money, property, wealth, and other material values. They greeted each other by "Oh Filotis," meaning "Hi my friend."

Ancient Greeks did a lot of activities with their friends: wrestling and gymnastics to keep up fitness as well as athletics, including boxing, discus, running, javelin, and long jump.

Other activities included knucklebones, playing music, and spending time talking with friends and telling stories, playing board games, playing with bow and arrows or slingshots, swimming, having dinner parties (symposia), and going to public gymnasiums.

Friendship was also more than evident in names. There were several such names (over 35) that had the prefix of "phil," denoting friendship (e.g., Phillip = lover of horses, Philomila = friend of harmony, Philiston, Philoklis, etc.) and which were given to the children of ancient Greeks by their parents. **Philotes** (or Filotis) was the semi-goddess (spirit) of friendship and affection.

Friendship Quotations

An example of Friendship quotations by noted ancient Greek thinkers is as follows:

> **Aristotle**: "A true friend is one soul in two bodies." "He who has many friends, has no friends at all." "Friendship is the basic substance of a good life."
>
> **Epicurus**: "The largest of the goods that wisdom creates for a happy life is friendship." "Friendship is the only capable condition for maintaining peace in life." "Every friendship is a virtue by itself. Its beginning, however, is based on good actions." "We should not accept hasty or lazy friends, even though we should, because of friendship, risk them both, in order to attain it." "Friendship moves the whole universe declaring to all people to get up and associate with each other with the best intentions." "We participate in the misfortunes of our friends not with grief but with actions."
>
> **Plato**: "Equality creates friendship." "All of us were not born only for ourselves. One of our parts belongs to our parents, one to our friends and one to our country." "Friendship, freedom, justice, wisdom, courage and moderation are the key values that define a good society." "The happiest people are those people who do not need anyone."

The Seven Sages: "Interact with everyone." "Behave always with courtesy." "Socialize with wise people." "Do not suspect anyone." "Do not acquire friends quickly. When, however, you acquire them, do not reject them quickly."

Friendship and AI

In the context of AI, the **Friendship Principle** is about applying aspects of friendship in practical AI scenarios, ensuring that AI actions contribute positively to human welfare and promote solidarity. This involves designing AI that can learn from past interactions and improve its ethical reasoning over time, aligning more closely with human values. AI heavily relies on vast amounts of data, often of a personal and sensitive nature. Ensure your use of AI does not harm the data privacy and security of individuals that may unknowingly have shared personal information to your AI systems/solutions. It would also make it crucial that decisions, outcomes, and results of AI systems/solutions support individual, social, and environmental well-being.

Friendship Measures (Example)

An example of measures related to *friendship* that may be implemented by companies to bolster AI deployments includes Family Support Policy, No False Advertising Policy, Nature Support Program, Data Protection Policy, Data Quality Policy, etc.

Principle 6: Kalokagathia (Goodness and Kindness)

Description of Kalokagathia (Goodness and Kindness)

Kalokagathia, as a principle, containing both Goodness and Kindness, in everyday personal life and business operations has to do with the aspects of good life, goodness, gratitude, kindness, peace and war, malice and badness, hate, anger, vice, and errors.

This is like a coin of two faces. Goodness defines the state or quality of being good. Kindness is a personal quality that enables an individual to be sensitive to the needs of others and to take personal action and do noble deeds on behalf of others to meet those needs.

It also encompasses personal virtue, courtesy, and moral excellence in character. It may be considered synonymous to the Greek term "christotes," meaning useful (from "chrao" = use), good, honest, upright, and magnanimous.

"Kalokagathia" is a word of Greek origin. It is an ideal of human upbringing, popular in ancient Greece. This meant a combination of both external and internal features, especially physical efficiency and mind and character development. It involves notions of **symmetry** important to Greeks. The word *"kalokagathia"* means the character and conduct of *"kalos kagathos,"* that is, of the perfect and just man; thus, it includes kindness, uprightness, and honesty, attributes that finally lead to happiness.

In classical Greek, the meaning of the word *"kalos"* is linked with the human physique rather than human character; thus, *"kalos"* has to do with the beauty, the harmony, of the body, attained through physical exercise. The word *"agathos"* means the good and virtuous man, who is wise, brave, and just.

Kalokagathia was the semi-goddess (spirit) of nobility and goodness. She was associated with virtue (Greek *"areti"*) and excellence (Greek *"eukleia"*).

Kalokagathia (Goodness and Kindness) Quotations

An example of Kalokagathia (Goodness and Kindness) quotations by noted ancient Greek thinkers is as follows:

> **Aristotle**: "Every art and every inquiry, and similarly every action and pursuit, is thought to aim at some good; and for this reason the good has rightly been declared to be that at which all things aim."

> "Let us again return to the good we are seeking, and ask what it can be. It seems different in different actions and arts; it is different in medicine, in strategy, and in the other arts likewise. What then is the good of each? Surely that for whose sake everything else is done. In medicine this is health, in strategy victory, in architecture a house, in any other sphere something else, and in every action and pursuit the end; for it is for the sake of this that all men do whatever else they do. Therefore, if there is an end for all that we do, this will be the good achievable by action, and if there are more than one, these will be the goods achievable by action."

> **Democritus**: 'Good means not merely to do wrong, but rather not to desire to do wrong.'

> **Epictetus**: "It takes more than just a good-looking body. You've got to have the heart and soul to go with it."

34

The Seven Sages: "Your words should be words of kindness and respect." "Pursue harmonic co-existence." "Praise the good." "Struggle without losing your good reputation." "Do not beautify your external appearance, but you should look to become good in your behavior."

Kalokagathia (Goodness and Kindness) and AI

In the context of AI, the **Kalokagathia (Goodness and Kindness) Principle** translates to the ability of algorithms to make decisions based on goodness and kindness and their manifestations. This principle guides AI to evaluate all potential consequences of its actions, guiding users toward choices that serve long-term benefits.

This would ensure that investment suggestions are not only profitable but also sustainable and ethical. It would also make it necessary that decisions, outcomes, and results of AI systems/solutions support community and social cohesion and well-being in the most effective way.

Kalokagathia (Goodness and Kindness) Measures (Example)

An example of measures related to *Kalokagathia (Goodness and Kindness)* that may be implemented by companies to bolster AI deployments includes Community Relations Policy, Corporate Social Responsibility Policy (see example in Chapter 3), Philanthropic Support Policy, etc.

Principle 7: Courage

Description of Courage

Courage, as a principle, in everyday personal life and business operations has to do with the aspects of Courage, Adjustment, Acceptance, Perseverance and Vitality, Contingency Planning, Bravery and Valor, Risk Management, Decision-Making, Governance, Protection of Homeland, Managing Time and Work, Effectiveness, Education, Knowledge and Stress Coping Skills, Aging, Death, Health, Pleasures, Marriage, Family, Women, Children, Parents, and Conduct and Virtues in life.

Courage is one of the so-called "cardinal values," first identified by Socrates and noted by Plato, his disciple, in *Protagoras*:

Cardinal Value 1: Prudence = Ability to judge between actions at a given time

Cardinal Value 2: Temperance = Practicing self-control, abstention, and moderation

Cardinal Value 3: Courage = Endurance and ability to confront fear and uncertainty

Cardinal Value 4: Justice = Proper moderation between self-interest and the need of others

Plato says: "Friendship, freedom, justice, wisdom, courage and moderation are the key values that define a good society."

It is also one of the four cardinal virtues of the Stoic philosophy: Wisdom (*Sophia*), Courage (*Andreia*), Justice (*Dikaiosyne*), and Temperance (*Sophrosyne*).

Courage Quotations

An example of Courage quotations by noted ancient Greek thinkers is as follows:

Seven Sages: "Carry out your activities with no fear and without losing your courage."

Agesilaus the Second, 443–359 BC, King of Sparta (401–360 BC):

"Courage is of no value unless accompanied by justice; yet if all men became just, there would be no need for courage."

Aristotle: "The courageous man acts for the sake of the noble or the beautiful, but the ordinary courage of the citizen is undertaken in pursuit of honor, which is something noble, and for fear of shame." "You will never do anything in this world without courage. It is the greatest quality of the mind next to honor."

Epicurus: "You don't develop courage by being happy in your relationships every day. You develop it by surviving difficult times and challenging adversity."

Thucydides: "The secret of happiness is freedom. The secret of freedom is courage."

Courage and AI

In the context of AI, the **Courage Principle** involves AI developers and programmers to take ethical stands in developing AI systems, even when they are not the easiest or most popular paths. It means creating systems that can, for instance, flag unethical practices in corporate environments or challenge incorrect but widely accepted data.

In an AI context, courage inspires businesses to innovate and invest in disruptive technologies. It emboldens companies to adopt AI and transformative digital experiences (e.g., the shift to intelligent assistants) even when the outcomes are uncertain and the learning curve of teams is steep. Organizations need the courage to fail, learning from every experiment and viewing "failure" as a stepping-stone toward eventual success.

It would also make it paramount that inclusivity is considered and included in the design and operation of an AI system/solution to make all decisions, outcomes, and results of AI systems/solutions fair and just to humans.

Courage Measures (Example)

An example of measures related to *courage* that may be implemented by companies to bolster AI deployments includes AI Incident Management Procedure, AI Results Review Procedure, Business Continuity Plan, Staff Training Policy, etc. See examples in Part VII (Appendix).

Outcome, Results, and Outputs

The main outcome, result, and output of this chapter are the production of "**The Seven Ancient Greek Wisdom Principles handbook**" (in both printed and digital formats). This may be used for awareness, reference, and training purposes by company managers and staff, as well as compliance and auditing purposes by internal corporate functions and external regulatory authorities and audit partners.

Recommendations

As regards the better use of the above-described Seven Ancient Greek Wisdom Principles (Temperance, Faith, Justice, Harmony, Friendship, Kalokagathia (Goodness and Kindness), and Courage) for your AI environment, the following recommendations (REC) are proposed:

> REC 1. Review all these seven principles and consider how they impact your AI systems/solutions in your operating landscape and how you may utilize them.

REC 2. Prepare and issue them as a **product** with the title "Seven Ancient Greek Wisdom Principles handbook." See the examples of measures included in the description of each principle and ensure you consider them in Chapter 8, Step B1-6 (Determine AI ethical principles and values).

REC 3. Ensure all your AI staff and relevant managers and board members are fully aware of their concepts and principles and trained, as required, on applying them in your AI ecosystem and its AI systems/solutions.

Conclusion

In conclusion, when it comes to AI, ensure you use the Seven Ancient Greek Wisdom Principles (Temperance, Faith, Justice, Harmony, Friendship, Kalokagathia (Goodness and Kindness), and Courage) to develop a thoughtful, measured approach to implementing new AI technologies.

Instead of rushing to adopt every new AI tool, solution, model, or trend, you should thoroughly evaluate the potential benefits and risks, considering factors like cost, feasibility, ethical implications, and alignment with your broader business objectives. Develop a balanced portfolio for AI systems/solutions by diversifying risk instead of pouring all resources (and risk) into one AI project.

These principles may also play a role in managing the expectations and hype around AI. You must resist the temptation to see AI as a magic solution that can solve all your problems. Instead, you should recognize that while AI can be a powerful tool, it also has limitations and must be used wisely.

This chapter also described how the Seven Ancient Greek Wisdom Principles (Temperance, Faith, Justice, Harmony, Friendship, Kalokagathia (Goodness and Kindness), and Courage) may be applied in your AI environment with examples of measures, such as

Management Duty of Care Policies; Business Conduct Handbook; Employee Disciplinary Policy, Managing AI Expectations; Vision, Mission, and Values Statements; Corporate Ethics Policy; AI Ethics Policy; Environment Protection Policy; Employee Punishment Policy; Workplace Procedural Justice Policy; Anti-Discrimination

Policy; Diversity and Inclusion Policy; Wellness Policy; Stress
Reduction Policy; Health and Safety Policy; Data Quality Policy;
Family Support Policy; No False Advertising Policy; Nature
Support Program; Community Relations Policy; Corporate Social
Responsibility Policy; Philanthropic Support Policy; AI Incident
Management Procedure; AI Results Review Procedure; Business
Continuity Plan; Staff Training Policy; etc.

This is the first part of the **second** milestone (***Define a robust AI ethics framework***)
of your AI Ecosystem Journey. The next chapter continues this exciting journey by
describing several Corporate Philosophy Statements and Policies.

CHAPTER 3

Corporate Philosophy Statements and Policies

Albert Schweitzer: "The first step in the evolution of ethics is a sense of solidarity with other human beings."[1]

Overview: This chapter contains a set of three statements and seven policies on issues related to implementing and operating an AI ecosystem (infrastructure, systems, solutions, tools, etc.) in a beneficial way, such as AI Vision, AI Mission, and AI Values Statements; Conflict of Interest Policy; AI Ethical Standards Policy; Corporate Ethics Policy; Corporate Social Responsibility Policy; Corporate Diversity Policy; Environment Protection Policy; and Data Ethics Policy.

These statements and policies are the second part of *Component 1: Corporate Philosophical Framework (of the AI Management System)*.

More details about how these statements and policies are applied to support and permeate your AI ecosystem are included in Chapter 8.

Typical examples of such statements and policies are detailed next.

CPP01: AI Vision, AI Mission, and AI Values Statements

> **AI Vision**: "Establish an effective AI ecosystem to enable development of AI systems and solutions to benefit mankind for my business organization (Company AXZ (FICTITIOUS ENTITY))."

© John Kyriazoglou 2025
J. Kyriazoglou, *AI Management Framework*, https://doi.org/10.1007/979-8-8688-1536-2_3

AI Mission: "Craft and implement an AI strategy and relevant policies, procedures, and action plans to use AI to improve company operations and results, support customers better, and benefit the communities we belong to."

AI Values: "The company management and board will use the following values to manage our AI ecosystem (infrastructure, systems/solutions) as best as possible and align with the adopted Seven Ancient Greek Wisdom Principles (Temperance, Faith, Justice, Harmony, Friendship, Kalokagathia (Goodness and Kindness), and Courage)).

Value 1: Commitment. Commit to AI, our company's vision, our families, our country, and human wellness.

Value 2: Conviction. Align AI actions with corporate beliefs and convictions, the Supreme Being, and nature.

Value 3: Cooperation. Implement AI by cooperating with others for the greater good of all.

Value 4: Coexistence. Utilize AI to improve company operations, products, and services so that everyone lives better (our employees, customers, community members, and stakeholders)."

CPP02: Conflict of Interest Policy

Article 1. Prohibition declaration

1.1.   It is the policy of Organization "XYZ" (a fictitious company, "the Company") to prohibit its management and employees from engaging in any activity, practice, or conduct which conflicts with, or appears to conflict with, the interests of the Company (business, operations, projects, IT systems, AI systems/solutions, etc.), its customers, or its major suppliers.

1.2.   Since it is quite impossible to describe all of the situations that might cause or give the appearance of a conflict of interest, the prohibitions included in this policy are not intended to be exhaustive and include only some of the most clear and lucid examples.

Article 2. Representation

2.1.   All managers and employees are expected to represent the Company in a positive and ethical manner. Thus, managers and employees have an obligation to avoid conflicts of interest and to refer questions and concerns about potential conflicts to their manager.

Article 3. Policy acknowledgment

3.1.   Senior Management and others who have contact with customers and major suppliers may be required to sign a special statement acknowledging their understanding of and adherence to this policy.

Article 4. Staff conduct

4.1.   Managers and employees may not engage in, directly or indirectly either on or off the job, any conduct that is disloyal, disruptive, competitive, or damaging to the Company.

Article 5. Outside employment

5.1.   No employee, excluding the office of the Chairman and Vice Chairman, shall engage in any outside employment with a business organized for profit without first obtaining approval of the Director of Human Resources.

5.2.   Approval may not be given if the outside employment interferes in any manner with the proper and effective performance of the person's official duties, creates a conflict of interest, or involves rendering advice or exercising opinion that is based on information, reports, or analysis, access to or availability of which results primarily from or through employment with the Company.

Article 6. Application and Compliance Framework

6.1.   Compliance: Any violations, partial or full non-compliance, etc., of the rules, concepts, and principles embodied in this policy by the employees or anyone else will not be tolerated by the company.

6.2.   Correction: The company will quickly take all necessary administrative and legal measures to correct any issue that may arise.

6.3.   Violation: Anyone found to have violated or failed to comply with these principles (as set forth herein) may be subject to various penalties. These are defined in the internal operating regulations, policies, and procedures of the company and in other national legislative and regulatory frameworks. Indicatively, these penalties include the interruption of work, the dismissal of an employee, the cancellation of the work and contractual arrangements of partners, the resignation of a member of the board of directors, etc.

Article 7. Other complementary policies

Other policies that complement this policy include corporate ethics policy, wellness policies, environment protection policy, human rights policy, etc.

Revision History

Version Number: ... Original Creation Date: ...

Created By: ... Approved By: ... Created By: ...

Last Revised Date: ... Revised By: ... Approved By: ...

Journal of Changes: ...

CPP03: AI Ethical Standards Policy

Overview

The company's "Artificial Intelligence (AI) Ethical Standards Policy" (hereinafter "Policy"), <Company or Organization Logo, Title, Business Address, Website, etc.> (hereinafter referred to as "Company"), contains the framework and general rules, characteristics, and limitations that determine the use of ethics embodied in all AI solutions and their results used by all employees of the company at all corporate levels of the organization.

Objective

The objective of this policy is to define the ethical framework followed for the deployment and use of AI solutions by the company's personnel, in order to ensure that results and outcomes of all AI solutions are just, fair, beneficial, and cause no harm to any people, general society, or the environment.

Applicability

This policy applies to every employee, full-time or part-time, of the company, without discrimination of gender, position in the hierarchy, etc. This policy may also be applied to temporary employees only after management approval and does not apply to external partners or other specialist consultants for service, maintenance, etc.

Policy Principles (PP)

PP1. Our strategic vision is to apply the Harmony Mnemonic (see Annex 1) and use its AI Vision, Mission, and Values (see "CPP01: AI Vision, AI Mission, and AI Values Statements") and other aspects to deploy AI solutions to solve real-world problems, because we believe AI can create a better future for all.

PP2. Our commitment is to build a culture of responsible innovation with a governance architecture that brings the values and principles of ethical, fair, and safe AI to life, people, society, and environment.

PP3. We will ensure that the AI systems/solutions deployed will accomplish several goals:

> Goal 1: They will be ethically permissible by considering the impacts they may have on the well-being of affected stakeholders and communities.

> Goal 2: They will be just, fair, and non-discriminatory by accounting for their potential to have any discriminatory effects on individuals, social groups, and greater society.

> Goal 3: They will be worthy of public trust by guaranteeing to the maximum extent possible the privacy, safety, accuracy, reliability, and security of their outcomes and results.

Goal 4: They will be justifiable in terms of both the transparency of the process by which the AI models are designed and implemented and the transparency and interpretability of their decisions and behaviors.

PP4. When we use AI to create content, that content will be sourced from our own high-quality data and our own previously published work and will be carefully fact-checked by expert company staff to ensure accuracy and appropriateness.

PP5. Every piece of content we publish is factual, original, and edited by a human, whether it's created by a human alone or assisted by any AI tools and techniques.

PP6. Authors and creators are always credited for their work.

PP7. Any AI tools and techniques we may use, develop, deploy, test, or adopt will include staff training on processes that prioritize accurate sourcing and meet legitimate standards of citation.

PP8. Our use of AI is guided in part by a working group of corporate staff from across our organization who regularly meet to collaborate on principles of ethics (see Ancient Greek Wisdom Principles (Chapter 2) and AI Guidelines (Chapter 4)), relevant laws, regulations, and guidelines that establish how we work with new and emerging AI tools and techniques.

Application and Compliance Framework

Compliance: Any violations, partial or full non-compliance, etc., of the rules, concepts, and principles embodied in this document by the employees or anyone else will not be tolerated by the company.

Correction: The company will quickly take all necessary administrative and legal measures to correct any issue that may arise.

Violation: Anyone found to have violated or failed to comply with these principles (as set forth herein) may be subject to various penalties. These are defined in the internal operating regulations, policies, and procedures of the company and in other national legislative and regulatory frameworks. Indicatively, these penalties include the interruption of work, the dismissal of an employee, the cancellation of the work and contractual arrangements of partners, the resignation of a member of the board of directors, etc.

Other Complementary Policies

Other policies that complement this policy include corporate ethics policy, conflicts of interest, wellness policies, environment protection policy, human rights policy, etc.

Revision History

Version Number: ... Original Creation Date: ... Created By: ...

Approved By: ... Created By: ... Last Revised Date: ...

Revised By: ... Approved By: ... Journal of Changes: ...

Annex 1: Harmony Mnemonic

H: Harmonize: Use the Harmony Principle to deploy AI systems/ solutions that enable people at all levels of the company and in all walks of society to be able to act with a harmony between desires, thoughts, and actions, so that all people can live their lives with integrity at work and can take that model of an integrated life with them into all other aspects of their lives.

A: Act: Use the Faith Principle to deploy AI systems/solutions that continually make people to desire to be active, as Aristotle and other Greeks understood it: to develop and exercise as many of the natural activities of soul as possible; employees will be inspired to do their jobs well, to work well with others, to anticipate problems and prevent them, etc.

R: Resolve: Use the Temperance Principle to deploy AI systems/ solutions that support the ability to act well at the critical moment; everyone has good opinions, but it takes resolve to be able to know what to do in a given moment and to then do it; encourage this character trait throughout the organization.

M: Manage: Use the Kalokagathia Principle to deploy AI systems/ solutions that support the art of managing all aspects of one's life, private and public, with a view of exercising all the virtues and justice and benefit all.

O: Organize: Use the Justice Principle to deploy AI systems/ solutions that enable the ability to calculate the most efficient means to achieving a given goal; encourage employees to be continually thinking of better ways to do their jobs or to organize some aspect of the company (what they know most about) or some new way to respond to the external cultural climate (employees each know something different about the external culture; a good employer gains from listening to these views).

N: Nourish: Use the Friendship Principle to deploy AI systems/ solutions that enable people to take time to find out about all other aspects of the culture, to meet people from different walks of life, to nurture the young (children), and to mentor the youth, to relax, reflect, and engage in many different activities that are part of human flourishing.

Y: Yield: Use the Courage Principle to deploy AI systems/ solutions that facilitate people to acknowledge higher truths and powers beyond one's control, to learn to accept one's limits, and to acknowledge all types of excellence and truth and challenge decisions of AI systems/solutions, as needed.

CPP04: Corporate Ethics Policy

Article 1. The Ethics Policy of Company "XXX" sets forth the values and ethics of service to guide and support all Board Members, Executive Management, Middle and Lower Level, Non-executive Directors, Employees, External Consultants, and Maintenance Contractors (termed *Company parties*) in all their professional activities.

    Article 2. In carrying out the Company's business, all *Company parties* often learn and have access to sensitive, confidential, or proprietary data, information, trade secrets, IT systems, AI Systems/Solutions and their models and algorithms, and transactions about the Company, its activities, customers, suppliers, or joint venture and joint project partners. This Policy prohibits the unauthorized disclosure or use of sensitive, confidential, or proprietary data, trade secrets, and information about the Company, its customers, suppliers, or joint venture and joint project partners.

Article 3. No *Company party* entrusted with or otherwise knowledgeable about information of a sensitive, confidential, or proprietary nature shall disclose, give, or use that data, trade secret, information, or transactions outside the Company or for personal gain, either during or after employment or other service to the Company, without the valid and proper written Company authorization to do so given by a manager or employee with the authority to release sensitive, confidential, or proprietary information, data, or transactions. An unauthorized disclosure could be harmful to the Company or helpful to a competitor or third party.

Article 4. The Company also works with proprietary data owned by joint venture partners and suppliers and by customers. The protection of such data is of the highest importance and must be managed with the greatest attention and care for the Company to merit the continued confidence of such parties. No *Company party* shall disclose or use sensitive, confidential, or proprietary information owned by someone other than the Company to anyone without Company written authorization, nor shall any such person disclose the information to others unless a need-to-know basis is established and approved.

Article 5. All staff are required to sign at the time of employment a proprietary information agreement that restricts disclosure of proprietary, trade secrets, and certain other data and information about the Company, its joint venture partners, suppliers, and customers. This Policy applies to all *Company parties* without regard to whether such agreements have been formally signed.

Article 6. All *Company parties* should not have private interests, other than those permitted by these measures, that would be affected particularly or significantly by actions in which they participate.

Article 7. They should not solicit or accept transfers of economic benefit. They should not step out of their official roles to assist private persons in their dealings with the Company where this would result in undue preferential treatment to the persons.

Article 8. They should not knowingly take advantage of, or benefit from, information that is obtained in the course of their official duties and that is not generally available.

Article 9. All *Company parties* may engage in employment and business activities outside the Company only when they are specifically authorized to do so.

Article 10. All *Company parties* must perform all duties to the fullest extent of their capabilities, ensure that all confidential information that is made available to them by virtue of their position is not divulged without written permission, avail themselves of information and material that will improve their effectiveness for all matters relating to the business of the Company or their profession, and actively participate in all activities of their Professional Association including liaison with other members in the exchange of information and professional development.

Article 11. All *Company parties* must use their best judgment to avoid situations of real or perceived conflict. In doing so, they must not accept or solicit any gifts, hospitality, or other benefits that may have a real or apparent influence on their objectivity in carrying out their official duties or that may place them or the Company under obligation to the donor.

Article 12. Any *Company party* which wants to raise, inform, discuss, and clarify issues related to this policy should first talk with their manager or contact the senior official designated by the Board for ethics issues, according to the procedures and conditions established by the Board.

Article 13. All *Company parties* shall report, in person or in writing, any known or suspected violations of governmental laws, rules, and regulations or this Ethics Policy to the Company's President, Chief Financial Officer, or head of the Audit Committee.

Article 14. This Policy applies to all *Company parties* working for the Company.

Article 15. Other complementary policies

Other policies that complement this policy include corporate ethics policy, conflicts of interest, wellness policies, environment protection policy, human rights policy, etc.

Revision History

Version Number: ... Original Creation Date: ...

Created By: ... Approved By: ... Created By: ...

Last Revised Date: ... Revised By: ...

Approved By: ... Journal of Changes: ...

CPP05: Corporate Social Responsibility Policy

Corporate Social Responsibility Policy – Example

"Our business is focused on delivering essential products and services to millions of people every day. By understanding our impact on society, the economy, and the wider environment, we can develop positive relationships with stakeholders to benefit both business and the community. Outlining our approach to corporate responsibility with details of the policies and initiatives that illustrate our commitments includes

1. **Market**: Ensure our core products and services (including IT systems and AI systems/solutions) as well as the way we buy and sell goods and services impact society in a beneficial way.

2. **Environment**: Ensure we have good impact on the environment and we always strive to reduce any impact our business has on the environment.

3. **Workplace**: Ensure we support our employees within our working environment to help them balance the competing demands of work (IT, AI, etc.) and their life.

4. **Community**: Ensure we achieve positive impact in local communities through our community investment program.

5. **Diversity**: Ensure we manage key diversity issues through developing a greater understanding of AI technology, customer, and employee needs.

6. **Alignment**: Ensure all corporate policies (HR, Sales, IT, AI, etc.) are aligned with our corporate strategic vision, mission, and values in order to serve all people in a better way."

CPP06: Corporate Diversity Policy

Your Corporate Diversity Policy might be as follows:

"We appreciate the importance of creating an environment in which all of our employees can feel valued, included, and empowered to bring great ideas to our workplace and to the way we do business. It is the policy of our company not to discriminate against or harass any person employed or seeking employment with our company on the basis of race, color, national origin, religion, sex, gender identity, pregnancy, physical or mental disability, medical condition, ancestry, marital status, age, sexual orientation, citizenship, or military status.

This policy applies to all employment practices, including personnel recruitment, selection, promotion, transfer, merit increase, salary, training and development, demotion, and separation.

Our diversity and inclusion efforts will therefore focus on

1. Leading, managing, and embracing different cultures, ethnicities, genders, and sexual orientations.

2. Creating a work environment that fosters growth and advancement.

3. Engaging with our customers in a way that reflects and respects their unique perspectives and experiences.

4. Monitoring our company performance as regards our diversity objectives on a continuous basis and report our progress toward achieving them on an annual basis."[2]

CPP07: Environment Protection Policy

A typical example of such a policy is
"The Company shall"

1. Meet or surpass all environmental legislation, regulations, and other applicable requirements and continuously improve the company's environmental performance consistent with defined goals.

2. Fully integrate environmental and economic considerations into the company's processes of planning, constructing, operating, and decommissioning.

3. Ensure that the environmental impacts and risks of company activities are identified, assessed, and managed.

4. Proactively advocate socially responsible laws and regulations and, where appropriate, market-based and voluntary approaches for achieving environmental objectives.

5. Inform and encourage meaningful consultation and collaboration with employees, customers, contractors, and the public related to the company's operations and its impact on the environment.

6. Be an environmentally responsible neighbor in the communities in which the company operates.

7. The company will act promptly and responsibly to correct incidents or conditions that endanger the environment and inform those who may be affected; achieve ongoing improvements in eco-efficiency through reductions in wastes and emissions per unit of electrical and thermal energy produced and delivered.

8. Identify and develop new business practices, AI systems/solutions, and business opportunities which represent solutions to environmental problems and create value for shareholders.

9. Use a performance assurance process to assess compliance with this policy and the company's environmental management system.

10. Performance assurance results will be reported periodically to the board of directors.

11. Use an environmental protection management system to set environmental protection objectives and targets that support this policy and regularly review performance against these objectives with senior management.

12. Make all staff aware and ensure they are trained on ways to protect the environment.

CPP08: Data Ethics Policy

Overview

The company's "Data Ethics Policy" (hereinafter "Policy"), <Company or Organization Logo, Title, Business Address, Website, etc.> (hereinafter referred to as "Company"), contains the framework and general rules, characteristics, and limitations that determine the use of ethics in collecting, managing, and using data in all information systems and all AI systems/solutions of the company. The principles of data ethics are described in two parts: Principles of Data Ethics for AI and Data Ethics Principles for Personal Data.

Objective

The objective of this policy is to formally state the data ethics principles of "XYZ Fictitious Company S.A." (herein, the "Company") and describe the overall ways on how the company process data (personal and other) to develop and operate AI systems/solutions.

Applicability

This policy applies to all aspects of data collected, used, and processed by the Company and to every employee, full-time or part-time, of the company, without discrimination of gender, position in the hierarchy, etc. This policy may also be applied to temporary employees only after management approval and does not apply to external partners or other specialist consultants for service, maintenance, etc.

Definition of Data Ethics

Data ethics refers to the principles behind how organizations gather, protect, and use data. It's a field of ethics that focuses on the moral obligations that entities have (or should have) when collecting and disseminating information about us. In a world where data is more valuable and ubiquitous than ever, data ethics issues are more pressing now than at any time in history.

Data ethics is about responsible and sustainable use of data. It is about doing the right thing for people and society. Data processes should be designed as sustainable solutions benefitting first and foremost humans.

Data ethics refer and adhere to the principles and values on which human rights and personal data protection laws are based.

Data ethics is the step further than mere compliance with personal data protection laws: all data processing therefore respects as a minimum the requirements set out in the EU's General Data Protection Regulation (GDPR), the Charter of Fundamental Rights of the European Union, and the European Convention on Human Rights.[3]

Part A: Principles of Data Ethics for AI

According to the independent European Data Ethics Think Tank,[4] the following data ethics principles should be taken into consideration in designing, developing, and deploying AI systems/solutions: the Human Being at the Center, Individual Data Control, Transparency, Accountability, and Equality.

Principle A1. The Human Being at the Center

Human interests always prevail for institutional and commercial interests. People are not computer processes or pieces of software, but unique with empathy, self-determination, unpredictability, intuition, and creativity and therefore have a higher status than machines. The human being is at the center and has the primary benefit of data processing.

Principle A2. Individual Data Control

Humans should be in control of their data and empowered by their data. A person's self-determination should be prioritized in all data processes, and the person should be actively involved in regard to the data recorded about them. The individual has the primary control over the usage of their data, the context in which their data is processed, and how it is activated.

Principle A3. Transparency

Data processing activities and automated decisions must make sense for the individual. They must be truly transparent and explainable. The purpose and interests of data processing must be clearly understood by the individual in terms of understanding risks, as well as social, ethical, and societal consequences.

Principle A4. Accountability

Accountability is an organization's reflective, reasonable, and systematic use and protection of personal data. Accountability is an integral part of all aspects of data processing, and efforts are being made to reduce the risks for the individual and to mitigate social and ethical implications. Sustainable personal data processing is embedded throughout the organization and ensures ethical accountability in the short, medium, and long term. An organization's accountability should also apply to subcontractor's and partners' processing of data.

Principle A5. Equality

Democratic data processing is based on an awareness of the societal power relations that data systems sustain, reproduce, or create. When processing data, special attention should be paid to vulnerable people, who are particularly vulnerable to profiling that may adversely affect their self-determination and control or expose them to discrimination or stigmatization, for example, due to their financial, social, or health-related conditions. Paying attention to vulnerable people also involves working actively to reduce bias in the development of self-learning algorithms.

Part B: Data Ethics Principles for Personal Data

When the Company processes personal data (PD) or designs, develops, acquires, or implements technologies for processing of PD, the principles for data ethics outlined below must be reviewed, considered, evaluated, and included in the considerations during the whole process (design, develop, acquire, implement) before the initiation of this process.

Principle B1. Legality. The processing of PD shall, at all times, comply with applicable privacy legislation and their related processing principles (e.g., GDPR (Articles 5–13), LGPD (Articles 2, 6–14), PIPEDA, etc.). PD shall be processed in ways that are consistent with the purpose stated to data subjects at the time of collection. PD may be processed for new purposes only upon the consent of the data subjects involved, unless legal requirements prevail.

Principle B2. Necessity. Only PD which are necessary to fulfill the purpose of the processing activity shall be collected and processed.

Principle B3. Transparency. PD shall always be processed in a way which ensures transparency, especially where algorithms are used for the processing. Furthermore, when the processing activity includes automated decision-making for decisions which have legal or similarly significant effects, the results shall be subject to human review.

Principle B4. Impact. The consequences of the processing activity and the technology used for the processing activity shall be considered, especially where new technology is used for the processing of PD. In such cases, the consequences for the individuals, both on short term and long term, shall be taken into effect, on the basis of a Privacy or Data Protection Impact Assessment on the risks involved and the potential harm to individuals.

Principle B5. Security. A sufficient level of security technical and organizational measures shall be implemented in the processing of PD. The sufficient level of security shall be assessed based on a risk assessment of the specific processing activity and the technology used for the processing of PD. PD will only be stored as long as necessary and deleted safely, thereafter, as per relevant Data Protection Regime applicable to the Company.

Principle B6. Human Rights. Processing of PD and the technologies used for processing of PD shall ensure that human rights are respected so that the risks of discrimination, marginalization, or stigmatization against individuals are completely avoided.

Principle B7. Staff Training. The Company ensures that employees, who, as a part of their job with the Company, process PD or are engaged in designing, developing, acquiring, or implementing technologies for the processing of PD, receive training in the principles for data ethics described above, at least once a year.

Review and Changes

The Board of Directors shall review and assess the adequacy of this policy, as required and, at least, on an annual basis, to ensure that it always reflects the Company's data ethics considerations.

Other Complementary Policies

Other policies that complement this policy include Data Governance Policy (Appendix 13), Data Quality Policy (Appendix 14), Data Quality Improvement Procedure (Appendix 15), Corporate Ethics Policy, conflicts of interest, wellness policies, environment protection policy, human rights policy, etc.

Outcomes, Results, and Outputs

The main outcomes, results, and outputs of this chapter include the following types of products:

> **Type 5. Administrative support controls**. This includes issuing, sharing, and retaining on file: AI Vision, AI Mission, and AI Values Statements.
>
> **Type 6. AI governance, development, and operations support controls**. This includes issuing, sharing, using, implementing, and keeping current policies and procedures, such as Conflict of Interest Policy, AI Ethical Standards Policy, Corporate Ethics Policy, Corporate Social Responsibility Policy, Corporate Diversity Policy, Environment Protection Policy, and Data Ethics Policy.

All these may be implemented at the appropriate AI Implementation phase. Also, they may be used for awareness, reference, and training purposes by company managers and staff, as well as compliance and auditing purposes by internal corporate functions and external regulatory authorities and audit partners.

Recommendations

As regards the better use of the above-described three statements (AI Vision, AI Mission, and AI Values Statements) and seven policies (Conflict of Interest Policy, AI Ethical Standards Policy, Corporate Ethics Policy, Corporate Social Responsibility Policy, Corporate Diversity Policy, Environment Protection Policy, and Data Ethics Policy), the following recommendations (REC) are proposed:

REC 1. Review all these statements and policies and consider how they impact your AI systems/solutions in your operating landscape and how you may utilize them.

REC 2. Prepare and issue them as a set of products with the title **"Corporate Philosophy Statements and Policies handbook."** This will include

Product 1: AI Vision, AI Mission, and AI Values Statements

Product 2: Conflict of Interest Policy

Product 3: AI Ethical Standards Policy

Product 4: Corporate Ethics Policy

Product 5: Corporate Social Responsibility Policy

Product 6: Corporate Diversity Policy

Product 7: Environment Protection Policy

Product 8: Data Ethics Policy

REC 3. Ensure you consider them in Chapter 8 (Establish AI Governance), Step B1-6 (Determine AI ethical principles and values), and use them as defined above or improve them, as required.

REC 4. Ensure all your AI staff and relevant managers and board members are fully aware of their concepts and principles and trained, as required, on applying them in your AI ecosystem and its AI systems/solutions.

REC 5. Ensure you keep current all above statements and policies, by reviewing them and updating them every two to three years or as needs, expectations, and operating conditions and circumstances warrant.

Conclusion

This chapter described three statements and seven policies on issues related to implementing and operating an AI ecosystem (infrastructure, systems, solutions, tools, etc.) in a beneficial way, such as AI Vision, AI Mission, and AI Values Statements, Conflict of Interest Policy, AI Ethical Standards Policy, Corporate Ethics Policy, Corporate Social Responsibility Policy, Corporate Diversity Policy, Environment Protection Policy, and Data Ethics Policy. Also, several recommendations regarding their best application were made.

These statements and policies are complemented by other relevant policies, as described in the previous chapter, such as Management Duty of Care Policies, Managing AI Expectations, Wellness Policy, Stress Reduction Policy, Health and Safety Policy, Data Quality Policy, etc.

This and the previous chapter supported you to achieve your **second** milestone in your AI Ecosystem Journey: ***Define a robust AI ethics framework***. This is deemed to be the first prerequisite for preparing for AI and developing, deploying, and improving AI systems/solutions for your company's AI ecosystem.

The next three chapters (Part III) continue this exciting journey by describing several AI Global Standards and Guidelines (Chapter 4), Major Data Protection Laws and Privacy by Design Framework Principles (Chapter 5), and Digital and Secure AI System Development Guidelines (Chapter 6).

PART III

AI Regulations and Standards

Part III contains

Reviewing the impact of AI standards, AI guidelines, and related privacy and digital guidelines and considering compliance and development actions required to be taken in relation to AI supports you to achieve the **third** milestone (***Consider impact of AI regulations and standards***) of your AI Ecosystem Journey.

All these (contents of Chapters 4–6) compose the second component (Legal and Regulatory Environment (external legal and regulatory frameworks and controls)) related to AI of your AI Management System.

CHAPTER 4

AI Global Standards and Guidelines

Gray Scott:[1] "Who gets to decide the robotic bill of rights? It's going to be controversial."

Overview: This chapter presents a summary of the major global AI guidelines, such as ISO/IEC 42001 AI Management System, Australia's AI Ethics Principles, NIST AI Risk Management Framework, Universal Guidelines for Artificial Intelligence, the OECD AI Principles, the EU AI Act, the EU AI Act System Development Principles, and the Responsible AI Principles of three global IT vendors (Microsoft, Google, and IBM).

These guidelines are the first part of *Component 2: Legal and Regulatory Environment (of the AI Management System).*

ISO/IEC 42001 AI Management System

Applicable to all types of company in any industry, ISO/IEC 42001 is the first international management system standard for AI.[2]

The ISO 42001 standard is structured around several core components that are essential for the effective management of AI systems:

- **AI Management Systems (AIMS):** Integration with organizational processes to ensure continuous improvement and alignment with other ISO standards

- **AI Risk Assessment:** A systematic approach to identifying and mitigating risks throughout the AI life cycle

© John Kyriazoglou 2025
J. Kyriazoglou, *AI Management Framework*, https://doi.org/10.1007/979-8-8688-1536-2_4

- **AI Impact Assessment**: Evaluation of the consequences of AI on individuals and societies

- **Data Protection and AI Security**: Emphasis on compliance with privacy laws and safeguarding AI systems against threats

ISO 42001 Standard Responsible AI Principles

A commitment to responsible AI is not a one-time act, but a sustained effort involving vigilance and adaptation, according to ISO 42001: 2023.[3]

Some key principles of responsible AI ethics are

Fairness: Datasets used for training the AI system must be given careful consideration to avoid discrimination.

Transparency: AI systems should be designed in a way that allows users to understand how the algorithms work.

Non-maleficence: AI systems should avoid harming individuals, society, or the environment.

Accountability: Developers, organizations, and policymakers must ensure AI is developed and used responsibly.

Privacy: AI must protect people's personal data, which involves developing mechanisms for individuals to control how their data is collected and used.

Robustness: AI systems should be secure – that is, resilient to errors, adversarial attacks, and unexpected inputs.

Inclusiveness: Engaging with diverse perspectives helps identify potential ethical concerns of AI and ensures a collective effort to address them.

Australia's AI Ethics Principles

Australia's AI Ethics Principles[4] include

- **Human, Societal, and Environmental Well-Being**: AI systems should benefit individuals, society, and the environment.

- **Human-Centered Values**: AI systems should respect human rights, diversity, and the autonomy of individuals.

- **Fairness**: AI systems should be inclusive and accessible and should not involve or result in unfair discrimination against individuals, communities, or groups.

- **Privacy Protection and Security**: AI systems should respect and uphold privacy rights and data protection and ensure the security of data.

- **Reliability and Safety**: AI systems should reliably operate in accordance with their intended purpose.

- **Transparency and Explainability**: There should be transparency and responsible disclosure so people can understand when they are being significantly impacted by AI and can find out when an AI system is engaging with them.

- **Contestability**: When an AI system significantly impacts a person, community, group, or environment, there should be a timely process to allow people to challenge the use or outcomes of the AI system.

- **Accountability**: People responsible for the different phases of the AI system life cycle should be identifiable and accountable for the outcomes of the AI systems, and human oversight of AI systems should be enabled.

NIST AI Risk Management Framework

Formally released on January 26, 2023, the NIST AI Risk Management Framework[5] is a four-part, voluntary framework intended to guide the responsible development and use of AI systems.

The core of the framework is recommendations divided into four overarching functions:

(1) **Govern**, which covers overarching policy decisions and organizational culture around AI development

(2) **Map**, which covers efforts to contextualize AI risks and potential benefits

(3) **Measure**, which covers efforts to assess and quantify AI risks

(4) **Manage**, which covers the active steps an organization should take to mitigate risks and prioritize elements of trustworthy AI systems

Universal Guidelines for Artificial Intelligence

In October 2018, over 250 experts and 60 organizations, representing more than 40 countries, endorsed the Universal Guidelines for Artificial Intelligence ("UGAI"). The guidelines were organized by the Public Voice.[6]

The guidelines in full are

1. **Right to Transparency**: All individuals have the right to know the basis of an AI decision that concerns them. This includes access to the factors, the logic, and techniques that produced the outcome.

2. **Right to Human Determination**: All individuals have the right to a final determination made by a person.

3. **Identification Obligation**: The institution responsible for an AI system must be made known to the public.

4. **Fairness Obligation**: Institutions must ensure that AI systems do not reflect unfair bias or make impermissible discriminatory decisions.

5. **Assessment and Accountability Obligation**: An AI system should be deployed only after an adequate evaluation of its purpose and objectives, its benefits, as well as its risks. Institutions must be responsible for decisions made by an AI system.

6. **Accuracy, Reliability, and Validity Obligations**: Institutions must ensure the accuracy, reliability, and validity of decisions.

7. **Data Quality Obligation**: Institutions must establish data provenance and assure quality and relevance for the data input into algorithms.

8. **Public Safety Obligation**: Institutions must assess the public safety risks that arise from the deployment of AI systems that direct or control physical devices and implement safety controls.

9. **Cybersecurity Obligation**: Institutions must secure AI systems against cybersecurity threats.

10. **Prohibition on Secret Profiling**: No institution shall establish or maintain a secret profiling system.

11. **Prohibition on Unitary Scoring**: No national government shall establish or maintain a general-purpose score on its citizens or residents.

12. **Termination Obligation**: An institution that has established an AI system has an affirmative obligation to terminate the system if human control of the system is no longer possible.

The OECD AI Principles

The OECD AI Principles were adopted in 2019 and endorsed by 42 countries – including the United States, several European countries, and the G20 nations.[7]

The OECD AI Principles establish international standards for AI use:

1. **Inclusive Growth, Sustainable Development, and Well-Being**: AI should benefit people and the planet.

2. **Human-Centered Values and Fairness**: AI systems should be designed in a way that respects the rule of law, human rights, democratic values, and diversity, and they should include appropriate safeguards – for example, enabling human intervention when necessary – to ensure a fair and just society.

3. **Transparency and Explainability**: There should be transparency and a responsible disclosure around AI systems to ensure that people understand AI-based outcomes and can challenge them.

4. **Robustness, Security, and Safety**: AI systems must function in a robust, secure, and safe way throughout their life cycles, and potential risks should be continually assessed and managed.

5. **Accountability**: Organizations and individuals developing, deploying, or operating AI systems should be held accountable for their proper functioning in line with the above principles.

EU AI Act

The EU AI Act is an EU-wide legal framework (Regulation) that sets out clear transparency and reporting obligations for any company placing an AI system on the EU market or companies whose system outputs are used within the EU (regardless of where systems are developed or deployed.[8]

At a minimum, developers and implementers whose technology falls within the high-risk category should be prepared to comply with the following requirements of the AI Act:

1. Register with the centralized EU database

2. Have a compliant quality management system in place

3. Maintain adequate documentation and logs

4. Undergo relevant conformity assessments

5. Comply with restrictions on the use of high-risk AI

6. Continue to ensure regulatory compliance and be prepared to demonstrate such compliance upon request

Fines are expected for

1. Non-compliance with prohibited AI violations resulting in up to 7% of total worldwide annual turnover for the preceding financial year or €35M (whichever is higher)

2. Non-compliance with most other violations resulting in up to 3% of total worldwide annual turnover for the preceding financial year or €15M (whichever is higher)

3. Supplying incorrect, incomplete, or misleading information to notified bodies and national competent authorities in response to a request resulting in up to 1.5% of total worldwide global annual turnover or €7.5M (whichever is higher)

Depending on the risk threshold of your systems, enterprises will have some level of responsibilities that could include

1. **Registration**: Registration of all use cases in the EU database before placing the AI solution on the market or putting it into service.

2. **Classification**: Identification of all high-risk AI use cases.

3. **Risk Management**: Adoption of appropriate and targeted risk management measures to mitigate identified risks.

4. **Data Governance**: Confirmation of the use of high-quality training data, adherence to appropriate data governance practices, and assurance that datasets are relevant and unbiased.

5. **Technical Documentation**: Keeping records containing information which is necessary to assess the compliance of the AI system with the relevant requirements and facilitate post-market monitoring (i.e., the general characteristics, capabilities, and limitations of the system, algorithms, data, training, testing, and validation processes used as well as documentation on the relevant risk management system and should be drawn in a clear and comprehensive form). The technical documentation should be kept up to date, appropriately throughout the lifetime of the AI system (note: high-risk AI systems should technically allow for automatic recording of events (logs) over the duration of the lifetime of the system).

6. **Human Oversight**: Incorporate human-machine interface tools to prevent or minimize risks upfront, enabling users to understand, interpret, and confidently use these tools.

7. **Accuracy, Robustness, and Security**: Ensure consistent accuracy, robustness, and cybersecurity measures throughout the AI system's life cycle.

8. **Quality Management**: Providers of high-risk AI systems must have a quality management system in place documented in a systematic and orderly manner in the form of written policies, procedures, and instructions.

9. **EU Declaration of Conformity**: Draft the declaration of conformity for each high-risk AI system, asserting compliance (kept up to date for 10 years, submitting copies to national authorities, and updating as necessary).

10. **CE Marking**: Ensure that the CE marking is affixed in a visible, legible, and indelible manner or digitally accessible for digital systems, thereby indicating compliance with the general principles and applicable European Union laws.

11. **Incident Reporting**: Providers of high-risk AI systems placed on the European Union market must report any "serious incident" to the market surveillance authorities of the EU Member States where that incident occurred (immediately after the provider has established a causal link between the AI system and the serious incident or the reasonable likelihood of such a link and, in any event, not later than 15 days after the provider or, where applicable, the deployer becomes aware of the serious incident).

EU AI Act System Development Principles

Overview: The EU AI Act includes several AI System Development Principles. These are contained in numerous recitals related to protection of personal data, AI literacy, technical robustness and safety, AI system performance monitoring, etc.

These are described in summary next.

List of Recitals

Recital (2) Protection (persons, law, environment)

Recital (10) Protection of personal data

Recital (20) AI literacy

Recital (27) Technical robustness and safety; privacy and data governance; transparency; diversity, non-discrimination, and fairness; social and environmental well-being; accountability

Recital (42) Natural persons should always be judged on their actual behavior

Recital (48) Protection of fundamental rights

Recital (65) Risk management system

Recital (67) Data governance

Recital (69) Protecting the privacy of personal data

Recital (71) Traceability and compliance

Recital (75) Technical robustness

Recital (76) Cybersecurity

Recital (81) Quality management system

Recital (91) AI system performance monitoring

Description of Recitals (in summary)

Recital (2) Protection of natural persons, undertakings, democracy, the rule of law, and environment

This Regulation should be applied in accordance with the values of the Union enshrined as in the Charter, facilitating the **protection of natural persons**, undertakings, democracy, the rule of law, and environmental protection, while boosting innovation and employment and making the Union a leader in the uptake of trustworthy AI.

Recital (10) Protection of personal data

The fundamental right to the **protection of personal data** is safeguarded in particular by Regulations (EU) 2016/679 and (EU) 2018/172 of the European Parliament and of the Council and Directive (EU) 2016/680 of the European Parliament and of the Council. Directive 2002/58/EC of the European Parliament and of the Council additionally protects private life and the confidentiality of communications, including by way of providing conditions for any storing of personal and non-personal data in and access from terminal equipment, etc. It also does not affect the obligations of providers and deployers of AI systems in their role as data controllers or processors stemming from Union or national law on the protection of personal data insofar as the design, the development, or the use of AI systems involves the processing of personal data.

Recital (20) AI literacy (including interpreting the AI system's output and the knowledge necessary to understand how decisions are taken)

In order to obtain the greatest benefits from AI systems while protecting fundamental rights, health, and safety and to enable democratic control, **AI literacy** should equip providers, deployers, and affected persons with the necessary notions to make informed decisions regarding AI systems. This includes understanding the correct application of technical elements during the AI system's development phase, the measures to be applied during its use, the suitable ways in which to interpret the AI system's output, and, in the case of affected persons, the knowledge necessary to understand how decisions taken with the assistance of AI will have an impact on them, etc.

Recital (27) Technical robustness and safety; privacy and data governance; transparency; diversity, non-discrimination, and fairness; social and environmental well-being; accountability

Technical robustness and safety mean that AI systems are developed and used in a way that allows robustness in the case of problems and resilience against attempts to alter the use or performance of the AI system so as to allow unlawful use by third parties and minimize unintended harm.

Privacy and data governance mean that AI systems are developed and used in accordance with privacy and data protection rules while processing data that meets high standards in terms of quality and integrity.

Transparency means that AI systems are developed and used in a way that allows appropriate traceability and explainability while making humans aware that they communicate or interact with an AI system, as well as duly informing deployers of the capabilities and limitations of that AI system and affected persons about their rights.

Diversity, non-discrimination, and fairness mean that AI systems are developed and used in a way that includes diverse actors and promotes equal access, gender equality, and cultural diversity while avoiding discriminatory impacts and unfair biases that are prohibited by Union or national law.

Social and environmental well-being means that AI systems are developed and used in a sustainable and environmentally friendly manner as well as in a way to benefit all human beings while monitoring and assessing the long-term impacts on the individual, society, and democracy.

Accountability means that the application of those principles should be translated, when possible, in the design and use of AI models. They should in any case serve as a basis for the drafting of codes of conduct under this Regulation. All stakeholders, including industry, academia, civil society, and standardization organizations, are encouraged to take into account as appropriate the ethical principles for the development of voluntary best practices and standards.

Recital (42) Natural persons should always be judged on their actual behavior

In line with the presumption of innocence, natural persons in the Union should always be judged on their actual behavior. Natural persons should never be judged on AI-predicted behavior based solely on their profiling, personality traits, or characteristics, such as nationality, place of birth, place of residence, number of children, level of debt, or type of car, without a reasonable suspicion of that person being involved in a criminal activity based on objective verifiable facts and without human assessment thereof.

Recital (48) Protection of fundamental rights

The extent of the adverse impact caused by the AI system on the fundamental rights protected by the Charter is of particular relevance when classifying an AI system as high risk. Those rights include the right to human dignity, respect for private and family life, protection of personal data, freedom of expression and information, freedom of assembly and of association, non-discrimination, right to education, consumer protection, workers' rights, rights of persons with disabilities, gender equality, intellectual property rights, right to an effective remedy and to a fair trial, right of defense and the presumption of innocence, right to good administration, etc.

Recital (65) Risk management system

The **risk management system** should consist of a continuous, iterative process that is planned and run throughout the entire life cycle of a high-risk AI system. This process should be aimed at identifying and mitigating the relevant risks of AI systems on health, safety, and fundamental rights. The risk management system should be regularly reviewed and updated to ensure its continuing effectiveness, as well as justification and documentation of any significant decisions and actions taken subject to this Regulation, etc.

Recital (67) Data governance

High-quality data and access to high-quality data play a vital role in providing structure and in ensuring the performance of many AI systems, especially when techniques involving the training of models are used, with a view to ensure that the high-risk AI system performs as intended and safely and it does not become a source of discrimination prohibited by Union law. High-quality datasets for training, validation, and testing require the implementation of appropriate data governance and management practices. Datasets for training, validation, and testing, including the labels, should be relevant, sufficiently representative, and to the best extent possible free of errors and complete in view of the intended purpose of the system. In order to facilitate compliance with Union data protection law, such as Regulation (EU) 2016/679, data governance and management practices should include, in the case of personal data, transparency about the original purpose of the data collection, etc.

Recital (69) Protecting the privacy of personal data

The right to **privacy and to protection of personal data** must be guaranteed throughout the entire life cycle of the AI system. In this regard, the principles of data minimization and data protection by design and by default, as set out in Union data protection law, are applicable when personal data are processed. Measures taken by providers to ensure compliance with those principles may include not only anonymization and encryption but also the use of technology that permits algorithms to be brought to the data and allows training of AI systems without the transmission between parties or copying of the raw or structured data themselves, without prejudice to the requirements on data governance provided for in this Regulation, etc.

Recital (71) Traceability and compliance

Having comprehensible information on how high-risk AI systems have been developed and how they perform throughout their lifetime is essential to **enable traceability** of those systems, **verify compliance** with the requirements under this Regulation, as well as monitoring of their operations and post-market monitoring. This requires **keeping records and the availability of a technical documentation, containing information which is necessary to assess the compliance of the AI system** with the relevant requirements and facilitate post-market monitoring. Such information should include the general characteristics, capabilities, and limitations of the system, algorithms, data, training, testing, and validation processes used as well as documentation on the relevant risk management system and should be drawn in a clear and comprehensive form, etc.

Recital (75) Technical robustness

The **technical robustness** is a key requirement for high-risk AI systems. They should be resilient in relation to harmful or otherwise undesirable behavior that may result from limitations within the systems or the environment in which the systems operate (e.g., errors, faults, inconsistencies, unexpected situations). Therefore, technical and organizational measures should be taken to ensure robustness of high-risk AI systems, for example, by designing and developing appropriate technical solutions to prevent or minimize harmful or otherwise undesirable behavior. Those technical solutions may include, for instance, mechanisms enabling the system to **safely interrupt its operation (fail-safe plans)** in the presence of certain anomalies or when operation takes place outside certain predetermined boundaries, etc.

Recital (76) Cybersecurity

Cybersecurity plays a crucial role in ensuring that AI systems are resilient against attempts to alter their use, behavior, or performance or compromise their security properties by malicious third parties exploiting the system's vulnerabilities. Cyberattacks against AI systems can leverage AI-specific assets, such as training datasets (e.g., data poisoning) or trained models (e.g., adversarial attacks or membership inference), or exploit vulnerabilities in the AI system's digital assets or the underlying ICT infrastructure. To ensure a level of cybersecurity appropriate to the risks, suitable measures, such as security controls, should therefore be taken by the providers of high-risk AI systems, also taking into account as appropriate the underlying ICT infrastructure, etc.

Recital (81) Quality management system

The provider should establish a sound **quality management system**, ensure the accomplishment of the required conformity assessment procedure, draw up the relevant documentation, and establish a robust post-market monitoring system. Providers of high-risk AI systems that are subject to obligations regarding quality management systems under relevant sectorial Union law should have the possibility to include the elements of the quality management system provided for in this Regulation as part of the existing quality management system provided for in that other sectoral Union law, etc.

Recital (91) AI system performance monitoring

Given the nature of AI systems and the risks to safety and fundamental rights possibly associated with their use, including as regards the need to ensure proper **monitoring of the performance of an AI system** in a real-life setting, it is appropriate to set specific responsibilities for deployers. Deployers should in particular take appropriate technical and organizational measures to ensure they use high-risk AI systems in accordance with the instructions of use, and certain other obligations should be provided for with regard to monitoring of the functioning of the AI systems and with regard to recordkeeping, as appropriate. Furthermore, deployers should ensure that the **persons** assigned to implement the instructions for use and human oversight as set out in this Regulation have the necessary competence, in particular, an adequate level of AI literacy, training, and authority to properly fulfill those tasks, etc.

Microsoft Responsible AI Standard Principles

The principles of responsible AI, according to Microsoft,[9] are

> **Fairness and Inclusiveness**: AI systems should treat everyone fairly and avoid affecting similarly situated groups of people in different ways. For example, when AI systems provide guidance on medical treatment, loan applications, or employment, they should make the same recommendations to everyone who has similar symptoms, financial circumstances, or professional qualifications.

> **Reliability and Safety**: To build trust, it's critical that AI systems operate reliably, safely, and consistently. These systems should be able to operate as they were originally designed, respond safely to unanticipated conditions, and resist harmful manipulation. How they behave and the variety of conditions they can handle reflect the range of situations and circumstances that developers anticipated during design and testing.

> **Transparency**: When AI systems help inform decisions that have tremendous impacts on people's lives, it's critical that people understand how those decisions were made. For example, a bank might use an AI system to decide whether a person is creditworthy. A company might use an AI system to determine the most qualified candidates to hire.

> **Privacy and Security**: As AI becomes more prevalent, protecting privacy and securing personal and business information are becoming more important and complex. With AI, privacy and

data security require close attention because access to data is essential for AI systems to make accurate and informed predictions and decisions about people. AI systems must comply with relevant privacy laws.

Accountability: The people who design and deploy AI systems must be accountable for how their systems operate. Organizations should draw upon industry standards to develop accountability norms. These norms can ensure that AI systems aren't the final authority on any decision that affects people's lives. They can also ensure that humans maintain meaningful control over otherwise highly autonomous AI systems.

Google Responsible AI Practices

The principles of responsible AI, according to Google,[10] are as follows:

Use a human-centered design approach

Example of actions:

Design features with appropriate built-in disclosures: clarity and control are crucial to a good user experience.

Engage with a diverse set of users and use-case scenarios, and incorporate feedback before and throughout project development. This will build a rich variety of user perspectives into the project and increase the number of people who benefit from the technology.

Identify multiple metrics to assess training and monitoring

Example of actions:

Consider metrics including feedback from user surveys, quantities that track overall system performance and short- and long-term product health (e.g., click-through rate and customer lifetime value, respectively), and false positive and false negative rates sliced across different subgroups.

Ensure that your metrics are appropriate for the context and goals of your system, for example, a fire alarm system should have high recall, even if that means the occasional false alarm.

When possible, directly examine your raw data

Example of actions:

Note that ML models will reflect the data they are trained on, so analyze your raw data carefully to ensure you understand it. In cases where this is not possible, for example, with sensitive raw data, understand your input data as much as possible while respecting privacy, for example, by computing aggregate, anonymized summaries.

Understand the limitations of your dataset and model

Example of actions:

Note that a model trained to detect correlations should not be used to make causal inferences or imply that it can. For example, your model may learn that people who buy basketball shoes are taller on average, but this does not mean that a user who buys basketball shoes will become taller as a result.

Test, test, test

Example of actions:

Learn from software engineering best test practices and quality engineering to make sure the AI system is working as intended and can be trusted.

Conduct rigorous unit tests to test each component of the system in isolation.

Conduct integration tests to understand how individual ML components interact with other parts of the overall system.

Continue to monitor and update the system after deployment

Example of actions:

Issues will occur: any model of the world is imperfect almost by definition. Build time into your product road map to allow you to address issues.

Consider both short- and long-term solutions to issues. A simple fix (e.g., blocklisting) may help to solve a problem quickly, but may not be the optimal solution in the long run. Balance short-term simple fixes with longer-term learned solutions.

IBM Responsible AI Practices

The principles of responsible AI practices, according to IBM,[11] are as follows:

Explainability

Machine learning models such as deep neural networks are achieving impressive accuracy on various tasks. But explainability and interpretability are ever more essential for the development of trustworthy AI. Three principles comprise IBM's approach to explainability:

Prediction Accuracy: Accuracy is a key component of how successful the use of AI is in everyday operation.

Traceability: Traceability is a property of AI that signifies whether it allows users to track its predictions and processes.

Decision Understanding: This is the human factor. Practitioners need to be able to understand how and why AI derives conclusions. This is accomplished through continuous education.

Fairness

Machine learning models are increasingly used to inform high-stakes decision-making that relates to people. Although machine learning, by its very nature, is a form of statistical discrimination, the discrimination becomes objectionable when it places privileged groups at systematic advantage and certain unprivileged groups at systematic disadvantage, potentially causing varied harms. Biases in training data, due to either prejudice in labels or under-/oversampling, yield models with unwanted bias.

Diverse and representative data

Ensure that the training data used to build AI models is diverse and representative of the population it is meant to serve. Include data inputs from various demographic groups to avoid underrepresentation or bias. Regularly check and assess training data for biases. Use tools and methods to identify and correct biases in the dataset before training the model.

Bias-aware algorithms

Incorporate fairness metrics into the development process to assess how different subgroups are affected by the model's predictions. Monitor and minimize disparities in outcomes across various demographic groups. Apply constraints in the algorithm to ensure that the model adheres to predefined fairness criteria during training and deployment.

Bias mitigation techniques

Apply techniques like resampling, reweighting, and adversarial training to mitigate biases in the model's predictions.

Diverse development teams

Assemble interdisciplinary and diverse teams involved in AI development. Diverse teams can bring different perspectives to the table, helping to identify and rectify biases that may be overlooked by homogeneous teams.

Ethical AI review boards

Establish review boards or committees to evaluate the potential biases and ethical implications of AI projects. These boards can provide guidance on ethical considerations throughout the development life cycle.

Robustness

Robust AI effectively handles exceptional conditions, such as abnormalities in input or malicious attacks, without causing unintentional harm. It is also built to withstand intentional and unintentional interference by protecting against exposed vulnerabilities. Our increased reliance on these models and the value they represent as an accumulation of confidential and proprietary knowledge are at increasing risk for attack. These models pose unique security risks that must be accounted for and mitigated.

Transparency

Users must be able to see how the service works, evaluate its functionality, and comprehend its strengths and limitations. Increased transparency provides information for AI consumers to better understand how the AI model or service was created. This helps a user of the model to determine whether it is appropriate for a given use case or to evaluate how an AI produced inaccurate or biased conclusions.

Privacy

Many regulatory frameworks, including GDPR, mandate that organizations abide by certain privacy principles when processing personal information. A malicious third party with access to a trained ML model, even without access to the training data itself, can still reveal sensitive personal information about the people whose data was used to train the model. It is crucial to be able to protect AI models that may contain personal information and control what data goes into the model in the first place.

Outcomes, Results, and Outputs

The main outcome, result, and output of this chapter are the production of "**The AI Global Standards and Guidelines handbook**" (in both printed and digital formats). This may be used for awareness, reference, and training purposes by company managers and staff, as well as compliance and auditing purposes by internal corporate functions and external regulatory authorities and audit partners.

Recommendations

As regards the better use of the above-described guidelines for your AI environment, the following recommendations (REC) are proposed:

REC 1. Document all these guidelines and create a product with the title "AI Global Standards and Guidelines handbook."

REC 2. Review all these guidelines and consider how they impact your AI systems/solutions in your operating landscape and how you may utilize them. See also **Step A2 (Carry Out AI Regulations and Standards Analysis) in Phase A in Chapter 7 (Prepare for AI).**

REC 3. Especially if you offer AI systems/solutions within EU countries, you will definitely need to review and comprehend fully all aspects of the EU AI Act, etc.

REC 4. Ensure all your AI staff and relevant managers and board members are fully aware of the concepts and principles of AI contained in the above product and trained on applying them in your AI ecosystem and its AI systems/solutions.

REC 5. Ensure you keep current the above product, by reviewing it and updating it every two to three years or as needs, expectations, and operating conditions and circumstances warrant.

Conclusion

This chapter described a summary of the major global AI guidelines, such as ISO/IEC 42001 AI Management System, Australia's AI Ethics Principles, NIST AI Risk Management Framework, Universal Guidelines for Artificial Intelligence, the OECD AI Principles, the EU AI Act, and IBM, Google, and Microsoft principles.

This is the first part of your **third** milestone (***Consider impact of AI regulations and standards***) of your AI Ecosystem Journey. The next chapter continues this exciting journey by describing Major Data Protection Laws and Privacy by Design Framework Principles.

Other Data Privacy Regulations (e.g., those of Canada, China, etc.) and various ISO Standards (Information Security, Management, Environment Protection, etc.) as well as laws relevant to AI (e.g., National Health, Employment Protection, Labor, and other laws) are beyond the scope of this book and will not be discussed further.

CHAPTER 5

Major Data Protection Laws and Privacy by Design Framework Principles

Richard Perle:[1] "Law-abiding citizens value privacy. Terrorists require invisibility. The two are not the same, and they should not be confused."

Overview: This chapter presents a summary of the two major global data protection and privacy laws (GDPR (for EU) and LGPD (for Brazil)) and the Privacy by Design Framework Principles with an example of three to four recommended actions to achieve the intent of each principle and which level of management is responsible for carrying out the actions to fulfill each principle.

These laws are the second part of *Component 2: Legal and Regulatory Environment (of the AI Management System)*.

GDPR (for EU)

Introduction

On May 25, 2018, the EU General Data Protection Regulation ("GDPR" or "the Regulation") came into force, without the need for national laws to implement its provisions.

The EU General Data Protection Regulation (GDPR[2]) represents a major change and radical improvement in the personal data protection compliance regime for data controllers and data processors for companies and organizations, called "enterprises" in GDPR terms.

© John Kyriazoglou 2025
J. Kyriazoglou, *AI Management Framework*, https://doi.org/10.1007/979-8-8688-1536-2_5

Central in personal data protection is privacy protection of the rights of persons, called data subjects in the language of GDPR. They must know what data are maintained on them, correct and improve their accuracy, limit their use, and be assured that confidentiality and integrity are maintained at all times.

These data may be processed by enterprises in manual and computerized systems that maintain and process valuable information or provide services to multiple users concurrently, on the basis of the provision of security safeguards against unauthorized access, use, or modifications of any data.

Enterprises must protect manual and computerized systems against all types of security and privacy risks, abuse of personal data, unauthorized use, errors, illegal intrusions, disruption of operations, and physical damage, among other things.

The growing number of computer applications processing business transactions that involve using valuable information or assets and the ever-increasing number of criminal actions directed against them underscore the need for finding efficient and effective solutions to the computer security and privacy issues.

In the future, concerns for privacy and security of personal data must become integral in the planning and design of manual and computer systems and their applications.

People will appreciate doing business with companies and organizations that demonstrate a respect for their privacy rights. This will ultimately lead to a competitive advantage for businesses. Companies and organizations can see this as an opportunity to review and improve their personal information handling practices.

GDPR Highlights

The major highlights of this regulation relate to

1. **Data protection principles**

   Organizations must ensure that all processing operations of personal data must adhere to and comply with the following principles:

   1. "Lawfulness, fairness, and transparency"

   2. "Purpose limitation"

   3. "Data minimization"

   4. "Accuracy"

5. "Storage limitation"

6. "Integrity and confidentiality"

7. "Accountability"

2. **Data Protection Impact Assessments (DPIAs)**

Organizations must undertake DPIAs when conducting risky or large-scale processing of personal data.

3. **Consent**

   3.1. Consent to process data must be freely given and for specific purposes by data subjects.

   3.2. Data subjects must be informed of their right to withdraw their consent.

   3.3. Consent must be explicit in the case of sensitive personal data or trans-border data flows.

4. **Mandatory breach notification**

   4.1. Organizations must notify supervisory authority of data breaches "without undue delay" or within 72 hours, unless the breach is unlikely to be a risk to individuals.

   4.2. If there is a high risk to data subjects, then such data subjects should also be informed.

5. **Data subject rights**

There are several rights, such as

   5.1. The right to be forgotten, that is, the right to ask data controllers to erase all personal data without undue delay in certain circumstances.

   5.2. The right to data portability, that is, the right of individuals that have provided personal data to a service provider to require the provider to transfer or "port" the data to another service provider provided this is feasible.

   5.3. The right to object to profiling, that is, the right not to be subject to a decision based solely on automated processing, etc.

6. **Data Protection by Design and by Default**

   6.1. Organizations should design data protection into the development of business processes and new systems.

7. **Personal data definitions**

   7.1. The GDPR applies to all personal data that is collected in the EU, regardless of where in the world it is processed. Any database containing personal or sensitive data collected within the EU will be in scope, as will any media containing personal or sensitive data. Any organization that has such data in its systems, regardless of business size or sector, will have to comply with the GDPR.

   7.2. Personal data is anything that can identify a "natural person" ("data subject") and can include information such as a name, a photo, an email address (including work email address), bank details, posts on social networking websites, medical information, or even an IP address.

   7.3. This definition is critical because EU data protection law only applies to personal data. Information that does not fall within the definition of "personal data" is not subject to EU data protection law.

   7.4. "Sensitive Personal Data" are personal data revealing racial or ethnic origin, political opinions, religious or philosophical beliefs, or trade-union membership; data concerning health or sex life and sexual orientation; genetic data; or biometric data.

8. **Administrative fines for GDPR non-compliance**

   Article 83 GDPR includes requirements concerning penalties. When DPAs decide whether to impose an administrative fine and decide on the amount of the administrative fine in each individual case, due regard shall be given to the following:

- Nature, gravity, and duration of the infringement, the number of data subjects affected, and the level of damage suffered by them

- Intent or negligence

- Action taken to mitigate the damage

- Degree of responsibility

- Any previous infringements

- Degree of cooperation with supervisory authority

- Categories of personal data affected

- Manner in which the infringement became known to the supervisory authority

- Compliance with previously ordered measures

- Adherence to approved codes of conduct pursuant or approved certification mechanisms

- Any other aggravating or mitigating factor

Administrative fines are up to €10,000,000 or, in the case of an undertaking, up to 2% of the total worldwide annual turnover of the preceding financial year, whichever is higher, in case of a violation of

- Obligations of the controller and the processor pursuant to Articles 8, 11, 25, 26, 27, 28, 29, 30, 31, 32, 33, 34, 35, 36, 37, 38, 39, 42, and 43

- Obligations of the certification body pursuant to Articles 42 and 43

- Obligations of the monitoring body pursuant to Article 41(4)

Administrative fines are up to €20,000,000 or, in the case of an undertaking, up to 4% of the total worldwide annual turnover of the preceding financial year, whichever is higher, in case of a violation of

- The basic principles for processing, including conditions for consent, pursuant to Articles 5, 6, 7, and 9

- The data subjects' rights pursuant to Articles 12 to 22

- The transfers of personal data to a recipient in a third country or an international organization pursuant to Articles 44 to 49

- Any obligations pursuant to Member State law adopted under Chapter IX (specific processing situations)

- Non-compliance with an order or a temporary or definitive limitation on processing or the suspension of data flows by the supervisory authority

LGPD (for Brazil)

Introduction

LGPD[3] is the first comprehensive general data protection law in Latin America.

Besides the LGPD, other sectoral laws and statutes in Brazil also address privacy and data protection rights and, in many cases, support and complement the privacy requirements of LGPD.

These include the Civil Code, the Internet Act, the Consumer Protection Code, the Wiretap Act, etc.

According to recent statistics, Brazil had a population of **213.3 million** in January 2021. Brazil has 160 million Internet users (the population of the tenth largest country in the world), making it one of the largest Internet markets in Latin America and the fourth largest market in the world. Internet penetration in Brazil stood at **75.0%** in January 2021.

In previous years, Brazil has drafted over 40 legal regulations with regard to data privacy on a federal level, some of which established general guidelines and some were sector specific, leading to many overlaps and conflict between different laws across industries.

The negative aspect of these sectoral laws is that they are applicable to specific industries and do not provide Brazilian Internet users and consumers comprehensive protections. Also, for organizations and businesses involved in multi-sectoral operations, complying with all of these different laws and their requirements is an expensive and difficult affair.

This is why the new data protection law of Brazil known as the LGPD (Lei Geral de Proteção de Dados Pessoais) was set into motion to provide a more comprehensive and overall regulatory framework to data privacy.

Law 13.709 of Brazil is the General Law for the Protection of Personal Data, or in Portuguese the Lei Geral de Proteção de Dados Pessoais ("LGPD"), and was sanctioned by the former president of Brazil, Michel Temer, in August of 2018.

In August 2020, the President of Brazil approved the creation of the federal independent regulatory authority – The Autoridade Nacional de Proteção de Dados (ANPD) – to interpret and enforce the LGPD and act as the national supervisory authority.

The LGPD was signed into law on September 18, 2020, and it is in effect since then. The sanctions under the law are now in full effect.

1. LGPD: Applicability

The LGPD applies to all personal data that is collected in Brazil, regardless of where in the world it is processed. Any database containing personal or sensitive data collected within Brazil will be in scope, as will any media containing personal or sensitive data. Any organization that has such data in its systems, regardless of business size or sector, will have to comply with the LGPD.

2. LGPD: Definition of Terms

There are 20 definitions in LGPD. The first 19 are included in Article 5, and the last one is defined in Article 13, paragraph 4.

(1) **Personal Data**: Information regarding an identified or identifiable natural person

(2) **Sensitive Personal Data**: Personal data concerning racial or ethnic origin, religious belief, political opinion, trade union, or religious, philosophical, or political organization membership; data concerning health or sex life; genetic or biometric data, when related to a natural person

3. LGPD Major Highlights

The major highlights of this law, in summary, are outlined next.

3.1. Data protection principles

Organizations must ensure that all processing operations of personal data must adhere to and comply with the following principles (LGPD Article 6):

Principle 1. Purpose: You must ensure that you carry out the processing of personal data for legitimate, specific, and explicit purposes of which the data subject (holder) is informed, with no possibility of subsequent processing that is incompatible with these purposes.

Principle 2. Adequacy: You must ensure that there is compatibility of the processing of personal data with the purposes communicated to the data subject (holder), in accordance with the context of the processing.

Principle 3. Necessity: You must only process personal data that is necessary for the fulfillment of your stated purposes of processing.

Principle 4. Free Access: Data subjects (holders) must be able to freely exercise their rights under the law and have unencumbered, easy access to any information about the processing of their personal data, without any charge.

Principle 5. Quality of the Data: You, the controller, must ensure the data subjects of integrity and accuracy of the personal data processed and keep it updated and relevant, in accordance with the purpose for processing such personal data.

Principle 6. Transparency: Information about your processing of personal data must be clear, accurate, and easily available to data subjects (holders). Data subjects must also be able to access information about the third parties that you, the controller, share their personal data with.

Principle 7. Security: Both the controller and any processors must be sure to implement technical and administrative measures in order to protect personal data from unauthorized access, accidental or unlawful destruction, loss, alteration, and unauthorized communication or dissemination.

Principle 8. Prevention: It's the responsibility of both the controller and the processor to adopt technical and organizational measures to prevent any damage being caused by the processing of personal data.

Principle 9. Non-discrimination: No processing of personal data should occur for discriminatory purposes.

Principle 10. Responsibility and Accountability: As the controller, or processor, you must comply with the law and must be able to prove it. Also, you must review and improve the effectiveness of the protection measures implemented for the personal data you process.

3.2. Legal basis for processing of personal data

Under the LGPD (Article 7), personal data can only be processed if there's at least one legal basis for doing so.

The legal bases are

- Consent of the data subject

- Compliance with laws or regulations

- Public interest

- Research studies

- Contract execution

- Judicial, administrative, or arbitration procedures

- Protection of life or physical safety of persons

- Protection of health

- Legitimate interests of the controller or a third party

- Credit protection

3.3. Consent

According to LGPD (Articles 8, 11, and 14)

1. Consent to process data must be freely given and for specific purposes by data subjects.

2. Data subjects must be informed of their right to withdraw their consent.

3. Consent must be explicit in the case of sensitive personal data or trans-border data flows.

4. The controller shall bear the burden of proving that consent was obtained in accordance with the provisions of this Law, etc.

5. The processing of sensitive personal data shall only occur in certain cases, such as consent of data subjects, controller's compliance with a legal or regulatory obligation, shared processing of data by public entities, etc.

3.4. Transparency

Under the LGPD (Article 9), data subjects have the right to be informed of the nature of the processing of their personal data in a clear, adequate, and overt way.

3.5. Data subject rights

Under the LGPD (Articles 17 to 22), data subjects have rights (DSR), such as

DSR1. Confirmation of the existence of the processing.

DSR2. Access to the data.

DSR3. Correction of incomplete, inaccurate, or out-of-date data.

DSR4. Anonymization, blocking, or deletion of unnecessary or excessive data or data processed in non-compliance with the provisions of this Law.

DSR5. Portability of the data to another service or product provider, by means of an express request, etc.

DSR6. Deletion of personal data processed with the consent of the data subject, except in the cases provided for in Article 16 of this Law.

DSR7. Information about public and private entities with which the controller has shared data.

DSR8. Information about the possibility of denying consent and the consequences of such denial.

DSR9. Revocation or withdrawal of consent.

DSR10. Lodging a complaint with the Data Protection Authority (DPA).

DSR11. Opposing the processing of their personal data where there is non-compliance with the provisions of the law.

DSR12. Requesting the review of decisions made solely on the basis of automated processing of personal data which affect their interests. This includes decisions used to define their personal, professional, consumer and credit profile, or the aspects of their personality.

3.6. Data security measures and breach notification

According to LGPD (Articles 46 to 49), both controllers and processors must adopt technical and administrative data security measures to protect personal data from unauthorized access, accidents, destruction, and loss and must develop secure information systems.

Also, the controller must communicate to the national authority and to the data subjects the occurrence of a security incident that may create risk or relevant damage to the data subjects and other relevant details, etc.

3.7. International transfer of data

According to LGPD (Articles 33 to 36), to transfer LGPD protected data outside of Brazil, there are some guidelines to keep in mind. The LGPD allows the cross-border transfer of personal data if an *adequate level* of protection of the personal data is provided and under certain other conditions, such as data subject consent, contracts, global corporate rules, codes of conduct, etc.

3.8. Data Protection Officer

According to LGPD (Article 41), companies and public organizations must appoint a Data Protection Officer (DPO) to be the "channel of communication" between the controller, the data subjects, and regulators. Also, the DPO's details will be disclosed publicly; they will accept complaints and communications from data subjects, providing explanations and adopting measures, etc.

3.9. Data Protection Impact Assessments

Under the law (LGPD Article 38), the national authority may determine that the controller must prepare an impact report on protection of personal data (DPIA: Data Protection Impact Assessment).

The DPIA document (impact report) must at least include

(1)   A description of the categories of data processed

(2)   The methods used to collect the data

(3)   The security measures used

(4)   A description of the measures used to mitigate the risks involved in processing the personal data, etc.

3.10. Non-compliance fines and sanctions

According to LGPD (Articles 52 to 54), the legal consequences for non-compliance can include fines of 2% of a company's annual turnover, up to 50 million Brazilian reais, per violation. Also, the Brazilian Data Protection Authority may take actions against those who are found to be in violation, such as issue warnings, request the blocking or deletion of the processing activities or personal data to which the infraction refers to, demand the suspension of the database, etc.

Additionally, the LGPD allows data subjects with a cause for action to seek civil damages for violation of the privacy law, etc.

Privacy by Design Principle Framework

Introduction

The Privacy by Design Principle Framework includes seven principles aimed at embedding privacy into the development process of technologies and systems from the very beginning. In terms of AI, this approach ensures that privacy considerations are an integral part of the system life cycle, rather than an afterthought, fostering a balance between individual privacy rights and the utility of AI applications. By prioritizing privacy at every stage, these principles help create more trustworthy AI systems that respect user data while still providing valuable services. These principles can enhance the overall utility of AI applications by fostering user confidence, which can lead to increased usage and acceptance of these technologies.[4]

The Privacy by Design Principle Framework of seven principles and an example of three to four recommended actions to achieve the intent of each principle and which level of management is responsible for carrying out the actions to fulfill each principle are outlined next.[5]

List of Principles

Principle 1. Proactive not reactive; preventative not remedial

Principle 2. Privacy as default setting

Principle 3. Embedded privacy in design

Principle 4. Full functionality – positive-sum instead of zero-sum

Principle 5. End-to-end security – full lifespan protection

Principle 6. Transparency and visibility – make it open

Principle 7. Respect for the privacy of the user – make it user-centric

Description of Principles and Examples of Actions
Principle 1. Proactive not reactive; preventative not remedial

The Privacy by Design approach is characterized by proactive rather than reactive measures. It anticipates and prevents privacy invasive events before they happen. Privacy by Design does not wait for privacy risks to materialize, nor does it offer remedies for resolving privacy infractions once they have occurred – it aims to prevent them from occurring. In short, Privacy by Design comes before the fact, not after. The focus is on the role played by organizational leadership/senior management in the formation, execution, and measurement of an actionable privacy program.

Actions (a small example)

1. Affirm senior leadership commitment to a strong, proactive privacy program.

2. Ensure that concrete actions, not just policies, reflect a commitment to privacy.

3. For AI systems/solutions, monitor through a system of regularly reviewed metrics.

4. Develop systematic methods to assess privacy and security risks in AI systems/solutions and to correct any negative impacts well before they occur.

Responsibility: Leadership/Senior Management (e.g., Board of Directors, CEO, CIO, COO, CSO, Company Owner(s)).

Principle 2. Privacy as default setting

Privacy is irrespective of any action; if an individual remains inactive, their privacy still remains intact. Privacy by default is also becoming a requirement with the GDPR. As an example, this principle would especially be crucial when designing AI systems, where the individuals may not know that their personal data have been collected and used.

Actions (a small example)

1. Adopt as narrow and as specific a purpose for AI data collection as possible.

2. Minimize the collection of AI data at the outset to only what is strictly necessary for the AI system/solution.

3. Do not use email addresses for marketing and do not share transaction records with other companies without affirmative customer, employee, or user consent.

4. Obtain explicit consent from new customers and new employees for uses of their personal data in any way (e.g., AI system/ solution).

Responsibility: Software Engineers, AI Developers, AI Application Owners, Line of Business and Process Owners/Managers.

Principle 3. Embedded privacy in design

Privacy by Design is embedded into the design and architecture of IT systems, AI systems/solutions, and business practices. It is not bolted on as an add-on, after the fact. The result is that privacy becomes an essential component of the core functionality being delivered. Privacy is integral to every system, product, or service, without diminishing functionality.

As part of their initial design, AI systems/solutions, mobile apps, and web pages could be programmed to process such transfer requests.

Actions (a small example)

1. Make a Privacy Risk Assessment or Data Protection Impact Assessment an integral part of the design stage of any initiative, for example, IT Application System, AI system/solution, AI product, service, etc.

2. Develop and use your own or employ a ready-made identity metasystem to authenticate an Internet user's identity just as a driver's license and credit card serve as two forms of ID in day-to-day life.

3. Consider privacy in IT and AI system development life cycles and organizational engineering processes.

Responsibility: Software Engineers, AI Developers, AI Application Owners, Line of Business and Process Owners/Managers, and Regulators.

Principle 4. Full functionality – positive-sum instead of zero-sum

Privacy by Design seeks to accommodate all legitimate interests and objectives in a positive-sum "win-win" manner, not through a dated, zero-sum approach, where unnecessary trade-offs are made.

The essence of Privacy by Design is that multiple, legitimate business interests must coexist with privacy. The notion that privacy requirements must be traded off against others (e.g., security vs. privacy or performance vs. privacy) is discarded as a dated formulation from the past. Innovative privacy solutions must prevail.

Actions (a small example)

1. Acknowledge that multiple, legitimate business interests must coexist.

2. Understand, engage, and partner.

3. Practice the 3Cs – communication, consultation, and collaboration – to better understand multiple and, at times, divergent interests.

Responsibility: Leaders/Senior Management, Software Engineers, AI Developers, AI Application Owners, Line of Business and Process Owners/Managers.

Principle 5. End-to-end security – full lifespan protection

Privacy by Design, having been embedded into the system prior to the first element of information being collected, extends securely throughout the entire life cycle of the data involved – strong security measures are essential to privacy, from start to finish. This ensures that all data are securely retained and then securely destroyed at the end of the process in a timely fashion. Thus, Privacy by Design ensures cradle to grave, secure life cycle management of information, end-to-end.

Actions (a small example)

1. All personal information collected is protected during the intake process, and the lifespan and expected destruction period are determined before the data is initially collected.

2. For all data collected (customer, marketing, sales, service, support, etc.) that may be necessary to process the transaction, consider how long it is really needed before collecting it. Destroy the data as soon as the business purpose no longer exists.

3. Employ encryption by default to mitigate the security concerns associated with the loss, theft, or disposal of electronic devices such as laptops, tablets, smartphones, USB memory keys, and other external media and devices. The default state of data, if breached, must be "unreadable."

4. Ensure IT and AI infrastructures are being designed and built on the basis of Threat and Risk Assessment prior to live operations (and preferably prior to implementation) to ensure that they work as expected.

Responsibility: Software Engineers, AI Developers, AI Application Owners, Line of Business and Process Owners/Managers.

Principle 6. Transparency and visibility – make it open

Privacy by Design seeks to assure all stakeholders that whatever the business practice or technology involved, it is, in fact, operating according to the stated promises and objectives, subject to independent verification. Its component parts and operations remain visible and transparent to users and providers alike. Remember, trust but verify. Even if privacy policies often go unread by customers and users, they can still serve as a standard for companies to meet and be evaluated against.

Actions (a small example)

1. Make the identity and contact information of the individual(s) responsible for privacy and security available to the public and well known within the organization.

2. Implement a policy that requires all "public-facing" documents to be written in "plain language" that is easily understood by the individuals whose information is the subject of the policies and procedures.

3. Make information about the policies, procedures, and controls relating to the management of Personal Information readily available to all individuals.

4. Make tools available so that users can easily determine how their data is stored, protected, and used and how decisions and results are produced by an AI system/solution.

Responsibility: Leadership/Senior Management, Software Engineers, AI Developers, AI Application Owners, System Architect.

Principle 7. Respect for the privacy of the user – make it user-centric

Privacy by Design requires IT and AI system/solution architects and IT and AI operators to keep the interests of the individual uppermost by offering such measures as strong privacy defaults, appropriate notice, and empowering user-friendly options. The privacy interests of the end user, customer, or citizen are paramount. Privacy by Design demands that application and process developers undertake a collection of activities to ensure that an individual's privacy is protected even if they take no explicit steps to protect it. Privacy defaults are key; clear notice is equally important.

Actions (a small example)

1. Offer strong privacy defaults in all AI systems/solutions and products.

2. Provide access to the AI management practices of the organization.

3. Ensure that you implement measures to assure transparency, attain informed user consent in all areas of AI (cloud, social and mobile computing applications, online tracking and advertising services, online contracts, electronic health records, personal data vaults, etc.), provide rights of access and correction, and make effective redress mechanisms available.

4. Develop and implement AI systems/solutions that are easy to operate and allow users to find out how decisions affecting them are produced by the specific AI system/solution.

Responsibility: Leadership/Senior Management, Software Engineers, AI Developers, AI Application Owners, Line of Business and Process Owners/Managers.

Outcomes, Results, and Outputs

The main outcome, result, and output of this chapter are the production of "**The Major Data Protection Laws and Privacy by Design handbook**" (in both printed and digital formats). This may be used for awareness, reference, and training purposes by company managers and staff, as well as compliance and auditing purposes by internal corporate functions and external regulatory authorities and audit partners.

Recommendations

As regards the better use of the above-described data protection laws and privacy framework principles for your AI environment, the following recommendations (REC) are proposed:

REC 1. Document all these laws and guidelines and create a product with the title "Major Data Protection Laws and Privacy by Design handbook."

REC 2. Review these two laws and the privacy framework principles and consider how they impact your AI systems/ solutions in your operating landscape and how you may utilize them. See also **Step A2 (Carry Out AI Regulations and Standards Analysis) in Phase A in Chapter 7 (Prepare for AI)**.

REC 3. Especially if you offer AI systems/solutions within EU countries, you will definitely need to review and comprehend fully all aspects of the EU GDPR, etc. The same is also true (review LGPD) if you operate within Brazil or provide services and products in Brazil, etc.

REC 4. Ensure all your AI staff and relevant managers and board members are fully aware of the concepts and principles of data protection and privacy and trained on applying them in your AI ecosystem and its AI systems/solutions.

REC 5. Ensure you keep current the above product, by reviewing it and updating it every two to three years or as needs, expectations, and operating conditions and circumstances warrant.

Conclusion

This chapter described a summary of the two major global data protection laws (GDPR for EU and LGPD for Brazil) and a summary of the principles of the Privacy by Design Framework.

Other Data Privacy Regulations (e.g., those of Canada, China, etc.) and various ISO Standards (Information Security, Management, Environment Protection, etc.) as well as laws relevant to AI (e.g., National Health, Employment Protection, Labor, and other laws) are beyond the scope of this book and will not be discussed further.

For compliance measures related to both of these laws, see my books in "Additional Resources."

This is the second part of the **third** milestone (*Consider impact of AI regulations and standards*) of your AI Ecosystem Journey. The next chapter continues this exciting journey by describing several Digital and Secure AI System Development Guidelines.

CHAPTER 6

Digital and Secure AI System Development Guidelines

Douglas Engelbart:[1] "The digital revolution is far more significant than the invention of writing or even of printing."

Overview: This chapter presents a summary of digital principles, such as the Digital Nations Charter, EU's Digital Rights and Principles, the Principles for Digital Development, and the Guidelines for Secure AI System Development.

These principles are the third part of *Component 2: Legal and Regulatory Environment (of the AI Management System)*.

Digital Nations Charter[2]

1. The Treasury Board of Canada Secretariat; the Agency for Digitization of Denmark; the Ministry of Economic Affairs and Communications of the Republic of Estonia; the National Digital Affairs Directorate in the Ministry of Economy of Israel; the Ministry of the Interior and Safety of the Republic of Korea; the Office of the Presidency of Mexico; the Department of Internal Affairs of New Zealand; the Ministry of State Modernization and Public Administration of Portugal; the Department for Digital, Culture, Media and Sport of the United Kingdom; and the Office of the President of the Oriental Republic of Uruguay, hereinafter individually referred to as "the Participant" and collectively as "the Participants," have reached the following understanding:

© John Kyriazoglou 2025
J. Kyriazoglou, *AI Management Framework*, https://doi.org/10.1007/979-8-8688-1536-2_6

2. The Participants have mutually agreed to form the Digital Nations (DN), a group of the most digitally advanced governments in the world, to provide a focused forum to share best practices, identify how to improve the Participants' digital services, collaborate on common projects, and to support and champion our growing economies.

The Participants have committed to working toward fulfilling the following principles as we advance our digital development, acknowledging that they will not be able to meet all the criteria on joining:

3.1. **User Needs**: Strive to ensure that the design and delivery of public services through the use of data, digital, and other technologies takes a human-centered approach and promotes the global public good.

3.2. **Necessary Safeguards**: Strive to ensure that the design, development, and deployment of digital technologies, especially the use of data and artificial intelligence, are

a. Subject to adequate and necessary safeguards to uphold public trust and protect personal data

b. Underpinned by human rights and guided by effective ethical, legal, or other frameworks

3.3. **Open Standards**: Promote interoperability of digital technologies, including by adopting a credible royalty-free open standards policy.

3.4. **Open Source**: Strive to create future government systems, tradecraft, manuals, and standards as open source and shareable between Participants.

3.5. **Open Markets**: Promote competition in digital markets, for all enterprises regardless of size, including in government procurement, encourage and support a dynamic start-up/scale-up culture in the digital and technology sectors, and promote sustainable economic growth through open markets.

3.6. **Open Government**: Be a member of the Open Government Partnership, promote digital technologies to facilitate transparency and citizen participation, and use open licenses to produce and consume open data.

3.7. **Digital Inclusion and Accessibility**: Strive to ensure the opportunities and benefits offered by digital tools, technologies, and services are available to all by taking inclusive approaches to tackle digital divides, including through efforts to improve connectivity, promote access to digital infrastructure, and support high-quality web and other accessibility standards.

3.8. **Digital Skills and Training**: Strive to support children, young people, and adults in developing digital competencies and skills and also promote innovative learning environments for public servants.

3.9. **Co-creation and Experimentation**: Promote a culture of innovation and experimentation where new ideas and experiences take place, including through a multi-stakeholder approach inclusive of industry, academia, and civil society's engagement and participation.

3.10. **Sustainability**: Promote a sustainable approach to digital government, make effective use of digital technologies to contribute to climate targets, and strive to reduce the negative environmental impacts of digital operations while delivering responsible and resilient digital services.

EU Digital Rights and Principles

The European Declaration on Digital Rights and Principles promotes a digital transition shaped by European values.

The EU wants to empower people to fully enjoy the opportunities that the digital transition is bringing. It has adopted a set of digital rights and principles that reflect EU values and promote a human-centric, secure, and sustainable vision for the digital transformation. The Declaration also includes commitments for the EU and Member States to act in a number of digital matters.[3]

The digital rights and principles are shaped around six themes.

Theme 1. Putting people and their rights at the center of the digital transformation

Technology should serve and benefit all people living in the EU and empower them to pursue their aspirations. It should not infringe upon their security or fundamental rights.

The EU and its Member States commit to making sure that the digital transformation benefits everyone and improves the lives of all people living in the EU. They take measures to ensure our rights are respected online as well as offline and promote this approach both at home and on the international stage.

Theme 2. Supporting solidarity and inclusion

Universal access to inclusive technology that upholds EU rights is essential. Everyone should

- Have access to affordable and high-speed digital connectivity

- Be able to acquire the education and skills necessary to enjoy the benefits of digital technology

- Have fair and just working conditions

- Have access to key digital public services

The EU and its Member States have been committed to leaving no one behind, supporting efforts to equip all education and training institutions, ensuring the right to disconnect from work, and providing a digital identity that gives access to a broad range of online services.

Theme 3. Ensuring freedom of choice online

Everyone should be empowered to make their own, informed choices online. This includes when interacting with artificial intelligence systems, which should serve as a tool for people, with the ultimate aim to increase human well-being.

The EU and Member States notably commit to promote human-centric, trustworthy, and ethical artificial intelligence systems, which are used in a transparent way and in line with EU values.

Freedom of choice also includes being free to choose which online services we use, based on objective, transparent, and reliable information. This in turn involves making sure businesses are empowered to compete and innovate in the digital world.

Theme 4. Fostering participation in the digital public space

Everyone should have access to a trustworthy, diverse, and multilingual online environment and should know who owns or controls the services they are using. This encourages pluralistic public debate and participation in democracy.

The Declaration also highlights the need to create a digital environment that protects people from disinformation, information manipulation, and other forms of harmful content, including harassment and gender-based violence. It recognizes the role of very large online platforms in this context and asks them to mitigate the risks stemming from the functioning and use of their services.

The EU and Member States notably commit to support effective access to digital content that reflects cultural and linguistic diversity in the EU.

Theme 5. Increasing safety, security, and empowerment of individuals (especially young people)

Everyone should have access to safe, secure, and privacy-protective digital technologies, products, and services. The EU and Member States notably commit to protect the interests of people, businesses, and public services against cybercrime and to ensure that everyone has effective control over their personal and non-personal data in line with EU law.

Children and young people should be empowered to make safe and informed choices and express their creativity in the digital environment. The EU and Member States also commit to promote positive experiences for children and young people in an age-appropriate and safe digital environment and to protect them against harmful and illegal content, exploitation, manipulation, and abuse online.

Theme 6. Promoting the sustainability of the digital future

The digital and green transitions are closely linked. While digital technologies offer many solutions for climate change, we must ensure they do not contribute to the problem themselves. Digital products and services should be designed, produced, and disposed of in a sustainable way.

The EU and Member States commit to supporting digital technologies with minimal negative environmental and social effects. The aim is to promote digital technologies that have a positive impact on the environment and climate, contributing to the green transition. They also commit to promote sustainability standards and labels for digital products and services, to provide people with more information regarding their environmental impact.

The European Declaration on Digital Rights and Principles offers citizens a bridge to Union digital laws and policies, as it indicates the direction of travel of the Union on its journey to digital transformation.

The Commission monitors the application of digital rights and principles across the EU and publishes its annual monitoring together with the State of the Digital Decade Report. The monitoring report aims to show how much the EU and Member States stay on course during this journey. Through Member States best practices, it aims to inspire further action across the EU.

The Principles for Digital Development

The Principles for Digital Development[4] serve as a compass for those working to promote sustainable and inclusive development in today's complex digital landscape. Using these Principles as a starting point, policymakers, practitioners, and technologists will be better equipped to ensure that all people can benefit from digital initiatives and from the broader digital society.

Originally developed in 2014, the Principles are officially endorsed by more than 300 organizations, including donors, international organizations, and civil society organizations. During the first decade (2014–2024), they widely influenced funder procurement policies and the design and implementation of development programs.

In 2024, the Principles were updated in consultation with a diverse set of individuals and organizations. Through this effort, the community expressed the need for the Principles to better reflect that people today largely interact with technology outside of development programs.

Today, all people – even those who do not yet have access to or use technology – live in societies that are increasingly shaped by digital ecosystems that can bring both immense benefit and immense harm.

Therefore, the refreshed Principles recognize the need for radical inclusion and local ownership, elevate issues arising from the generation and use of digital data, emphasize that open approaches to innovation can support the realization of the nine Principles, and intentionally speak to the original audience while resonating further with the full diversity of individuals and organizations that exert power over the design, deployment, and governance of digital systems and solutions.

The Principles are mutually reinforcing, as they emphasize the actions needed to ensure no one is left behind in an increasingly digital world.

Ultimately, when designing and implementing a policy, solution, system, or intervention, endorsers of these Principles commit, at minimum, to do no harm and, at best, to ensure their work maximizes the agency of people and communities to drive their own development. To achieve these objectives, each endorser will define how these Principles can be operationalized in their work, sphere of influence, and specific initiative.

Principle 1. Understand the existing ecosystem

Trust starts with a thorough understanding of the dynamic cultural, social, and economic context in which you are operating.

Principle 2. Share, reuse, and improve

Build on what works, improve what works, and share so that others can do the same.

Principle 3. Design with people

Good design starts and ends with people that will manage, use, and ideally benefit from a given digital initiative.

Principle 4. Design for inclusion

Consider the full range of human diversity to maximize impact and mitigate harm.

Principle 5. Build for sustainability

Build for the long term by intentionally addressing financial, operational, and ecological sustainability.

Principle 6. Establish people-first data practices

People-first data practices prioritize transparency, consent, and redressal while allowing people and communities to retain control of and derive value from their own data.

Principle 7. Create open and transparent practices

Effective digital initiatives establish confidence and good governance through measures that promote open innovation and collaboration.

Principle 8. Anticipate and mitigate harms

Harm is always possible when it comes to technology. To avoid negative outcomes, plan for the worst while working to create the best outcomes.

Principle 9. Use evidence to improve outcomes

Evidence drives impact: continually gather, analyze, and use feedback.

The Guidelines for Secure AI System Development

Introduction

The US Cybersecurity and Infrastructure Security Agency (CISA) and the UK National Cyber Security Centre (NCSC) released the Guidelines for Secure AI System Development to address the integration of artificial intelligence (AI), cybersecurity, and critical infrastructure.[5]

These guidelines and examples of actions to support the achievement of each guideline are presented in summary in the following paragraphs.

Secure Design Guidelines

Four guidelines for the design phase of the AI system development life cycle are included in this section. These are presented in summary next.

Secure Design Guideline 1: Raise staff awareness of threats and risks

Action 1. Ensure AI system owners and senior corporate leaders understand threats to secure AI and their mitigations.

Action 2. Ensure company data scientists and AI developers maintain an awareness of relevant security threats and failure modes and help risk owners to make informed decisions.

Action 3. Ensure you provide users with guidance on the unique security risks facing AI systems.

Action 4. Ensure you train AI developers in secure coding techniques and secure and responsible AI practices.

Secure Design Guideline 2: Model the threats to your system

Action 1. Ensure you apply a holistic process to assess the threats to your AI system, which includes understanding the potential impacts to the AI system, users, organizations, and wider society if an AI component is compromised or behaves unexpectedly.

Action 2. Ensure you assess the impact of AI-specific threats and document your decision-making.

Action 3. Ensure you recognize that the sensitivity and types of data used in your system may influence its value as a target to an attacker.

Action 4. Ensure your assessment considers that some threats may grow as AI systems increasingly become viewed as high-value targets and as AI itself enables new, automated attack vectors.

Secure Design Guideline 3: Design your system for security as well as functionality and performance

Action 1. Ensure that the task at hand is most appropriately addressed using AI.

Action 2. Ensure you assess the appropriateness of your AI-specific design choices by considering your threat model and associated security mitigations alongside functionality, user experience, deployment environment, performance, assurance, oversight, and ethical and legal requirements, among other considerations.

Action 3. Ensure you consider supply chain security when choosing whether to develop in-house or use external components, for example, a model, etc.

Action 4. Ensure, if using an external library, you complete a due diligence evaluation.

Action 5. Ensure you implement scanning and isolation/sandboxing when importing third-party models or serialized weights, which should be treated as untrusted third-party code and could enable remote code execution, etc.

Action 6. Ensure your system provides users with usable outputs without revealing unnecessary levels of detail to a potential attacker.

Secure Design Guideline 4: Consider security benefits and trade-offs when selecting your AI model

Action 1. Ensure your choice of AI model will involve balancing a range of requirements. This includes considering your threat model, AI security research advances, choice of model architecture, configuration, training data, training algorithm, and hyperparameters.

Action 2. When choosing an AI model, your considerations will likely include, but are not limited to

- The complexity of the model you are using, that is, the chosen architecture and number of parameters.

- Your model's chosen architecture and number of parameters will, among other factors, affect how much training data it requires and how robust it is to changes in input data when in use.

- The appropriateness of the model for your use case and/or feasibility of adapting it to your specific need (e.g., by fine-tuning).

- The ability to align, interpret, and explain your model's outputs (e.g., for debugging, audit, or regulatory compliance).

Secure Development Guidelines

Four guidelines for the development stage of the AI system development life cycle are included in this section. These are presented in summary next.

Secure Development Guideline 1: Secure your supply chain

Action 1. Ensure you assess and monitor the security of your AI supply chains across a system's life cycle and require suppliers to adhere to the same standards your own organization applies to other software.

Action 2. Ensure, if suppliers cannot adhere to your organization's standards, that you act in accordance with your existing risk management policies.

Action 3. Ensure you acquire and maintain well-secured and well-documented hardware and software components (e.g., models, data, software libraries, modules, middleware, frameworks, and external APIs) from verified commercial, open source, and other third-party developers to ensure robust security in your systems, etc.

Secure Development Guideline 2: Identify, track, and protect your assets

Action 1. Ensure you understand the value to your organization of your AI-related assets, including models, data (including user feedback), prompts, software, documentation, logs, and assessments (including information about potentially unsafe capabilities and failure modes), recognizing where they represent significant investment and where access to them enables an attacker.

Action 2. Ensure you treat logs as sensitive data and implement controls to protect their confidentiality, integrity, and availability.

Action 3. Ensure you know where your assets reside and have assessed and accepted any associated risks.

Action 4. Ensure you have processes and tools to track, authenticate, version control, and secure your assets and can restore to a known good state in the event of compromise.

Action 5. Ensure you have processes and controls in place to manage what data AI systems can access and to manage content generated by AI according to its sensitivity (and the sensitivity of the inputs that went into generating it).

Secure Development Guideline 3: Document your data, models, and prompts

Action 1. Ensure you document the creation, operation, and life cycle management of any models, datasets, and meta or system prompts.

Action 2. Ensure your documentation includes security-relevant information such as the sources of training data (including fine-tuning data and human or other operational feedback), intended scope and limitations, guardrails, cryptographic hashes or signatures, retention time, suggested review frequency, and potential failure modes.

Secure Development Guideline 4: Manage your technical debt

Action 1. Ensure you identify, track, and manage your "technical debt" throughout an AI system's life cycle (technical debt is where engineering decisions that fall short of best practices to achieve short-term results are made, at the expense of longer-term benefits).

Action 2. Ensure your life cycle plans (including processes to decommission AI systems) assess, acknowledge, and mitigate risks to future similar systems.

Secure Deployment Guidelines

Five guidelines for the deployment stage of the AI system development life cycle are included in this section. These are presented in summary next.

Secure Deployment Guideline 1: Secure your infrastructure

Action 1. Ensure you apply good infrastructure security principles to the infrastructure used in every part of your system's life cycle.

Action 2. Ensure you apply appropriate access controls to your APIs, models, and data and to their training and processing pipelines in research and development as well as deployment.

Action 3. Ensure you implement appropriate segregation of environments holding sensitive code or data.

Secure Deployment Guideline 2: Protect your model continuously

Action 1. Ensure you protect the model and data from direct and indirect access, respectively, by implementing standard cyber security best practices and implementing controls on the query interface to detect and prevent attempts to access, modify, and exfiltrate confidential information, etc.

Secure Deployment Guideline 3: Develop incident management procedures

Action 1. Ensure the inevitability of security incidents affecting your AI systems is reflected in your incident response, escalation, and remediation plans.

Action 2. Ensure your plans reflect different scenarios and are regularly reassessed as the system and wider research evolves.

Action 3. Ensure you store critical company digital resources in offline backups.

Action 4. Ensure responders have been trained to assess and address AI-related incidents.

Action 5. Ensure you provide high-quality audit logs and other security features or information to customers and users at no extra charge to enable their incident response processes.

Secure Deployment Guideline 4: Release AI responsibly

Action 1. Ensure you release AI models, AI applications, or AI systems only after subjecting them to appropriate and effective security evaluation such as benchmarking and red teaming (as well as other tests that are out of scope for these guidelines, such as safety or fairness), and you are clear to your users about known limitations or potential failure modes.

Secure Deployment Guideline 5: Make it easy for users to do the right things

Action 1. Ensure you recognize that each new setting or configuration option is to be assessed in conjunction with the business benefit it derives and any security risks it introduces.

Action 2. Ensure that the most secure setting will be integrated into the system as the only option.

Action 3. Ensure, when configuration is necessary, the default option should be broadly secure against common threats (i.e., secure by default).

Action 4. Ensure you apply controls to prevent the use or deployment of your AI system in malicious ways.

Action 5. Ensure you provide users with guidance on the appropriate use of your AI model or AI system, which includes highlighting limitations and potential failure modes.

Action 6. Ensure you inform users which aspects of security they are responsible for and are transparent about where (and how) their data might be used, accessed, stored, etc.

Secure Operation and Maintenance Guidelines

Four guidelines for the operation and maintenance stage of the AI system development life cycle are included in this section. These are presented in summary next.

Secure Operation and Maintenance Guideline 1: Monitor your system's behavior

Action 1. Ensure you measure the outputs and performance of your AI model and AI system such that you can observe sudden and gradual changes in behavior affecting security.

Action 2. Ensure you can account for and identify potential intrusions and compromises, as well as natural data drift.

Secure Operation and Maintenance Guideline 2: Monitor your system's input

Action 1. Ensure that, in line with privacy and data protection requirements, you monitor and log inputs to your system (such as inference requests, queries, or prompts) to enable compliance obligations, audit, investigation, and remediation in the case of compromise or misuse.

Secure Operation and Maintenance Guideline 3: Follow a secure-by-design approach to updates

Action 1. Ensure you include automated updates by default in every product and use secure, modular update procedures to distribute them.

Action 2. Ensure you update processes (including testing and evaluation regimes) to reflect the fact that changes to data, models, or prompts can lead to changes in system behavior (e.g., you treat major updates like new versions).

Action 3. Ensure you support users to evaluate and respond to model changes (e.g., by providing preview access and versioned APIs).

Secure Operation and Maintenance Guideline 4: Collect and share lessons learned

Action 1. Ensure you participate in information-sharing communities, collaborating across the global ecosystem of industry, academia, and governments to share best practice as appropriate.

Action 2. Ensure you maintain open lines of communication for feedback regarding system security, both internally and externally to your organization, including providing consent to security researchers to research and report vulnerabilities.

Action 3. Ensure that, when needed, you escalate issues to the wider community, for example, publishing bulletins responding to vulnerability disclosures, including detailed and complete common vulnerability enumeration.

Action 4. Ensure you take action to mitigate and remediate issues quickly and appropriately.

Outcomes, Results, and Outputs

The main outcome, result, and output of this chapter are the production of **"The Digital and Secure AI System Development Guidelines handbook"** (in both printed and digital formats). This may be used for awareness, reference, and training purposes by company managers and staff, as well as compliance and auditing purposes by internal corporate functions and external regulatory authorities and audit partners.

Recommendations

As regards the better use of the above-described digital principles for your AI environment, the following recommendations (REC) are proposed:

> REC 1. Document all these digital principles and create a product with the title "Digital and Secure AI System Development Guidelines handbook." This will include the Digital Nations Charter, EU's Digital Rights and Principles, the Principles for Digital Development, and the Guidelines for Secure AI System Development.

> REC 2. Review these and consider how they impact your AI systems/solutions in your operating landscape and how you may utilize them. For example, you may need to upgrade your digital transformation policies and practices before you develop and deploy effective AI systems/solutions. See also **Step A2 (Carry Out AI Regulations and Standards Analysis) in Phase A in Chapters 7,** 11, and 12.

REC 3. Ensure all your AI staff and relevant managers and board members are fully aware of these digital principles and trained on applying them in your AI ecosystem and its AI systems/solutions.

REC 4. Ensure you keep current the above product by reviewing it and updating it every two to three years or as needs, expectations, and operating conditions and circumstances warrant.

Conclusion

This chapter described a summary of the following digital principles: the Digital Nations Charter, EU's Digital Rights and Principles, and the Principles for Digital Development. Other Data Privacy Regulations (e.g., those of Canada, China, etc.) and various ISO Standards (Information Security, Management, Environment Protection, etc.) as well as laws relevant to AI (e.g., National Health, Employment Protection, Labor, and other laws) are beyond the scope of this book and will not be discussed further.

This and the previous two chapters supported you to achieve your **third** milestone (***Consider impact of AI regulations and standards***) in your AI Ecosystem Journey.

AI Global Standards and Guidelines (Chapter 4), Major Data Protection Laws and Privacy by Design Framework Principles (Chapter 5), and Digital and Secure AI System Development Guidelines (this chapter) are deemed to be the second prerequisite for preparing for AI and developing, deploying, and improving AI systems/solutions for your company's AI ecosystem.

The next chapters (Part IV) continue this exciting journey by describing how to establish an AI infrastructure management framework. Chapter 7 describes how to prepare the organization for AI, Chapter 8 describes how to establish an AI Governance Structure, Chapter 9 describes how to establish a Data Governance Structure, and Chapter 10 describes how to manage IT Governance and Privacy Controls.

PART IV

AI Infrastructure Management

Part IV contains

Managing the process of establishing and operating an AI infrastructure supports you to achieve the **fourth** milestone (***Establish AI infrastructure management framework***) of your AI Ecosystem Journey.

All these (actions of Chapters 7–10) compose the **first constituent** element of the **third** component (**AI Implementation Approach**) of your **AI Management System**.

The overall purpose of these four chapters is to prepare the organization better so that it could develop and operate more effective and ethical AI systems/solutions in your AI Ecosystem.

CHAPTER 7

Prepare the Organization for AI

Abraham Lincoln:[1] "Give me six hours to chop down a tree and I will spend the first four sharpening the axe."

Overview: This chapter describes how to prepare your organization for AI. It includes (a) **seven steps**, (b) over **25 actions**, (c) over **18 products** (outcomes, results, and outputs, such as organizational functions/HR resources; assessment reports; reference documentation; AI/ICT infrastructure; administrative support controls; AI governance, development, and operations support controls; and live AI systems/ solutions/tools), and (d) **five assurance tasks** to enable you to support, achieve, and ensure the good and effective development and operation (deployment) of AI systems/ solutions. The goal, objectives, steps, actions, products, and assurance tasks presented below form Phase A (AI Preparation), the first phase of the AI Implementation Approach.

Phases of the AI Implementation Approach

The AI Implementation Approach (Component 3 of the AI Management System) includes five phases:

- AI Preparation (*Phase A*, *this chapter*)
- AI Management Framework (Phase B)
- AI Systems Development (Phase C)
- AI Systems Operation (Phase D)
- AI Infrastructure and Systems Assessment (Phase E)

© John Kyriazoglou 2025
J. Kyriazoglou, *AI Management Framework*, https://doi.org/10.1007/979-8-8688-1536-2_7

Goal and Objectives of Phase A (AI Preparation)

The **goal of Phase A** is to "Prepare the company better for AI."

The objectives that support the achievement of this goal are

Objective 1: Evaluate AI corporate readiness

Objective 2: Engage top management in AI

Steps of Phase A (AI Preparation)

The seven steps to support the achievement of the goal and objectives of Phase A are

Step A1: Conduct AI Needs and Gap Analysis

Step A2: Carry Out AI Regulations and Standards Analysis

Step A3: Perform AI Readiness and Awareness Assessment

Step A4: Establish AI Steering Committee

Step A5: Appoint AI Project Manager

Step A6: Draft AI Budget

Step A7: Educate Board and Senior Management

Each step will contain one or more actions (and in some cases a questionnaire) to manage and resolve specific implementation issues. Also, each step will generate one or more products to achieve the specific step's purpose. These are listed in "**Products of Phase A (AI Preparation)**" later in this Chapter.

Step A1: Conduct AI Needs and Gap Analysis

Action 1. Carry out an analysis of the AI needs of your company. It is very crucial to be clear from the outset on what you are looking to achieve with AI, why it matters to your enterprise, and how you can be sure it will deliver. If you have not yet identified the primary opportunities to benefit from AI, then you should assess where AI can make the most immediate difference. The following actions and questions will support you in this task.

Action 2. Identify areas, uses, cases, or topics where AI can have the most substantial impact, such as managing e-mails, employee screening and hiring, loan approvals, marketing, research in new company products or services, cybersecurity, automating manual tasks, bolstering data analysis, improving fraud detection, etc.

Action 3. Consider what others in your industry are doing with AI.

Action 4. Work with internal or external experts, as needed.

Action 5. Ensure the problem you are looking to solve by AI is clear and that you can measure its success.

Action 6. Check if other systems/solutions have been tried, already considered, or deployed to deal with this problem and what the outcome has been.

Action 7. Ensure the scope of the AI opportunity is well-defined.

Action 8. Ensure the availability of the funds and technology resources required to develop, operate, and maintain an AI system/solution.

You may also use the following questions:

> Question 1. Can you access the data sources you need, without technological, contractual, or other impediments?

> Question 2. Is the business impact significant enough to merit the effort?

> Question 3. Is executive management supportive of AI?

> Question 4. Are the affected business functions fully committed to AI?

> Question 5. Is the AI team clearly defined, with sufficient time, skills, and motivation to make it happen?

> Question 6. Does the company have a data science function, infrastructure, and expertise?

> Question 7. Does the company have an AI strategy with specific goals?

> Question 8. Is your IT function aware and trained on AI and willing as well as ready to participate?

Action 9. Conduct gap analysis. Implementing compliance requires a gap analysis to recognize areas for improvement and suggest desirable changes necessary for complying with regulations. Therefore, Artificial Intelligence compliance demands gap analysis at the initial stage to identify organizations' weaknesses and plan for measures accordingly. The product of this action will be **an AI Needs and Gap Analysis Report**.

Action 10. Assess AI risks. Execute the required steps to support you in assessing AI risks in your corporate environment and take the relevant actions to remedy any risks identified. For more details, see Appendix 6.

Step A2: Carry Out AI Regulations and Standards Analysis

Action 1. Collect and review the statutes, laws, and regulations related to AI affecting all functions of the business the company is involved in and the countries or states (provinces if you also operate in Canada) it operates in. See also Chapters 4–6.

Action 2. Create an AI List of Standards and Regulations.

Step A3: Perform AI Readiness and Awareness Assessment

Action 1. Carry out an analysis and assessment of the readiness and awareness of your company (board, management staff, etc.) on AI and privacy issues.

You may use the "AI Readiness Assessment Questionnaire" (see Appendix 2) and the "Privacy Readiness Assessment Questionnaire" (see Appendix 3) for this purpose.

Action 2. Record the results in a report (AI Readiness Report).

Step A4: Establish AI Steering Committee

Action 1. Form a steering committee, working group, or task force of managers and relevant professionals to lead and provide support and guidance to your AI projects.

Action 2. Ensure this group or committee includes corporate compliance experts, data science professionals, IT experts, data protection officers, HR professionals, legal advisors, business unit managers, etc.

Action 3. This group or committee will oversee policy creation, gather necessary expertise, and ensure representation from various departments and stakeholders. The chair of this committee will ensure that minutes of meeting of each working meeting of this group will be maintained and distributed to all approved parties within the company.

Action 4. This group or committee will, in many cases, establish two additional committees and oversee their actions. These are an AI Ethics Committee and a Data Governance Committee.

The primary purpose of the AI Ethics Committee[2] is to advise the company's leadership on AI-related research priorities, commercialization strategies, strategic partnerships, and fundraising activities. The Committee is essentially a gauge of balance pointing at how well profit motives are aligned with ethical standards, preventing any negative impact that could be caused by aggressive market tactics.

The responsibilities of the Data Governance Committee[3] include all aspects of data governance, such as establishing and enforcing data governance policies, strategic planning, decision-making, risk management, communication and advocacy, oversight of data roles and responsibilities, and review and improvement.

Action 5. Ensure the role of this is approved by the board and that its establishment and operation is announced to all company staff and functions.

Step A5: Appoint AI Project Manager

Action 1. Appoint an AI Project Manager. Specify the duties of this manager, such as

(a) Manage, develop, and implement collection mechanisms, strategy, policies, and procedures for all AI data (internal and external) for the AI projects of the organization

(b) Work closely with corporate management to determine needs and support the use of AI solutions

(c) Provide technical assistance for the development and deployment of AI systems and solutions

(d) Monitor emerging trends and technologies in AI and data governance technologies

(e) Participate in the needs identification, evaluation, design, and implementation of new AI solutions and sources of data

Action 2. Ensure the duties of the appointed AI Project Manager are included in a job description and added to the person's employment agreement.

Action 3. Ensure the appointed AI Project Manager is effectively supported by several, depending on the AI system, personnel which will perform the tasks of human oversight for verifying the results and outputs of each AI system/solution.

It should be noted that in some cases and in large organizations, additional roles that may be considered are AI System Owner and AI Solution Owner.

Step A6: Draft AI Budget

Action 1. Draft an AI Project Budget. This should contain all that are required for the AI project or the AI solutions to be implemented, such as personnel, funds, systems and tools, office space, equipment, subscriptions to external data bases, etc.

Also, it must include all necessary AI computer infrastructure (i.e., Hardware Components (GPU (Graphics Processing Unit) Servers, AI Accelerators, TPUs (Tensor Processing Units), High-Performance Computing (HPC) Systems, etc.) and Software Components (Machine Learning Frameworks; Data Processing Libraries that are used for handling and processing large datasets; Storage Solutions, such as cloud storage, data lakes, and distributed file systems; etc.).

Action 2. Obtain board approval for the AI budget.

Action 3. Acquire the needed AI Infrastructure listed above via the corporate procurement process.

Step A7: Educate Board and Senior Management

Action 1. Ensure all board members and senior managers are aware and have a good understanding of AI, its risks, and benefits, as well as its operational considerations and ethical implications.

Action 2. Prepare an AI Awareness presentation.

Action 3. Use this presentation to give board members and senior managers awareness and training sessions or workshops to familiarize themselves with essential AI concepts, such as algorithmic bias, privacy concerns, and AI's potential impact on business operations and customer service.

For more details, see Appendix 4.

Action 4. Keep a record of all minutes of awareness meetings and presentations.

Products of Phase A (AI Preparation)

The products (outcomes, results, and outputs) define (a) what's required (i.e., organizational functions, HR resources, ICT hardware and software, policies, etc.) to establish, develop, operate, implement, and assess AI infrastructure and systems/solutions and (b) what outputs and results (i.e., reference documentation, assessment reports, decisions of live AI systems, AI data, etc.) are produced, managed, used, and maintained by AI systems/solutions and their developmental, implementation, operational, and assessment aspects.

The main outcomes, results, and outputs of this chapter include the following types of products:

Type 1. Organizational Functions/HR Resources: These include (a) establishing an AI Steering Committee, an AI Ethics Committee, and a Data Governance Committee and (b) appointing an AI Project Manager.

Type 2. Assessment Reports: These include carrying out the necessary assessment and review actions and issuing the following analyses and reports – AI Needs Analysis Report, AI Gap Analysis Report, AI Risk Assessment Report, AI Readiness Report, and Privacy Readiness Report.

Type 3. Reference Documentation: This includes crafting and issuing reference documentation, such as AI Regulations and Standards handbook, Board and Senior Managers' AI Awareness presentation, List of AI Standards and Regulations, AI opportunities areas and scope statement.

Type 4. AI/ICT Infrastructure: This includes the installation and operation of specialized computer servers, storage units, and other AI equipment and software to enable the effective development and operation of AI systems/solution.

Type 5. Administrative Support Controls: These include issuing, sharing, and retaining on file AI Steering Committee Announcement and Minutes of Meetings, AI Project Manager's updated (with AI duties) employment agreement, AI Budget, and Procurement order for AI Infrastructure components.

Type 6. AI Governance, Development, and Operations Support Controls: These include issuing, sharing, using, implementing, and keeping current policies and procedures, such as AI Awareness Action Plan and AI Risk Assessment Procedure.

Type 7. Live AI Systems/Solutions/Tools: These include issuing, managing, using, sharing, and retaining on file Board and Senior Managers' AI presentation (digital).

All these may be used and implemented at the appropriate AI Implementation phase. Also, they may be used for awareness, reference, and training purposes by company board members, managers, and staff, as well as compliance and auditing purposes by internal corporate functions and external regulatory authorities and audit partners.

Phase A (AI Preparation) Recommended Assurance Tasks

In order to have the best results and outcomes and achieve the **goal of preparation** more effectively, the following assurance tasks (RAT) are recommended:

RAT1. Assess Actions Taken: Assess the actions taken of the above seven steps of Phase A and improve the process of preparation, as required.

RAT2. Review Products: Review the *eleven products* generated of this phase and consider their potential impact on your company's operations, production, and support processes, your employees and customers, and greater society, as needed. More specifically, you must review the findings of the "AI Needs Analysis Report" (Product P01, Step A1) and decide where you want to use AI (business area, use, or application) and how you want to develop, implement, and deploy AI for your company.

A typical example would be to manage e-mails, manage AI data, manage employee screening and hiring, improve customer support, and bolster data analysis of business intelligence to improve and change the strategic objectives of the company.

RAT3. Implement Measures: Plan, improve, and implement any measures or controls identified during the above seven steps (of Phase A) and by the review activities of RAT1 and RAT2 above, as required. For example, if the company has no AI skills, plan to acquire or develop them. Also, if the company has no privacy controls implemented, plan to develop and implement the relevant GDPR compliance measures for your personal data, which you will use in AI implementations.

RAT4. Report: Communicate results of your actions to AI Steering Committee and Board, as required.

RAT5. Document: Document all activities carried out and retain full documentation in organized digital and paper files for transparency, accountability, and compliance purposes.

RAT6. Keep Products Current: Ensure you keep current the above products, by reviewing them and updating them every two to three years or as needs, expectations, and operating conditions and circumstances warrant.

Concluding Remarks

Executing the seven steps and 26+ actions of this chapter supported you to better achieve your first goal (*Prepare the company better for AI*) and its two objectives (evaluate AI corporate readiness and engage top management in AI).

The most crucial tasks you have achieved so far were the following:

(1) Assessing your company's AI readiness

(2) Issuing a procurement order for obtaining the required AI Infrastructure components

(3) Identifying a set of potential Artificial Intelligence (AI) Projects, such as Manage e-mails, Manage AI data, Manage employee screening and hiring, Improve customer support, and Bolster data analysis of business intelligence to improve and change the strategic objectives of the company.

This is the first part of the **fourth** milestone (***Establish AI infrastructure management framework***) of your AI Management System Implementation Journey. The next chapter continues this exciting journey by describing how to establish your AI Governance Structure.

CHAPTER 8

Establish AI Governance Framework

Sam Altman,[1] CEO of OpenAI: "AI is a fundamental tool for productivity and transformation in various industries."

Overview: This chapter describes how to establish an AI Governance Structure for your organization. It includes (a) **seven steps**, (b) over **34 actions**, (c) over **19 products** (outcomes, results, and outputs, such as organizational functions/HR resources; assessment reports; reference documentation; AI/ICT infrastructure; administrative support controls; AI governance, development, and operations support controls; and live AI systems/solutions/tools), and (d) **five** assurance tasks to enable you to support, achieve, and ensure the good and effective development and operation (deployment) of your AI ecosystem.

The goal, objectives, steps, actions, products, and assurance tasks presented below form Phase B (AI Management Framework, Part 1: AI Governance Structure) of the AI Implementation Approach.

Phases of the AI Implementation Approach

The AI Implementation Approach (Component 3 of the AI Management System) includes five phases:

- AI Preparation (Phase A, previous chapter)

- AI Management Framework (Phase B-Part 1: AI Governance, this chapter; Parts 2 and 3 in the next chapters)

- AI Systems Development (Phase C)

131

J. Kyriazoglou, *AI Management Framework*, https://doi.org/10.1007/979-8-8688-1536-2_8

- AI Systems Operation (Phase D)

- AI Infrastructure and Systems Assessment (Phase E)

Goal and Objectives of Phase B (AI Management Framework, Part 1: AI Governance Structure)

The **goal of Phase** B-**Part 1** is to "Establish AI Governance Framework."

The objectives that support the achievement of this goal are

Objective 1: Establish AI Governance Controls

Objective 2: Establish AI Strategy and Ethics

Objective 3: Train Staff on AI

Steps of Phase B (AI Management Framework, Part 1: AI Governance Structure)

The seven steps to support the achievement of the goal and objectives of Phase B-Part 1 are

Step B1-1: Ensure Corporate Governance Controls Operation

Step B1-2: Establish AI Governance Roles and Responsibilities

Step B1-3: Establish AI Governance Framework

Step B1-4: Develop and Issue AI Strategy

Step B1-5: Establish AI Third-Party Controls

Step B1-6: Determine AI Ethical Principles and Values

Step B1-7: Educate and Train Employees on AI

Each step will contain one or more actions (and in some cases a questionnaire) to manage and resolve specific implementation issues. Also, each step will generate one or more products to achieve the specific step's purpose. These are listed in "Products of Phase B (AI Governance)" later in this chapter.

Step B1-1: Ensure Corporate Governance Controls Operation

Action 1. Ensure the following controls are established and operate effectively:

- Board, management, and committee roles, structure, and responsibilities

- Business functions and resources

- Standards, policies, and procedures

- Internal Controls Framework

- Corporate culture, ethics, vision, mission, and values

- Business strategy, goals, objectives, and targets

- Performance Framework and Management

- GRC (Governance, Risk, and Compliance) controls

- Operational controls (purchasing, finance, IT, data, security, fraud, etc.)

- Personnel administration, including segregation of duties, compensating controls, etc.

- Management and compliance reporting

- Monitoring controls

- Internal audits

- Self-assessments

- External audits

- Regulatory audits

Action 2. Ensure the above are updated with any AI requirements. For example: Add progress of AI projects in Corporate Reports.

Action 3. Ensure you revise and upgrade the corporate performance management system and include AI Performance Metrics (see Appendix 5) in the performance management process.

Action 4. Ensure human resource requirements include needs of AI staff and skills.

Step B1-2: Establish AI Governance Roles and Responsibilities

Action 1. Establish your AI Governance Roles and Responsibilities and other Governance Controls by executing the actions outlined in the next paragraphs, taking into consideration the actions, assessments, and products of Phase A (Preparation), such as AI Needs Analysis Report, AI Gap Analysis Report, AI Regulations and Standards, AI Readiness Report, Privacy Readiness Report, and AI Budget.

Action 2. Establish an *AI Steering Committee* (details in Step A4, Chapter 7) and an *AI project team* with specific roles and responsibilities (details in Step A5, Chapter 7). Ensure this team includes data science staff, knowledge engineering staff, IT experts, HR, compliance and risk personnel, legal staff, etc. In certain cases, and depending on the particulars of the specific organization, the role of an AI System Owner or AI Solution Owner may be established. Other complementary roles (e.g., data engineer) are described in Chapter 9.

Action 3. Ensure the duties of the appointed AI Project Manager are included in a job description and added to the person's employment agreement.

Action 4. Ensure the duties of the members of the appointed AI Project Team (and AI System Owner(s)) are included in job descriptions and added to their employment agreements.

Step B1-3: Establish AI Governance Framework

Action 1. Establish an *AI governance framework*. Ensure it includes

(1) An *AI governance body* to oversee the implementation, monitoring, and improvement of AI policies, procedures, and practices. This is a board mechanism and focuses on oversight activities, while the AI Steering Committee (see Phase A) is a working committee and concentrates on the day-to-day AI tasks.

(2) An *AI program* with specific AI projects (and systems, solutions, etc.) to be developed (internally or externally) and implemented. An example of an AI Program is, as per AI Needs Analysis Report (of Phase A)

(2.1) AI Project 1: Manage emails

(2.2) AI Project 2: Manage AI data

(2.3) AI Project 3: Manage employee screening and hiring

(2.4) AI Project 4: Improve customer support

(2.5) AI Project 5: Bolster data analysis of business intelligence

(3) An *AI Risk Assessment Methodology* that ensures overviewing, managing, and resolving of AI risks and controls for all key areas, including the AI solutions, self-learning capabilities, interfaces, management processes, KPIs, etc. See also "**NIST Risk Implementation Approach**."[2]

You may use your corporate risk assessment process to assess AI risks or a specific AI risk assessment procedure (see example in Appendix 6) and produce an AI Risk Assessment Report. On the basis of this, you should prepare better by developing and implementing a set of measures for the identified risks. See also "Step A1: Conduct AI Needs and Gap Analysis" and its products: AI Needs Analysis Report, AI Gap Analysis Report, and AI Risk Assessment Report.

(4) An *AI Audit Methodology* with the relevant tools (audit programs, audit plan, assessment questionnaires, audit report, etc.) that ensures the execution of an effective process of reviewing, assessing, and improving all areas of AI (see Chapter 13). To support you in crafting your own AI Audit Methodology, you may use the material and tools included in my Audit books in "Additional Resources." More details related to assessing AI audit areas are contained in Chapters 13–18. An example of an AI Audit Report is presented in Appendix 39.

Action 2. Ensure you establish an *AI Operating Model* that specifies a set of interrelated components, such as

(2.1) Data sources (external and internal).

(2.2) IT operational infrastructures that underpin data flows and processing and dedicated personnel to ensure the smooth running of the AI solution development, deployment, and integration.

(2.3) Data science and AI tools and skilled resources; data and AI governance controls for the data stored and processed within the AI system, solution, or platform.

(2.4) Business process owners and end users who will benefit from the AI system or solution.

(2.5) An AI performance management system is established, metrics are selected, performance data are collected and monitored, resolution actions are taken when performance issues arrive, etc. For an example of AI Performance Metrics, see Appendix 5.

(2.6) AI service delivery management mechanisms (e.g., a centralized function to qualify and plan the data science and AI projects in order to drive projects forward, etc.).

Action 3. Adequate documentation on the AI Operating Model should be maintained and kept current at all times. You may want to use an Enterprise Architecture Approach (framework and platform software tools, such as TOGAF, etc.) to document and manage all these entities.

Also, you may want to acquire and use, as needed, AI Governance Tools (specific software) to manage, detect, and mitigate bias (e.g., IBM AI Fairness 360), to ensure "Explainability" (e.g., LIME, SHAP), assess risks (e.g., NIST Risk framework and tool), evaluate EU AI Act Compliance (e.g., EU AI Act Compliance Checker), etc.

Action 4. Establish an AI architecture and development methodology. Ensure it includes

(4.1) Multiple models for different types of solutions, covering preferred technologies, design concepts such as logging, security controls and monitoring requirements, and "portability

(4.2) All relevant components (e.g., organizational, information, business, application, and technological)

(4.3) Implementing AI Capability Controls to ensure that AI systems operate safely, ethically, and responsibly. These controls may contain

(4.3.1) Establishing clear objectives for their AI systems and set boundaries to prevent misuse on the types of data the system can access, the tasks it can perform, or the decisions it can make

(4.3.2) Regular monitoring and evaluation of AI systems

(4.3.3) Effective security measures for their AI systems

(4.3.4) Promoting a culture of AI ethics and responsibility, etc.

(4.3.5) Developing clear and accessible policies outlining their approach to AI operations, including guidelines for data usage, privacy, fairness, and accountability

Action 5. Ensure responsible AI managers and staff (e.g., AI developers, AI system owner, IT manager, CEO, DPO, Chief Data Officer, etc.) are covered by a professional indemnity insurance policy to guard the company against potential AI related lawsuits.

Step B1-4: Develop and Issue AI Strategy

Establish your AI Strategy by considering the AI Risk Assessment Report (see "Step A1: Conduct AI Needs and Gap Analysis," in Chapter 7) and by executing the actions outlined in the next paragraphs, taking into consideration the outputs of Step B1 (Establish AI Governance Controls) and the actions, assessments, and products of Phase A (Preparation), such as AI Needs Analysis Report, AI Gap Analysis Report, AI Regulations and Standards, AI Readiness Report, Privacy Readiness Report, and AI Budget.

Action 1. **Set Clear AI Vision, Mission, Values, Policy Goals, Objectives, and Use Cases**

This could include promoting responsible AI use, ensuring compliance with relevant regulations, protecting data privacy, mitigating AI-related risks, etc.

These AI Objectives and AI Use Cases (see example in Appendix 8) will shape the overall direction of the policy.

Action 2. **Craft an AI Strategy**

Use the "AI Strategy Questionnaire" (Appendix 7) and develop an AI Strategy (for an example, see Appendix 8).

Action 3. Ensure this is formally issued and communicated to all staff and managers, stakeholders, and relevant third parties.

Action 4. Ensure the AI strategy supports the development and use of AI, providing direction to apply AI to deliver business value as well as achieve benefits for the organization itself as well as the people involved.

Action 5. Ensure the AI strategy is aligned with other corporate strategies (e.g., business, sales, data protection, IT, etc.).

Action 6. Manage AI expectations by carrying out the following tasks (T):

> T01. Ensure company management know the limitations of AI technologies, the human elements in AI, as well as the AI state of maturity to avoid unreal high expectations and overconfidence in the implementation effort of the AI solutions deployed within the specific company.

> T02. Ensure company CEO is educated on the risks, costs, and potential benefits of AI solutions.

> T03. Ensure there is an AI plan with a budget, resources, and pilot projects before full AI implementation.

> T04. Ensure the company requests and uses the advice and support of an external AI consultant to manage its AI expectations effectively.

You may also update and use the AI Awareness Action Plan (Appendix 4) for this purpose.

Step B1-5: Establish AI Third-Party Controls

Action 1. Ensure you establish AI third-party controls to ensure the organization's risk exposure or performance is not negatively impacted by AI third-party solutions that operate (now or in the future, AI project "Manage emails") at a lower level of control maturity and/or security standards. For more details, see Appendix 10.

Step B1-6: Determine AI Ethical Principles and Values

Action 1. Determine the **ethical principles** (e.g., Seven Ancient Greek Wisdom Principles, Chapter 2) and values that guide AI development and deployment within your company. It would help if you considered fairness, transparency, accountability, and human well-being concepts. These principles will help establish a solid foundation for AI Ethics. This includes reviewing, crafting, and implementing a set of relevant statements and policies, such as AI Vision, AI Mission, and AI Values Statements, Conflict of Interest Policy, AI Ethical Standards Policy, Corporate Ethics Policy, Corporate Social Responsibility Policy, Corporate Diversity Policy, Environment Protection Policy, and Data Ethics Policy. For more details, also see Chapters 2 and 3.

Action 2. Ensure all relevant managers are aware of and review the EU AI Act (see Chapter 4) and its clear transparency and reporting obligations if you are placing an AI system on the EU market.

Action 3. Ensure all relevant managers are aware of and review the Universal Guidelines for Artificial Intelligence, as per Chapter 4 (e.g., Right to Transparency, Right to Human Determination, Identification Obligation, Fairness Obligation, Assessment and Accountability Obligation, etc.) and their potential impact to company operations.

Action 4. Ensure all relevant managers are aware of and review the OECD AI Principles (see Chapter 4) that establish international standards for AI use (e.g., inclusive growth, sustainable development, and well-being; human-centered values and fairness; transparency and explainability; robustness, security, and safety; and accountability) and their potential impact to your company's operations.

Action 5. Ensure all relevant managers are aware of and review the Harmony Mnemonic Approach (Chapter 3) and the Seven Principles (Chapter 2) and consider its aspects in your task to craft an AI Ethics Policy for your company.

Action 6. Craft an AI Ethics Policy. Review the AI Ethical Standards Policy (see example in Chapter 3), the Harmony Mnemonic Approach (Chapter 2), and the Seven Principles (Chapter 3) and develop your own AI Ethics Policy. All people should sign commitment to this policy.

Action 7. Craft an AI Acceptable Use Policy. On the basis of all the above, craft an "AI Acceptable Use Policy" (see Appendix 9) and get all people to sign their commitment to it.

Action 8. Ensure these (AI Ethics Policy, AI Acceptable Use Policy) are formally issued, maintained, improved, and communicated to all staff and managers, stakeholders, and relevant third parties.

Action 9. Ensure you implement effective measures to protect your organization against the internal threats and IT sabotage that may occur by your staff. For more details, see "Annex 1" and "Annex 2."

Step B1-7: Educate and Train Employees on AI

Action 1. Prepare a presentation and conduct AI awareness sessions for all relevant staff (see Appendix 4 for more details). You may use gaming, quizzes, and case studies to enrich the learning experience of the participants.

Action 2. Keep a record of all minutes of awareness meetings and presentations.

Action 3. Ensure the company has crafted a glossary with common AI language, terms, and definitions, and this is properly maintained and shared across all staff of the company.

For more details, see Appendix 1.

Action 4. Craft an AI training policy and implement it, making sure all relevant staff participate fully in all training activities.

For more details, see Appendix 11.

Action 5. Ensure all relevant company staff are developed and continuously trained on AI aspects to the required level of capability and capacity.

Action 6. Ensure company human resources include both AI-skilled people, for example, to develop AI solutions, and non-AI-skilled resources, for example, to retain business knowledge.

Action 7. Ensure these (awareness and training policy and procedure) develop the necessary skills to develop and maintain AI systems (e.g., general knowledge of AI, specific knowledge of AI models and tools, AI security, data privacy, data science skills, digital skills, programming language skills (in particular, Python)), big data analysis, data visualization, cloud computing, cognitive skills (creative problem-solving, analytical skills, problem-solving, critical thinking, judgment, etc., data literacy skills (read and understand data in various forms, such as graphs, charts, or reports; work, communicate, navigate, and reason with data; research; data analysis (collecting, formatting, cleaning, and processing data as well as analysis and interpretation)); data visualization; data management (data cleaning, data mining, data warehousing, etc.); programming languages (understanding and using programming languages).

Products of Phase B (AI Governance)

The products (outcomes, results, and outputs) define (a) what's required (i.e., organizational functions, HR resources, ICT hardware and software, policies, etc.) to establish, develop, operate, implement, and assess AI infrastructure and systems/solutions and (b) what outputs and results (i.e., reference documentation, assessment reports, decisions of live AI systems, AI data, etc.) are produced, managed, used, and maintained by AI systems/solutions and their developmental, implementation, operational, and assessment aspects.

The main outcomes, results, and outputs of this chapter include the following types of products:

Type 1. Organizational Functions/HR Resources: These include (a) establishing an AI Project Team and staffing it accordingly and (b) appointing an AI System Owner.

Type 2. Assessment Reports: These include carrying out the necessary assessment and review actions and issuing the following analyses and reports – AI Risk Assessment Report, AI Third-Party Risk Assessment Report, Updated Corporate Report with AI projects' performance.

Type 3. Reference Documentation: This includes crafting and issuing reference documentation, such as Updated (with AI) Corporate Governance Controls Documentation, AI Program (with a list of approved Projects), AI Operating Model Documentation, AI Glossary (printed), AI Training Presentation (printed).

Type 4. AI/ICT Infrastructure: This includes the installation and operation of the AI Glossary (digital), an Enterprise Architecture Framework platform, and numerous AI software tools (if used for AI purposes).

Type 5. Administrative Support Controls: These include issuing, sharing, and retaining on file AI Project Team job descriptions and agreements signed and filed in Employee Files, AI System Owner Assignment, AI Governance Body Minutes of Meetings, Notification of AI Strategy to Stakeholders, Employee-signed AI Ethics Commitment Statements, Updated AI Budget, AI Training Sessions – Minutes of Meeting, professional indemnity insurance policy for relevant AI managers and staff.

Type 6. AI Governance, Development, and Operations Support Controls: These include issuing, sharing, using, implementing, and keeping current policies and procedures, such as AI performance management system, AI Strategy, Updated AI Awareness Action Plan, AI Ethics Policy, AI Acceptable Use Policy, Insider Threats Action Plan, and IT Sabotage Prevention Plan.

Type 7. Live AI Systems/Solutions/Tools: These include issuing, managing, using, sharing, and retaining on file AI Glossary (digital), AI Training Presentation (digital), and Enterprise Architecture Platform loaded with specification data.

All these may be used and implemented at the appropriate AI Implementation phase. Also, they may be used for awareness, reference, and training purposes by company board members, managers, and staff, as well as compliance and auditing purposes by internal corporate functions and external regulatory authorities and audit partners.

Phase B (AI Governance) Recommended Assurance Actions

In order to have the best results and outcomes and achieve the goal of AI Governance more effectively, the following assurance actions (RAA) are recommended:

RAA1. Assess Actions Taken: Assess the actions taken in the above seven steps of Phase B and improve the process of AI Governance, as required.

RAA2. Review Products: Review the **19+ *products*** generated in this part of this phase and consider their potential impact on your company's operations, production, and support processes, your employees and customers, and greater society, as needed.

More specifically, it may prove beneficial to ensure that the relevant AI staff have reviewed the Ethics Policy and the seven principles, so that they become more ethical in their decisions, etc.

RAA3. Implement Measures: Plan, improve, and implement any measures or controls identified during the above seven steps (of Phase B) and by the review activities of RAA1 and RAA2 above, as required. It is critical to note that at least you must update the AI Budget and ensure it is still valid.

For example, ensure the AI operating model aligns well with the company's business model.

Also, ensure AI Training includes the requirements of all AI Projects (Manage emails, Manage AI data, Manage employee screening and hiring, Improve customer support, and Bolster data analysis of business intelligence to improve and change the strategic objectives of the company).

RAA4. Report: Communicate results of your actions to the AI Steering Committee and Board, as required.

RAA5. Document: Document all activities carried out and retain full documentation in organized digital and paper files for transparency, accountability, and compliance purposes.

RAA6. Keep Products Current: Ensure you keep current the above products by reviewing them and updating them every two to three years or as needs, expectations, and operating conditions and circumstances warrant.

Concluding Remarks

Executing the seven steps and 30+ actions of this chapter support you to better achieve your second goal (*Establish AI Governance Framework*) and its two objectives (Establish AI Governance Controls and Establish AI Strategy and Ethics).

The most crucial tasks you have achieved in this phase were the following:

(1) Establishing your company's AI Roles and Responsibilities

(2) Developing Ethics and Acceptable Use Policies

(3) Training all relevant staff for AI

This is the second part of your **fourth** milestone (***Establish AI infrastructure management framework***) of your AI Ecosystem Journey. The next chapter continues this exciting journey by describing how to establish your Data Governance Structure.

Annex 1: Insider Threats Action Plan

1. **Develop and implement Security Controls (SC)**

    SC1. Design, develop, and implement adequate security controls on the basis of a company-wide risk assessment of the threats and risks facing your specific company.

    SC2. Implement physical access and improve procedures for accessing protected information and recording all business transactional activities.

    SC3. Escort your visitors to all areas.

    SC4. Use computer passwords, safes, and locked file cabinets to restrict access to proprietary information, etc.

    SC5. Limit access to data and other critical resources and sensitive information to your employees. Your company should actively apply what is known as the "principle of least privilege," which implies that specific employees will only have the information privileges that are absolutely necessary to perform their job functions.

2. **Provide comprehensive security training for all staff**

   To mitigate the insider threat from careless and ignorant staff
   (management, operations) behavior, you should provide regular
   comprehensive training in proper Internet and email protocol and
   other data security processes and procedures to all your people.
   Your staff should be educated and aware of your company's
   acceptable use of computer equipment, systems, and social
   media. In addition, you should regularly update your managers
   and employees on the latest security threats and how they can
   avoid becoming a victim (avoid social engineering attacks, etc.).

3. **Pay attention to your employees' health, safety, and wellness**

   You should pay attention to the health, safety, wellness, morale,
   and well-being of your employees as a way to alleviate stress and
   improve performance at all levels. Your company should enforce
   mandatory vacations and provide stress management seminars
   and other vehicles to help employees manage anxiety and other
   issues at the workplace. These measures will help reduce the
   number of stressed and disgruntled employees at your workplace.
   For more details, see also my books in the "Additional Resources"
   paragraph.

4. **Establish clear company staff selection/dismissal processes**

   You should take the time to develop and execute clear selection,
   hiring, and dismissal processes and procedures for all your staff.
   One important policy is to carry out thorough background checks
   of all potential employees during the hiring process. In addition,
   your business should have clear procedures on how to access the
   Internet, social media, and emails and how to handle company
   data both in the office and remotely.

   Your company should carefully control and oversee the critical
   dismissal (or offboarding) process as this is when a disgruntled
   employee is most likely to act maliciously. As a result, access to
   your company's network should be immediately revoked as soon
   as a termination occurs, and the former employee should be
   monitored and given a strict time limit to exit company premises.

5. **Deploy and use data monitoring and auditing technology**

    You should take advantage of security and network monitoring technology to detect unusual inbound and outbound traffic. In addition, you should implement a log correlation tool to monitor and control your employees' data access and online activities.

6. **Have backup and recovery solutions in place**

    As with other forms of security events and data breaches, the last line of defense against insider threats and corporate espionage is to ensure that you have a comprehensive IT Disaster Recovery Plan with backups and recovery solutions well tested. With these solutions available, your company will be able to quickly recover and restore your operations in the event of partial or complete data loss. With the ability to quickly resume your operations, even in the face of the worst security events and data breaches, a malicious insider or outsider will not be able to hold your company hostage.

7. **Perform regular security reviews and tests**

    You should perform penetration tests, internal reviews, and external vulnerability assessments and configuration testing to ensure that your company's equipment settings and systems are as secure as possible.

Annex 2: IT Sabotage Prevention Plan

Action 1. Create and maintain good documentation for networks and IT resources used by all systems and networks. Ensure your documentation is clear and accurate and includes all systems infrastructure from top to bottom, on-premises, and off-premises. Control access to this documentation and consider encrypting it for additional security.

Action 2. Maintain "super administrator" access where possible so your company can maintain the highest level of control over your systems to prevent infiltration. Be sure that this is clearly documented and is controlled by only a few senior and trusted people in your organization.

Action 3. Have fast and clear change procedures for administrative passwords so that no worker can make system changes once they leave the company.

Action 4. Use IT tools that allow you to set thresholds and alerts when there are unexpected activities inside the network to aid in the detection of possible sabotage events.

Action 5. Manage unmet employee expectations (not receiving a promotion, failing to receive a salary increase or bonus, being put on "boring" projects, etc.).

Action 6. Manage and resolve employee disgruntlement.

Action 7. Implement employee monitoring, after consultation with the legal and labor relations function.

Action 8. Eliminate unknown access paths, including backdoor accounts, shared system administrator accounts, and other group accounts.

CHAPTER 9

Establish Data Governance Framework

Mark Twain:[1] "Data is like garbage. You'd better know what you are going to do with it before you collect it."

   Overview: This chapter describes how to establish a Data Governance Framework Structure for your organization. It includes (a) **seven steps**, (b) over **34 actions**, (c) over **25 products** (outcomes, results, and outputs, such as organizational functions/ HR resources; assessment reports; reference documentation; AI/ICT infrastructure; administrative support controls; AI governance, development, and operations support controls; and live AI systems/solutions/tools), and (d) **five assurance tasks** to enable you to support, achieve, and ensure the good and effective development and operation (deployment) of your AI ecosystem. The goal, objectives, steps, actions, products, and assurance tasks presented below form Phase B (AI Management Framework, Part 2: Data Governance Structure) of the AI Implementation Approach.

Phases of the AI Implementation Approach

The AI Implementation Approach (Component 3 of the AI Management System) includes five phases:

- AI Preparation (Phase A, Chapter 7)

- AI Management Framework (Phase B-Part 1: AI Governance, previous chapter; Phase B-Part 2, *this chapter*; and Phase B-Part 3, next chapter)

- AI Systems Development (Phase C)

© John Kyriazoglou 2025
J. Kyriazoglou, *AI Management Framework*, https://doi.org/10.1007/979-8-8688-1536-2_9

- AI Systems Operation (Phase D)

- AI Infrastructure and Systems Assessment (Phase E)

Goal and Objectives of Phase B (AI Management Framework, Part 2: Data Governance Structure)

The goal of Phase B-Part 2 is to "Establish Data Governance Framework."
   The objectives that support the achievement of this goal are

> Objective 1: Establish Data Management Controls
>
> Objective 2: Organize and manage corporate data
>
> Objective 3: Prepare data for AI projects

Steps of Phase B (AI Management Framework, Part 2: Data Governance Structure)

The seven steps to support the achievement of the goal and objectives of Phase B-Part 2 are

> Step B2-1: Establish Data Governance Function
>
> Step B2-2: Establish Data governance policies and procedures
>
> Step B2-3: Establish Big Data management policies and procedures
>
> Step B2-4: Manage Corporate Data Storage
>
> Step B2-5: Locate and organize AI data
>
> Step B2-6: Manage Business Records and Intelligence
>
> Step B2-7: Protect Intellectual Property (IP) Assets

Each step will contain one or more actions (and in some cases a questionnaire) to manage and resolve specific implementation issues. Also, each step will generate one or more products to achieve the specific step's purpose. These are listed in "Products of Phase B (AI Data Governance)" later in this chapter.

Step B2-1: Establish Data Governance Function

Establishing your Data Governance Function will require the full execution of the following actions:

Action 1. Establish a Data Management Office, which will be headed by a Chief Data Officer with responsibilities to define policies and procedures, train staff, and ensure data governance is connected with other relevant corporate functions.

Action 2. Assign dedicated staff to manage the daily data management activities.

Action 3. Establish a Corporate Data Steering Committee with the role to review progress, authorize funding, and resolve issues related to data.

Action 4. Establish AI Data Governance Roles and Responsibilities, such as AI Project Manager, AI System owner, AI solution owner, data owner, data steward, learning data owner, algorithm owner, AI engineer, AI software developer, data scientist, machine learning engineer, Chief Data Officer, etc.

Action 5. Ensure these roles and responsibilities are implemented effectively in employment or consulting agreement and job descriptions.

Action 6. Ensure all AI and Data Management staff sign a confidentiality statement.

Action 7. Ensure the company's DPO (Data Protection Officer) or Chief Privacy Officer is trained on all aspects of AI and its implications to the company.

For more details, see Appendix 12.

Step B2-2: Establish Data Governance Policies and Procedures

Action 1. Develop and implement data governance policies and procedures for managing and maintaining all aspects of data.

Action 2. Ensure these cover the complete life cycle of data quality aspects (i.e., availability, usability, integrity, and security) and administrative issues (e.g., data ownership rights, data collection, data labeling, data storage and security, and data management).

Action 3. Ensure these include best practices for maintaining data quality in AI (e.g., implement data governance policies, utilize data quality tools to ensure that AI models have access to high-quality data consistently, establish a dedicated team responsible for data quality, etc.).

Action 4. Ensure company management and staff, at all levels of the organization, operate within the framework and principles of data culture, that is, an organizational environment exists where all staff are literate with data, and data have high value in daily operations, are readily accessible and shared, and are used consistently to support and drive decision-making processes in the best way possible.

Action 5. Ensure company staff are trained in all aspects of data governance controls (e.g., data collection, data labeling, data storage and security, and data management).

Action 6. Ensure AI test data and AI "learning data" for all projects are effectively protected (e.g., access controls, encryption, separate servers, backup and restore controls, etc.).

Step B2-3: Establish Big Data Management Policies and Procedures

Action 1. Develop and implement policies and procedures for managing big data.

Action 2. Ensure these include assessing the potential risks of managing big data (e.g., data breaches, unauthorized access, data loss, and regulatory non-compliance) and developing adequate remedial measures (e.g., encrypting sensitive data, using access controls, and conducting regular audits) for their protection.

Action 3. Ensure staff are aware of data security issues and trained to handle them.

Action 4. Ensure big data controls are compliant with regulations like GDPR.

For more details, see Appendixes 13–15.

Step B2-4: Manage Corporate Data Storage

Action 1. Develop and implement policies and procedures for managing corporate data.

Action 2. Ensure these policies and procedures cover all incoming, processed, and outgoing data, information, and transactions of your company.

Action 3. Ensure all corporate data are kept:

    3.1.   In the original ("raw") format

    3.2.   In a well-protected, safe (from fire, etc.) storage

3.3.   Protected by access restriction rules in a location for as long as required by government regulations (tax, health, safety, etc.)

3.4.   Managed in accordance with industrial and other practices (stock exchange, banks, etc.) applicable to your business operation

Action 4. Ensure their attributes (data element description, type, format, validating and editing instructions, business processing rules, etc.) are maintained in a Corporate Data Register or Data Dictionary.[2]

Action 5. Develop and implement an Enterprise Data Repository.

Your corporate data usually will include classical databases (for legacy application systems) as well as data marts, data warehouses, and data lakes and unstructured data of all types, etc.

To make best use of all these data for AI and other corporate purposes, it is a good idea to establish, manage, and maintain an Enterprise Data Repository (see Annex 2 for an example of such a procedure).

Action 6. Assess and ensure your personnel have the necessary skills (e.g., knowledge engineering, data engineering, data validation, data science, business analysis, data analytics, etc.) to organize and manage your data storage systems (Enterprise Data Repository, data marts, data warehouses, data lakes,[3] etc.).

Action 7. Ensure your personnel have the necessary skills to manage and protect the Personal Data collected and processed by the company for various purposes, including your AI systems/solutions, etc. For more details, see Appendix 18.

Step B2-5: Locate and Organize AI Data

Action 1. Review the contents of your Enterprise Data Repository and decide whether they fit your purpose for the first AI Project (Manage emails). If required, obtain data from external legible sources and add them to your repository. Perform a due diligence assessment report on all external data providers before using their data.

Action 2. Identify and collect the data you need for this project by

2.1.   Selecting the method that is most suitable for your AI project (from internal and external data sources)

2.2.   Ensuring they are of high quality

2.3.   Transforming data (unstructured, audio, video, etc.) into numbers for machine learning

2.4.   Storing the data and taking into consideration privacy regulations

2.5.   Annotating the data by labeling or tagging them for machine readability

Data labeling requires the location and identification of raw data (i.e., images, text files, videos) and then the addition of one or more labels to that data to specify its context for the AI models, allowing the specific learning model to make accurate predictions.

It should be noted that some companies use synthetic data to avoid privacy regulations.

You may also use AI for this purpose, as per AI Needs Analysis Report (of Phase A), AI Project 2 (Manage AI data).

Action 3. Create AI test data and AI "learning data" for your first AI Project (Manage emails).

Action 4. Ensure your AI data are labeled for the use of the first AI Project (Manage emails).

Action 5. Document how the data was collected, the data sources utilized, any transformations applied to the data, and any other relevant metadata.

Action 6. For collecting data for your AI model, see Chapter 11, Step C5, and Appendix 31.

Step B2-6: Manage Business Records and Intelligence

Action 1. Ensure the company has implemented a corporate knowledge retention management process that includes

(1.1)   A strategy for managing knowledge related to decisions to be made – or supported – by the AI system or solution

(1.2)   The provision of subject matter expertise, thought leadership, and traditional business knowledge to support the organization in developing new AI capabilities effectively

Action 2. Resolve any potential conflicts arising from the data governance controls related to the development and deployment of AI systems or solutions.

Action 3. Develop and implement policies and procedures for managing the documentation of processing records and for gathering internal and external data and intelligence.

Action 4. Ensure these include the documentation for Personal Data Flows and Personal Data per company operation (function) and IT infrastructure (systems, equipment, devices, etc.).

Action 5. Ensure this documentation (PD, IT) includes all flows and all personal data that exist in all business functions, locations, systems, equipment, and devices.

Action 6. Ensure this documentation (PD, IT) is maintained in the required formats (in paper, in electronic form) and that it contains all the information required under EU GDPR.

For more details, see Appendix 16.

Step B2-7: Protect Intellectual Property (IP) Assets

Action 1. Ensure the company has implemented an Intellectual Property (IP) protection policy.

For more details, see Appendix 17.

Action 2. Ensure this policy includes all AI-related IP assets.

Action 3. Ensure there is a repository of all corporate IP assets related to an AI solution (i.e., data, code, models, and "learning data") set up and accessible in-house, secured, and protected.

Products of Phase B (AI Data Governance)

The products (outcomes, results, and outputs) define (a) what's required (i.e., organizational functions, HR resources, ICT hardware and software, policies, etc.) to establish, develop, operate, implement, and assess AI infrastructure and systems/solutions and (b) what outputs and results (i.e., reference documentation, assessment reports, decisions of live AI systems, AI data, etc.) are produced, managed, used, and maintained by AI systems/solutions and their developmental, implementation, operational, and assessment aspects.

The main outcomes, results, and outputs of this chapter include the following types of products:

Type 1. Organizational Functions/HR Resources: These include (a) establishing a Data Management Office and a Corporate Data Steering Committee and (b) appointing a Chief Data Officer and Data Management Staff.

Type 2. Assessment Reports: These include carrying out the necessary assessment and review actions and issuing the following analyses and reports – big data management risk assessment report, staff skills assessment report, and due diligence assessment report on all external data providers.

Type 3. Reference Documentation: This includes crafting and issuing reference documentation, such as Basic Personal Data Management Instructions, Data Handling Instructions, Data Management Employee Training Presentation, Data Management Employee and DPO or Privacy Officer Training Notes and additional material (games, quizzes, cases studies), AI Data Collection and Transformation Documentation, Business Records Documentation System, Personal Data Flows Inventory, Business Intelligence Documentation System, Repository of AI-related IT Assets (printed).

Type 4. AI/ICT Infrastructure: This includes the installation and operation of Big Data Repository, Corporate Data Storage, Corporate Data Dictionary, Enterprise Data Repository, AI Test Data for each AI Project, and AI "Learning Data" for each AI Project.

Type 5. Administrative Support Controls: These include issuing, sharing, and retaining on file Data Management Employee Training Records, Chief Data Officer (job description, employment agreement), Data Management Staff (job descriptions, employment agreements), Corporate Data Steering Committee Minutes of Meetings. AI and Data Management staff signed confidentiality statements.

Type 6. AI Governance, Development, and Operations Support Controls: These include issuing, sharing, using, implementing, and keeping current policies and procedures, such as Data Governance Policy, Data Quality Policy, Data Quality Improvement Procedure, Corporate Information and Business Intelligence Policy, AI Data Protection Guidelines, Enterprise Data Repository Management Procedure, and Intellectual Property Rights Protection Policy.

Type 7. Live AI Systems/Solutions/Tools: These include issuing, managing, using, sharing, and retaining on file Repository of AI-related IT Assets (digital), Live Enterprise Data Repository, Live Big Data Repository, Live Corporate Data Storage, Live Corporate Data Dictionary, Live AI Test Data for each AI Project, and Live AI "Learning Data" for each AI Project.

All these may be used and implemented at the appropriate AI Implementation phase. Also, they may be used for awareness, reference, and training purposes by company board members, managers, and staff, as well as compliance and auditing purposes by internal corporate functions and external regulatory authorities and audit partners.

Phase B (Data Governance) Recommended Assurance Actions

In order to have the best results and outcomes and achieve the goal of Data Governance more effectively, the following assurance actions (RAA) are recommended:

RAA1. Assess Actions Taken: Assess the actions taken of the above seven steps of Phase B and improve the process of preparation, as required.

RAA2. Review Products: Review the *18 products* generated of this phase and consider their potential impact on your company's operations, production, and support processes, your employees and customers, and greater society, as needed.

More specifically, it is a good idea to review the training of employees on data management and the data stores for the first AI project ("Manage emails") to ensure that everything is done properly and in accordance with the AI ethics policy of your company.

RAA3. Implement Measures: Plan, improve, and implement any measures or controls identified during the above seven steps (of Phase A) and by the review activities of RAA1 and RAA2 above, as required. It is critical to note that at least risk assessment, IT security, and data protection (GDPR) controls should be in place and operate effectively before you embark on any major AI system (application or solution) development and deployment and that AI data are effectively protected (see Annex 1).

Also, ensure data backups are included in the IT backup recovery process and the AI Budget is updated, as required.

RAA4. Report: Communicate results of your actions to AI Steering Committee and Board, as required.

RAA5. Document: Document all activities carried out and retain full documentation in organized digital and paper files for transparency, accountability, and compliance purposes.

RAA6. Keep Products Current: Ensure you keep current the above products, by reviewing them and updating them every two to three years or as needs, expectations, and operating conditions and circumstances warrant.

Concluding Remarks

Executing the seven steps and 34+ actions of this chapter supported you to better achieve your third goal (*Establish Data Governance Framework*) and its three objectives (establish Data Management Controls, organize and manage corporate data, and prepare data for AI projects).

The most crucial tasks you have achieved in this phase were the following:

(1) Establishing your company's Data Governance Roles and Responsibilities[4]

(2) Developing Data Governance policies and procedures[5]

(3) Organizing and managing corporate data in an Enterprise Data Repository

(4) Training all relevant staff on handling data

(5) Ensuring the required data (for testing and learning purposes) are prepared and ready for the first AI Project (Manage emails)

This is the third part of the **fourth** milestone (***Establish AI infrastructure management framework***) of your AI Ecosystem Journey. The next chapter continues this exciting journey by describing how to manage IT Governance and Privacy Controls.

Annex 1: AI Data Protection Guidelines

Data Protection Model

The Company has adopted and used the following data protection model, with the five dimensions: "Transparency," "Respecting Rights," "Understanding Needs," "Security," and "Treatment."

1. **Transparency**: We are open and clear about how data are collected, used, and processed for AI purposes.

2. **Respecting Rights**: We fully regard and respect the rights of data subjects (customers, employees, users, and persons in general).

3. **Understanding Needs**: We understand that data subjects are concerned about protecting their own data.

4. **Security**: We protect the data from misuse or unauthorized access, disclosure, loss, etc.

5. **Treatment**: We treat people on the basis of ethical values and respect and in a way that is consistent with our corporate values.

Security Safeguards

The Company uses the "Data Safe Haven" concept to establish a secure environment for personal data. This includes a secure office space, trained staff, security controls, security software, and privacy and security procedures for managing, storing, processing, and sharing data.

All Company systems and resources (including AI systems, tools, and resources) have appropriate safeguards to preserve privacy, security, confidentiality, integrity, and availability of all data according to major privacy and information security regulations.

These include physical, administrative, and technical controls such as secure storage facilities, key and password management procedures, firewalls, virus scanners, audit logging, and non-repudiation mechanisms. Safeguards (e.g., appropriate encryption) are implemented to protect data in transit, whether inside or outside the trust boundary of the Company.

Annex 2: Enterprise Data Repository Management Procedure

Step 1. Copy all these internal corporate data (raw, classical databases, data marts, data warehouses, and data lakes, unstructured data, etc.) and external data (from various sources, Internet, data providers, etc.).

Step 2. Organize and store them into a storage system.

Step 3. Clean them from any errors.

Step 4. Review them and ensure they comply with privacy regulations.

Step 5. Transform them into AI data by labeling them and running special software to translate text, sound, video, and text into numbers, etc.

Step 6. Establish your Enterprise Data Repository and store these data into this facility.

Step 7. Manage your Enterprise Data Repository effectively by maintaining quality, protecting all data stored in it via access and security controls, making the data available only to authorized persons and entities, cleaning and deleting damaged data, backing up data into archives according to backup policy, etc.

CHAPTER 10

Manage IT Governance and Privacy Controls

Narendra Modi:[1] "Good governance depends on ability to take responsibility by both administration as well as people."

Overview: This chapter describes how to ensure IT Governance and Privacy Controls[2] are effective for your organization's AI ecosystem. It includes (a) **15 steps**, (b) over **85 actions**, (c) over **22 products** (outcomes, results, and outputs, such as organizational functions/HR resources; assessment reports; reference documentation; AI/ICT infrastructure; administrative support controls; AI governance, development, and operations support controls; and live AI systems/solutions/tools), and (d) **five** assurance tasks to enable you to support, achieve, and ensure the good and effective development and operation (deployment) of your AI ecosystem and relevant AI Systems/Solutions. The goal, objectives, steps, actions, products, and assurance tasks presented below form Phase B (AI Management Framework, Part 3: IT Governance Controls) of the AI Implementation Approach.

Phases of the AI Implementation Approach

The AI Implementation Approach (Component 3 of the AI Management System) includes five phases:

- AI Preparation (Phase A, Chapter 7)

- AI Management Framework (Phase B-Part 1: AI Governance and Data Governance, Chapters 8 and 9, and Phase B-Part 3: IT Governance, *this chapter*)

- AI Systems Development (Phase C)

© John Kyriazoglou 2025
J. Kyriazoglou, *AI Management Framework*, https://doi.org/10.1007/979-8-8688-1536-2_10

- AI Systems Operation (Phase D)

- AI Infrastructure and Systems Assessment (Phase E)

Goal and Objectives of Phase B (AI Management Framework, Part 3: IT Governance Controls)

The **goal of Phase** B-**Part 2** is to "Support AI Environment and AI Systems Development and Operation."

The objectives that support the achievement of this goal are

Objective 1: Establish AI computer infrastructure

Objective 2: Ensure effective information security and privacy controls

Objective 3: Ensure critical IT controls include AI aspects

Steps of Phase B (AI Management Framework, Part 3: IT Governance Controls)

The 15 steps to support the achievement of the goal and objectives of Phase B-Part 3 are

Step B3-1: Manage AI computer infrastructure

Step B3-2: Manage information security and privacy policies and procedures

Step B3-3: Manage vulnerabilities and malware

Step B3-4: Manage robotic accounts

Step B3-5: Manage human accounts

Step B3-6: Manage account provisioning and revocation

Step B3-7: Manage password controls

Step B3-8: Manage segregation of IT duties

Step B3-9: Manage third-party access controls

Step B3-10: Manage IT changes

Step B3-11: Manage AI solutions inventory

Step B3-12: Manage IT resources

Step B3-13: Manage IT knowledge retention

Step B3-14: Manage IT configuration

Step B3-15: Manage backup and recovery process

Each step will contain one or more actions (and in some cases a questionnaire) to manage and resolve specific implementation issues. Also, each step will generate one or more products to achieve the specific step's purpose. These are listed in "IT Governance and Privacy Products" later in this chapter.

Step B3-1: AI Computer Infrastructure Management

Action 1. Ensure all necessary AI computer infrastructure components (i.e., hardware, software, etc.) are installed, tested, and operate effectively.

Action 2. Ensure this AI computer infrastructure includes

    (2.1)   Hardware Components (GPU (Graphics Processing Unit) Servers, AI Accelerators, TPUs (Tensor Processing Units), High-Performance Computing (HPC) Systems, etc.)

    (2.2)   Software Components (Machine Learning Frameworks, Data Processing Libraries that are used for handling and processing large datasets, etc.)

    (2.3)   Storage Solutions, such as cloud storage, data lakes, and distributed file systems

Action 3. Ensure AI computer infrastructure includes an integrated development environment with proper AI tools for research, learning, training, and experimental purposes.

Action 4. Ensure maintenance support is provided for all these components via proper Services Agreements with the vendor(s) of these hardware and software components.

Action 5. Ensure all the above are implemented fully before the first AI System (Manage emails) is developed and put in a production status.

Step B3-2: Information Security and Privacy Policies and Procedures Management

Action 1. Ensure your main information security and privacy management policies and procedures operate effectively and include all aspects of your AI environment.

Action 2. Ensure your AI environment complies fully with main information security and privacy policies, procedures, and daily practices.

Action 3. Ensure this approach is integrated with the "regular" security management controls to ensure a complete approach across the AI and related environments. This must apply to code, algorithms, configuration, IT infrastructure, applications, data structures, and data classification and related management processes.

Action 4. Ensure your information security management is aligned to good practice standards (e.g., ISO 27001).

Action 5. Ensure code and data storage as well as network communications to/from/ within the AI system/solution are adequately encrypted.

Action 6. Ensure penetration tests or "red team" reviews are performed to assess the AI environment's exposure to vulnerabilities.

Action 7. Ensure periodic security testing is performed to ensure security controls, sensors, and monitoring are effective and operational.

Action 8. Ensure you comply fully with privacy regulations for all your data (including AI data).

Action 9. Ensure all safety and security aspects of your data center by implementing relevant physical and environmental protection controls.

Action 10. Ensure your staff sign the IT Policies and Procedures Compliance Statement.

Action 11. Ensure all controls are implemented fully before the first AI System (Manage emails) is developed and put in a production status.

For more details, see Appendixes 19–22.

Also, see my IT and ISO 27001 books listed in "Additional Resources."

Step B3-3: Vulnerabilities and Malware Management

Action 1. Ensure malware protection is in place and includes all components and aspects of AI. This may include antimalware software, a bot manager (to classify web requests and allow the use of some bots while blocking others), and a firewall that can be configured to block bots and prevent certain traffic based on one or more IP addresses, behavior, etc.

Action 2. Ensure availability of new patches includes AI and is continuously monitored.

Action 3. Ensure an impact assessment is performed before the patch gets implemented in a timely manner.

Action 4. Ensure malware protection software applies to self-learning models and components, besides regular and AI hardware, AI application system software, and data.

Action 5. Ensure all the above are implemented fully before the first AI System (Manage emails) is developed and put in a production status.

For more details, see Appendix 23.

Step B3-4: Robotic Accounts Management

Action 1. Obtain and use a bot (robotic) manager (e.g., software product) to manage bots, such as blocking undesired or malicious Internet bot traffic while still allowing useful bots to access web properties.

Action 2. Ensure all Bot accounts used by AI systems are unique and have been assigned to a human with ultimate responsibility for these.

Action 3. Ensure that for each Bot, usage of its account is tracked in between applications and services and all activities are recorded in logs.

Action 4. Ensure the Bot's access rights to relevant systems are set up and assigned on a "need-to-have" basis.

Action 5. Ensure Bot access is constrained to applications and data required for specific, intended transactions only.

Action 6. Ensure the Bot's access accounts and their system privileges are reviewed periodically, the review results are documented, and any inappropriate uses investigated and corrected.

Action 7. Ensure access to all Bot accounts is monitored by proper management.

Action 8. Ensure all the above are implemented fully before the first AI System (Manage emails) is developed and put in a production status.

Step B3-5: Human Accounts Management

Action 1. Ensure human accounts to access the AI environment are personal and unique, and the individuals have ultimate responsibility for these.

Action 2. Ensure access to AI system logic and algorithms are appropriately restricted to authorized individuals.

Action 3. Ensure user access to the AI system/solution itself, additional (permanent or temporary) data storage facilities, log files, and other relevant components are set up and assigned on a "need-to-have" basis.

Action 4. Ensure user accounts and system privileges that have access to the AI system/solution itself, additional (permanent or temporary) data storage facilities, log files, and other relevant components are reviewed periodically, their results documented, and any findings acted upon.

Action 5. Ensure access to powerful user accounts (privileged accounts), which can be used to perform user access administration, change system configuration, or directly access interfaces or data, is restricted to a defined set of system administration personnel.

Action 6. Ensure access to all accounts is monitored by proper management.

Action 7. Ensure all the above are implemented fully before the first AI System (Manage emails) is developed and put in a production status.

For more details, see Appendix 24.

Step B3-6: Account Provisioning and Revocation Management

Action 1. Ensure an access provisioning procedure is in place for the creation of (human) user and Bot accounts and assigning user privileges to new or existing accounts.

Action 2. Ensure formal approval is required by appropriate business representatives for the establishment of users and granting of access rights, both the human and robotic accounts.

Action 3. Ensure an access revocation procedure is in place for the timely deletion or locking of user accounts and their privileges when an employee leaves or when the employee or the Bot no longer needs this access due to a change in role or decommissioning.

Action 4. Ensure all account approval and access revocations are monitored by proper management.

Action 5. Ensure all the above are implemented fully before the first AI System (Manage emails) is developed and put in a production status.

Step B3-7: Password Controls Management

Action 1. Ensure effective authentication controls (e.g., password controls policy) are in place, for example, through the use of password controls or biometrics, in line with the IT security policy for systems in scope across the IT environment (AI environment, network, OS, database, applications, and utilities).

Action 2. Ensure these controls apply to all user (robotic and human) accounts, including system administration accounts and automation authentication.

Action 3. Ensure compensating controls exist to mitigate the risk that unauthorized individuals can use the related accounts to access data or systems, in case certain accounts (e.g., system accounts or Bot accounts) do not have password controls in place or are required to use hard-coded passwords.

Action 4. Ensure all the above are implemented fully before the first AI System (Manage emails) is developed and put in a production status.

Step B3-8: Segregation of IT Duties Implementation

Action 1. Ensure that a segregation of IT duties policy that includes AI aspects is effectively upgraded (if it exists) and implemented.

Action 2. Ensure no single IT person can create user accounts (human, robotic) and assign access privileges to these accounts without approval by the IT manager.

Action 3. Ensure no single IT person can make changes to any IT components and the AI system(s) or its data directly in production.

Action 4. Ensure all changes to the AI environment are made in the development environment before these are applied to the AI production system.

Action 5. Ensure no single IT person can raise and approve the same change request.

Action 6. Ensure all the above are implemented fully before the first AI System (Manage emails) is developed and put in a production status.

Step B3-9: Third-Party Access Controls Implementation

Action 1. Ensure access by third-party users to corporate data or data processing facilities or any AI part is subject to the same level of controls as "regular" users, data, and data processing facilities.

Action 2. Ensure access by users to third-party data or data processing facilities is subject to the same level of controls as "regular" users, data, and data processing facilities.

Action 3. Ensure all the above are implemented fully before the first AI System (Manage emails) is developed and put in a production status.

For more details, see Appendix 10.

Step B3-10: IT Change Management

Action 1. Ensure changes to the AI environment follow a consistent change management approach with clear procedures and work instructions around changes to IT infrastructure, AI models and algorithms, data, etc.

Action 2. Ensure AI changes are integrated with the "regular" change management approach to enable a consistent approach across the AI and related environments.

Action 3. Ensure data governance inventories, including data classification policy, AI inventory, data asset flagging, and data flow maps, are maintained as part of the change management process.

Action 4. Ensure changes to production are not permitted, unless specific approval from the appropriate level of management is obtained.

Action 5. Ensure changes caused by the dynamic nature of machine learning are covered by additional measures, such as logging and review of any modifications and/or periodic comparison of the solutions at different time stamps to identify any changes made.

Action 6. Ensure the impact of changes to AI processing and outputs on other IT services is assessed and monitored.

Action 7. Ensure change management is aligned to good practice standards (e.g., ITIL) and versioning is in place for business processes, code, Bot configuration, applications, data structures, data classification, etc.

Action 8. Ensure all the above are implemented fully before the first AI System (Manage emails) is developed and put in a production status.

For more details, see Appendix 34.

Step B3-11: AI Solutions Inventory Management

Action 1. Ensure an inventory of all AI platforms, systems, tools, solutions, and use cases exists, is complete, and is kept up to date.

Action 2. Ensure the specific owner of each AI system or solution is captured in the inventory.

Action 3. Ensure the AI inventory is managed by a responsible IT person.

Action 4. Ensure all the above are implemented fully before the first AI System (Manage emails) is developed and put in a production status.

Step B3-12: IT Resource Management

Action 1. Ensure controls are in place to monitor IT resource demands more closely than other systems because AI systems might be more likely to be more unpredictable (need more resources on a dynamic basis, use of external systems or databases, etc.).

Action 2. Ensure IT knows or estimates the demand and use of IT resources (e.g., processing time, capacity, processes with other systems, etc.) by AI systems/solutions used.

Action 3. Ensure AI systems/solutions make decisions about the system resources they require that may impact the cost and efficacy of the overall system.

Action 4. Ensure all the above are implemented fully before the first AI System (Manage emails) is developed and put in a production status.

Step B3-13: IT Knowledge Retention Management

Action 1. Ensure AI system/solution and IT management processes, including process, technology, and data requirements, are well documented and maintained for the end-to-end process for each AI system/solution.

Action 2. Ensure sufficient IT knowledge (staff and/or skills) are retained and developed to effectively run and maintain the AI system/solution.

Action 3. Ensure development methodology, architectural standards, and other technical and data-related documentation are available to sufficiently skilled resources to support the development of new AI systems/solutions or new parts of existing systems/solutions.

Action 4. Ensure, in case external vendors are used to develop AI systems/solutions, adequate knowledge transfer has been designed and executed to retain relevant knowledge within the organization.

Action 5. Ensure documentation is kept up to date through automated logging and reporting of changes (e.g., through an audit trail of changes to decision logic).

Action 6. Ensure all the above are implemented fully before the first AI System (Manage emails) is developed and put in a production status.

Step B3-14: IT Configuration Management

Action 1. Ensure you understand the IT and data components of the overall AI environment and systems as well as their aspects (security, software licenses, IT operations, business continuity, capacity, availability, etc.).

Action 2. Ensure a configuration management database is established and maintained to ensure a complete understanding of all the IT and data components and their relationships.

Action 3. Ensure this repository includes all AI-related IT and data components.

Action 4. Ensure all the above are implemented fully before the first AI System (Manage emails) is developed and put in a production status.

For more details, see Appendix 25.

Step B3-15: Backup and Recovery Process Management

Action 1. Ensure effective business continuity plans (BCP) have been developed and approved, are being maintained adequately, and include AI solutions and data (process, learning).

Action 2. Ensure BCP roles and responsibilities, including AI, third parties, and external suppliers, are clearly defined and relevant staff are well trained in these.

Action 3. Ensure regular BCP simulations, including testing of alternative facilities, are performed to ensure plans and facilities are effective for all processing, regular and AI, and that staff are well trained to operate under such conditions (i.e., to ensure people, process, and technology are ready when needed).

Action 4. Ensure backup and recovery policy and procedures have been developed, documented, and tested fully.

Action 5. Ensure these (backup and recovery policy and procedures) include all AI systems and solutions and all their components (hardware, software, process and learning data, etc.).

Action 6. Ensure these (backup and recovery policy and procedures) cover all risks, such as IT infrastructure (i.e., not having core processing facilities available in time, access to data, etc.), solution (i.e., not having an alternative AI solution in place in time that provides the same functionality, learnings, access to the same data, etc.), and business (i.e., not being able to manually – or otherwise – operate relevant business processes without an effective AI solution in place).

Action 7. Ensure, if needed, the "Vault Principle" is applied, that is, an automated solution that securely stores any decision made by the AI system or solution, as well as the data the decision was based on and the latest version of the algorithm(s) and code.

Action 8. Ensure all the above are implemented fully before the first AI System (Manage emails) is developed and put in a production status.

IT Governance and Privacy Products

The products (outcomes, results, and outputs) define (a) what's required (i.e., organizational functions, HR resources, ICT hardware and software, policies, etc.) to establish, develop, operate, implement, and assess AI infrastructure and systems/solutions and (b) what outputs and results (i.e., reference documentation, assessment reports, decisions of live AI systems, AI data, etc.) are produced, managed, used, and maintained by AI systems/solutions and their developmental, implementation, operational, and assessment aspects.

The main outcomes, results, and outputs of this chapter include the following types of products:

> **Type 1. Organizational Functions/HR Resources**: These include (a) establishing an AI Incident Management Team, (b) staffing with relevant staff, and (c) appointing an IT person to manage the AI inventory.

> **Type 2. Assessment Reports**: These include carrying out the necessary assessment and review actions and issuing the following analyses and reports – AI penetration testing documentation, "red team" reviews for AI environment's exposure to vulnerabilities, AI compliance report (with main information security and privacy policies, procedures, and daily practices), and an impact assessment report for each software patch (before implementation).

> **Type 3. Reference Documentation**: This includes crafting and issuing reference documentation, such as AI computer infrastructure documentation; AI tools documentation; AI data privacy compliance documentation; Bot (robotic) manager (e.g., software product) documentation; Bot access accounts review notes; AI systems, tools, and solutions inventory; human accounts management procedure (to access the AI environment) documentation.

> **Type 4. AI/ICT Infrastructure**: This includes the installation and operation of AI computer hardware, software, and data storage units, malware protection software, software bot manager, and firewall management software.

> **Type 5. Administrative Support Controls**: These include issuing, sharing, and retaining on file AI Vendor Service Agreements, AI duties and responsibilities added to IT development and

operations staff, signed confidentiality statements by IT staff related to AI, and signed IT Policies and Procedures Compliance Statement.

Type 6. AI Governance, Development, and Operations Support Controls: These include issuing, sharing, using, implementing, and keeping current policies and procedures, such as main information security and privacy management policies and procedures (upgraded for AI), account provisioning and revocation procedure (upgraded for AI), password controls policy (upgraded for AI), segregation of IT duties policy (upgraded for AI), third-party access controls (upgraded for AI), IT change management policy (upgraded for AI), IT resource management controls (upgraded for AI), IT knowledge retention management (upgraded for AI), IT Configuration Management Policy (upgraded for AI), backup and recovery process management controls (upgraded for AI), and segregation of IT duties policy.

Type 7. Live AI Systems/Solutions/Tools: These include issuing, managing, using, sharing, and retaining on file AI integrated development environment; AI models, platforms, and tools; and firewalls.

All these may be used and implemented at the appropriate AI Implementation phase. Also, they may be used for awareness, reference, and training purposes by company board members, managers, and staff, as well as compliance and auditing purposes by internal corporate functions and external regulatory authorities and audit partners.

IT Governance Recommended Assurance Actions

In order to have the best results and outcomes and achieve the **goal of supporting the AI environment and the AI Systems Development and Operation** more effectively, the following assurance actions (RAA) are recommended:

RAA1. Assess Actions Taken: Assess the actions taken of the above IT controls and improve the process of preparation, as required.

RAA2. Review Products: Review the *22 products* generated of this phase and consider their potential impact on your company's operations, production and support processes, your employees and customers, and greater society, as needed.

More specifically, it is a good idea to review the operational aspects of these IT controls to ensure that the development and operation of the first AI project ("Manage emails") will be achieved in the most effective way.

RAA3. Implement Measures: Plan, improve, and implement all actions identified in the above controls (of Phase B-Part 3) and by the review activities of RAA1 and RAA2 above, as required. It is critical to note that full documentation of the AI System ("Manage emails") is in place before you transfer the AI system in production.

RAA4. Report: Communicate results of your actions to the AI Steering Committee and Board, as required.

RAA5. Document: Document all activities carried out and retain full documentation in organized digital and paper files for transparency, accountability, and compliance purposes.

RAA6. Keep Products Current: Ensure you keep current the above products by reviewing them and updating them every two to three years or as needs, expectations, and operating conditions and circumstances warrant.

Concluding Remarks

Executing the 85+ actions specified in the controls of this chapter supported you to better achieve your fourth goal (*Support AI environment and AI Systems Development and Operation*) and its three objectives (establish AI computer infrastructure, ensure effective information security and privacy controls, and ensure critical IT controls include AI aspects).

The most crucial tasks you have achieved in this phase were the following:

(1)   Establishing AI technical environment

(2)   Ensuring your IT critical controls include all relevant AI aspects

For more details related to a full and integrated set of IT controls for companies and organizations, see my IT and ISO 27K security books listed in "Additional Resources" at the end of this book.

This and the previous three chapters supported you to achieve your **fourth** milestone (***Establish AI infrastructure management framework***) in your AI Management System Implementation Journey.

Prepare the Organization for AI (Chapter 7), Establish AI Governance Framework (Chapter 8), Establish Data Governance Framework (Chapter 9), and Manage IT Governance and Privacy Controls (this chapter) are deemed to be the third prerequisite for developing, deploying, and improving AI systems/solutions for your company's AI ecosystem.

The next two chapters (Part V) continue this exciting journey by describing how to develop and operate AI Systems (Chapters 11 and 12).

PART V

AI Systems Development and Operations

Part V contains

Managing the process of developing and operating AI systems/solutions supports you to achieve the **fifth** milestone (***Develop and operate AI systems***) of your AI Ecosystem Journey.

All these (actions of Chapters 11 and 12) compose the **second constituent** element of the **third** component (**AI Implementation Approach**) of your **AI Management System**.

The overall purpose of these two chapters is to develop and operate (deploy) effective and ethical AI systems/solutions in your AI Ecosystem.

CHAPTER 11

Develop AI Systems

Bill Gates:[1] "Information technology and business are becoming inextricably interwoven. I don't think anybody can talk meaningfully about one without talking about the other."

Overview: This chapter describes how to develop effective AI Systems for your organization. It includes (a) **12 steps**, (b) over **51 actions**, (c) over **20 products** (outcomes, results, and outputs, such as organizational functions/HR resources; assessment reports; reference documentation; AI/ICT infrastructure; administrative support controls; AI governance, development, and operations support controls; and live AI systems/solutions/tools), and (d) **five assurance tasks to enable you to** support, achieve, and ensure the good and effective development of AI Systems/Solutions. The goal, objectives, steps, actions, products, and assurance tasks presented below form Phase C (AI Systems Development) of the AI Implementation Approach.

Phases of the AI Implementation Approach

The AI Implementation Approach (Component 3 of the AI Management System) includes five phases:

- AI Preparation (Phase A, Chapter 7)

- AI Management Framework (Phase B, Chapters 8–10)

- AI Systems Development (Phase C, *this chapter*)

- AI Systems Operation (Phase D)

- AI Infrastructure and Systems Assessment (Phase E)

179

J. Kyriazoglou, *AI Management Framework*, https://doi.org/10.1007/979-8-8688-1536-2_11

Goal and Objectives of Phase C (AI Systems Development)

The **goal of Phase C** is "Develop AI Systems."

The objectives that support the achievement of this goal are

Objective 1: Analyze and document AI System requirements and needs

Objective 2: Organize and manage hypotheses, algorithms, and the learning model of the AI System

Objective 3: Test the AI System and Learning Model

Steps of Phase C (AI Systems Development)

The 12 steps to support the achievement of the goal and objectives of Phase C are

Step C1: Establish AI Development Team

Step C2: Select AI Project to be developed and run

Step C3: Establish AI System Owner

Step C4: Perform AI System Regulatory Risk Analysis

Step C5: Develop AI System

Step C6: Check AI System's hypotheses, algorithms, and model

Step C7: Document Business Case for AI System

Step C8: Document Business Processes for AI System

Step C9: Include internal application controls in AI System

Step C10: Include "Explainability by design" in AI System

Step C11: Include Security and Privacy controls in AI System

Step C12: Test AI System

Each step will contain one or more actions (and in some cases a questionnaire) to manage and resolve specific implementation issues. Also, each step will generate one or more products to achieve the specific step's purpose. These are listed in "**Products of AI Systems Development**" later in this chapter.

Step C1: Establish AI Development Team

Establish an AI Develop Team, add relevant staff, and train them accordingly on all aspects of AI.

Step C2: Select AI Project to Be Developed and Run

Action 1. As per AI Needs Analysis Report (of Phase A), there were five projects identified in the AI Program to be implemented for this company:

(1)   AI Project 1: Manage emails

(2)   AI Project 2: Manage AI data

(3)   AI Project 3: Manage employee screening and hiring

(4)   AI Project 4: Improve customer support

(5)   AI Project 5: Bolster data analysis of business intelligence

Company management selected the first AI project (Manage emails) as a pilot example before implementing the rest of the AI projects.

Action 2. For this AI project (AI Project 1), management must decide whether to acquire a ready-made software solution or develop its own. Also, the learning model (e.g., LSTM, GRU, etc.[2]) to be used as well as the tools for email management.

The rest of the actions of this phase as well as of the other phases relate to both paradigms (internal development, external ready-made package) unless stated otherwise.

Action 3. Ensure the availability of the programming language (e.g., Python) and technical and other resources (e.g., AI techniques and methods).

Action 4. Ensure the establishment of a development and testing environment and an algorithmic framework required for internal development or procurement of the first AI project (Manage emails).

Use test data from the Enterprise Data Repository and external sources, as required. If a ready-made software is to be used for this AI project, then the IT Procurement steps (see example in Appendix 26) should be followed.

If you select a cloud platform, consider using a platform that offers all the cloud-based machine learning services, as it allows quick experimentation and scalable deployment, etc.

Action 5. Ensure proper use of test data from the Enterprise Data Repository (e.g., anonymize or mask to comply with privacy regulations, etc.).

Step C3: Establish AI System Owner

Action 1. Appoint an AI Solution or System Owner for the selected project (Manage emails) with responsibilities to oversee AI system development, AI Algorithm use, AI data use, and AI system deployment, operations, and retirement decisions, as needed.[3]

Action 2. Ensure the responsibilities of the AI Solution or System Owner are included in a job description and in a formal employment agreement.

Action 3. Ensure these responsibilities and role of the System Owner are communicated to all the relevant management positions and staff for the selected project (Manage emails).

Step C4: Perform AI System Regulatory Risk Analysis

Action 1. Ensure the AI System Owner, with the full support of the company's legal function and IT (as needed), conducts an in-depth analysis of the system and its regulatory environment to identify key regulatory risks, constraints, and design parameters.[4]

Action 2. Ensure the results of this risk assessment are taken into full consideration in developing the first system (Manage emails).

Action 3. Ensure your AI System (Manage emails) is trustworthy in terms of the three AI components:

(3.1) It should be lawful, ensuring compliance with all applicable laws and regulations.

(3.2) It should be ethical, demonstrating respect for, and ensuring adherence to, ethical principles and values.

(3.3) It should be robust, both from a technical and a social perspective, since, even with good intentions, AI systems can cause unintentional harm.

You may use Appendix 27 for this purpose.

Step C5: Develop AI System

Action 1. Create AI System by using the AI System Development and Operation Methodology. For more details, see Annex 2.

Action 2. In developing your AI System (Manage emails)

(2.1) Consider AI Ethics, AI Strategy, the Harmony Mnemonic, the Seven Ancient Greek Wisdom Principles, Ethics and other complementary policies (e.g., AI Vision, AI Mission, and AI Values Statements; Conflict of Interest Policy; AI Ethical Standards Policy; Corporate Ethics Policy; Corporate Social Responsibility Policy; Corporate Diversity Policy; and Environment Protection Policy), the EU Act System Development Principles, and the Guidelines for Secure AI System Development (see Chapters 2, 4–6, for more details).

(2.2) Ensure your AI System Development and Operation Methodology is integrated with the broader development of IT standards and is followed for all AI developments.

Action 3. Ensure your AI System Development and Operation Methodology includes steps, such as Risk Management, Problem Definition, Data Acquisition and Preparation, Model Development and Training, Model Evaluation and Refinement, Model Deployment, and Model Maintenance and Improvement.

Action 4. Ensure your AI development and operations staff review and follow the Human Aspects Improvement Guidelines (see Annex 3), where possible.

Action 5. Ensure your AI System (first AI Project "Manage emails") development products include two sets of documentation:

Set 1. Classical System Development Documentation: Feasibility Study, User/ Business Needs (see example in first AI Project "Manage emails" in Annex 1), Systems Analysis and Design Document, Software Code (source listing, source code, object code), and Application Documentation

Set 2. AI System Development Documentation: Learning Model, model data, machine learning algorithms, and hypotheses used for this first AI System (Manage emails).

In case the system ("Manage emails") is procured from an external supplier, the company will only have object code (and not source code), a software license, and a vendor agreement.

It should be noted that, before testing your AI system (Step C11), it is good practice to execute the assessment and assurance actions of the following steps: Step C5 to Step C10.

Action 5. Ensure you perform an algorithmic impact assessment of each AI system/ solution you are developing (see more details in Appendix 28). You may also want to use the HUDERIA (risk and impact assessment of AI systems) methodology of the Council of Europe.[5]

Action 6. Complete the writing of software code of your AI System. If you use or have included AI Prompts generated by an external AI Prompt Generation Software, ensure these are integrated and documented effectively into the specific AI system you are developing.

Action 7. You may want to use an Enterprise Architecture Approach (framework and platform software tools) to document and manage all development activities. Also, you may want to acquire and use, as needed, AI Governance Tools (specific software) to manage, detect, and mitigate bias (e.g., IBM AI Fairness 360), to ensure "Explainability" (e.g., LIME, SHAP), assess risks (e.g., NIST Risk framework and tool), evaluate EU AI Act Compliance (e.g., EU AI Act Compliance Checker), etc.

Step C6: Check AI System's Hypotheses, Algorithms, and Model

Action 1. Ensure the hypotheses for your AI System (Manage emails) remain relevant and appropriate throughout the complete life cycle of developing this system and that these hypotheses are documented properly and this documentation is kept current.

Action 2. Ensure the AI Algorithms for your AI System (Manage emails) are designed to process data that contain all aspects of data quality (e.g., accuracy, consistency, completeness, timeliness, and relevance) and that data quality is managed and improved by a relevant data quality program and organizational structure.

Action 3. Select or build a model[6] and manage AI model key components. Select, develop, build, and deploy your own model for your first AI System (Manage emails). For an example of a Model Development Procedure, see Appendix 31.

Ensure data, algorithms, parameters, and hyperparameters of the AI model you are using are documented; this documentation is encrypted; access and changes to all these documents and the key components are allowed to specific personnel, authorized by relevant management and monitored by a responsible officer.

Action 4. Ensure the AI Model Quality for your AI System (Manage emails) is based across five key categories:

(4.1) Model performance (model accuracy, stability, conceptual soundness, and robustness)

(4.2) Societal impact (fairness, transparency, privacy, and security)

(4.3) Operational compatibility (AI system effectiveness, model function, documentation, and collaborative capabilities)

(4.4) Data quality (capability to build and test models that impact model fitness, including missing data, and data representativeness, as well as the quality of production data)

(4.5) Also, ensure your AI Model Quality components are fully documented.

Step C7: Document Business Case for AI System

Action 1. Ensure a clear business case for the AI system or solution (first AI Project "Manage emails") is in place and formally approved by relevant stakeholders.

Action 2. Ensure all data related to the business case for the AI system or solution (first AI Project "Manage emails") are being kept up to date to reflect any changes in the expected total cost of ownership and/or benefits.

Action 3. Ensure individual AI system or solution (first AI Project "Manage emails") is assessed in the context of the organization's strategy.

Action 4. Ensure the expected costs and benefits of the AI systems or solutions (i.e., first AI Project "Manage emails") are clearly articulated and tracked during the course of the AI program initial and post-implementation tasks.

Step C8: Document Business Processes for AI System

Action 1. Ensure your company's "As-Is" and "To-Be" process narratives and flowcharts (especially for the first AI Project "Manage emails") are well documented and available, the impact of automation on current processes and internal controls have been assessed, and processes portray accurately the organization's transactions and data flows.

Action 2. Ensure "To-Be" process user stories (especially for the first AI Project "Manage emails"), including IT general and business process controls, are complete and accurate and have been approved by the appropriate management level.

Step C9: Include Internal Application Controls in AI System

Action 1. Ensure the AI development process has been set up to ensure that processes and internal controls are developed in line with the AI solution design.

Action 2. Ensure each AI Application (especially for the first AI Project "Manage emails") includes the relevant internal controls (input, output, processing, access, and integrity) as well as ethical principles which are either configured or hard-coded within the AI system or solution (first AI Project "Manage emails").

Action 3. Ensure AI's input datasets (especially for the first AI Project "Manage emails") are configured securely against human or machine intervention. Where relevant, completeness and accuracy checks are automatically performed on the data input.

Action 4. Ensure each AI Application (especially for the first AI Project "Manage emails") uses an audit trail to record all activities and actions.

Action 5. Ensure AI Application internal controls (especially for the first AI Project "Manage emails") are fully tested and documented for each AI Application.

For more details, see Appendix 29.

Step C10: Include "Explainability by Design" in AI System

Action 1. Ensure AI solutions used by the company (especially for the first AI Project "Manage emails") satisfy the four principles of explainable AI, as per NIST 8312 Standard, such as

(1.1) **Principle of Explanation**: A system (first AI Project "Manage emails") delivers or contains accompanying evidence or reason(s) for outputs and/or processes.

(1.2) **Principle of Meaningfulness**: A system (first AI Project "Manage emails") provides explanations that are understandable to the intended consumer(s).

(1.3) **Principle of Explanation Accuracy**: An explanation correctly reflects the reason for generating the output and/or accurately reflects the system's process (especially for the first AI Project "Manage emails").

(1.4) **Principle of Knowledge Limits**: A system (first AI Project "Manage emails") only operates under conditions for which it was designed and when it reaches sufficient confidence in its output).

Action 2. Ensure AI solutions (especially for the first AI Project "Manage emails") explain how they came to certain outcomes/decisions/advice and are not too complex for even their human designers to fully comprehend.

Action 3. Ensure the AI solution (especially for the first AI Project "Manage emails") generates the correct decision on the basis of the input, data, and process executed.

Step C11: Include Security and Privacy Controls in AI System

Action 1. Ensure "Security by design" principles are embedded in the AI architecture, approach, and development methodology of AI Systems as well as in the first AI Project ("Manage emails") to ensure appropriate and sustainable level of security.

Action 2. Ensure "Security by design" principles are embedded in all AI Systems as well as the first AI Project ("Manage emails"). These principles should include threat modeling, secure coding practices, access control (especially for sensitive data), secure communication, and continuous monitoring.

For more details, see Appendix 30.

Action 3. Ensure "Privacy by design and by default" principles are embedded in the first AI Project ("Manage emails") to maintain appropriate and sustainable level of privacy of personal data.

Action 4. Ensure "Privacy by design and by default" principles include data minimization, purpose limitation, user consent transparency in relation to data processing, etc. (Article 25 of the GDPR).

For more details, see Privacy by design and by default principles in Chapter 5.

Step C12: Test AI System

Action 1. Ensure data are used for AI System ("Manage emails") testing from the Enterprise Data Repository.

Action 2. Ensure adequate testing is carried out for the AI System ("Manage emails") application, resulting in a solution that meets business requirements and strategic objectives.

Action 3. Ensure automated testing packs (test cases, scripts, and test data) are in place, for example, for when major changes are introduced such as new data source to the AI solution or machine learning upgrade.

Action 4. Ensure adequate, automated testing of all new Bots and changes to Bots is in place, including testing of controls, using predefined test scripts, to help ensure that the AI solution ("Manage emails") remains valid.

Action 5. Ensure separate environments are available and are consistent, and used for development, test, and production (of the first AI System ("Manage emails")), to allow for testing being performed with a due diligence in the environment identical to production.

Action 6. Ensure testing and production strategy and approach are defined and followed, including data migration between environments and contingency planning.

Action 7. Ensure appropriate User Acceptance Testing (UAT) for the solution (first AI Project ("Manage emails")) is performed with appropriate consideration of business input for design, execute, and approve testing and signed off prior to be accepted.

Action 8. Ensure documentation of test cases and approvals for each AI solution as well as the first AI Project ("Manage emails") is retained.

Action 9. Ensure the AI model that will solve the defined problem for each AI System is trained well with the prepared data. This stage is iterative, often involving multiple rounds of model development and refinement based on the model's performance during training.

Action 10. Ensure, once the model has been trained, that it is evaluated to see how well it performs. This involves testing the model of the first AI Project ("Manage emails") on unseen data and analyzing its predictions. If the model's performance is not satisfactory, it's refined and tweaked. This could mean adjusting the model's parameters, changing the model's architecture, or even returning to the data acquisition phase to gather additional data.

Action 11. Ensure you separate the training data from the production data of each AI system to reduce the risk of compromising the training data.

Action 12. Ensure that the training data of each AI System is thoroughly validated and verified before it is used to train the model. This can be done by implementing data validation checks and employing multiple data labelers to validate the accuracy of the data labelling.

Action 13. Store the training data of each AI System in a secure manner, such as using encryption, secure data transfer protocols, and firewalls.

Action 14. Ensure all the above are implemented for all your AI Systems as well as for the first AI Project ("Manage emails") before it goes into production.

For more details, see Annex 4.

Products of AI Systems Development

The products (outcomes, results, and outputs) define (a) what's required (i.e., organizational functions, HR resources, ICT hardware and software, policies, etc.) to establish, develop, operate, implement, and assess AI infrastructure and systems/solutions and (b) what outputs and results (i.e., reference documentation, assessment reports, decisions of live AI systems, AI data, etc.) are produced, managed, used, and maintained by AI systems/solutions and their developmental, implementation, operational, and assessment aspects.

The main outcomes, results, and outputs of this chapter include the following types of products:

Type 1. Organizational Functions/HR Resources: These include (a) establishing an AI Development Team and adding relevant staff and (b) appointing an AI System Owner for each AI system.

Type 2. Assessment Reports: These include carrying out the necessary assessment and review actions and issuing the following analyses and reports: AI System Regulatory Risk Assessment Report for each system, AI System Trustworthiness Assessment Report for each system, and algorithmic impact assessment of each AI system/solution.

Type 3. Reference Documentation: This includes crafting and issuing reference documentation, such as the following: Set 1. Classical System Development Documentation (Feasibility Study, User/Business Needs, Systems Analysis and Design Document, Software Code (source listing, source code, object code), and Application Documentation for each system; Set 2. AI System Development Documentation (for Learning Model, model data, machine learning algorithms, and hypotheses used for each system); AI Model Quality Component Documentation for each system; AI System Business Case Documentation for each system; AI System Business Process Documentation for each system; AI System Internal Application Controls Documentation for each system; AI System "Explainability by Design" Documentation for each system; AI System "Security by Design" Documentation for each system; AI System "Privacy by Design" Documentation for each system; AI System Test Results Documentation for each system.

Type 4. AI/ICT Infrastructure: This includes the installation and operation of hardware and software for operating a technical environment for testing each AI System, programming language (e.g., Python), and other AI software tools to use an Enterprise Architecture Approach (framework and platform software tools) to document and manage all these entities and to use, as needed, AI Governance Tools (specific software) to manage, detect, and mitigate bias (e.g., IBM AI Fairness 360), to ensure "Explainability" (e.g., LIME, SHAP), assess risks (e.g., NIST Risk framework and tool), evaluate EU AI Act Compliance (e.g., EU AI Act Compliance Checker), etc.

Type 5. Administrative Support Controls: These include issuing, sharing, and retaining on file: AI System Development staff training notes; AI System Owner assignment job description and employment agreement for each system; Communication of the responsibilities and role of the System Owner to all the relevant management positions and staff for the AI systems/solutions.

Type 6. AI Governance, Development, and Operations Support Controls: These include issuing, sharing, using, implementing, and keeping current policies and procedures, such as AI Systems Development and Operation Methodology, Human Aspects Improvement Guidelines, AI system test procedure, AI Trustworthiness Assessment Questionnaire, algorithmic impact assessment, model development procedure, AI application controls, adding security in systems development plan.

Type 7. Live AI systems/solutions/tools. This includes issuing, managing, using, sharing, and retaining on file: AI System code; technical environment for testing each AI System; Learning Model, model data, machine learning algorithms, and hypotheses used for each system; AI System Model Training Data for each system; test data for each AI system; Tested AI System; Production AI System.

All these may be used and implemented at the appropriate AI Implementation phase. Also, they may be used for awareness, reference, and training purposes by company board members, managers, and staff, as well as compliance and auditing purposes by internal corporate functions and external regulatory authorities and audit partners.

AI Systems Development Recommended Assurance Actions

In order to have the best results and outcomes and achieve the goal of AI Systems Development more effectively, the following assurance actions (RAA) are recommended:

RAA1. Assess Actions Taken: Assess the actions taken of the above 12 steps of Phase C and improve the process of preparation, as required.

RAA2. Review Products: Review the *20 products* generated of this phase and consider their potential impact on your company's operations, production and support processes, your employees and customers, and greater society, as needed.

More specifically, it is a good idea to review the development of the first AI project ("Manage emails") to ensure that everything is done properly and in accordance with the AI ethics policy of your company.

RAA3. Implement Measures: Plan, improve, and implement any measures or controls identified in the above seven steps (of Phase A) and by the review activities of RAA1 and RAA2 above, as required. It is critical to note that full documentation of the AI System ("Manage emails") is in place before you transfer the AI system in production.

Also, ensure data backups of all development components are included in the IT Backup recovery process and the AI Budget is updated, as required.

RAA4. Report: Communicate results of your actions to AI Steering Committee and Board, as required.

RAA5. Document: Document all activities carried out and retain full documentation in organized digital and paper files for transparency, accountability, and compliance purposes.

RAA6. Keep Products Current: Ensure you keep current the above products, by reviewing them and updating them every two to three years or as needs, expectations, and operating conditions and circumstances warrant.

Concluding Remarks

Executing the 12 steps and over 51 actions of this chapter supported you to better achieve your fourth goal (*Develop AI System*) and its three objectives (analyze and document AI System requirements and needs; organize and manage hypotheses, algorithms, and the learning model of the AI System; and test the AI System and Learning Model).

The most crucial tasks you have achieved in this phase were the following:

(1)   Developing your first AI System ("Manage emails")

(2)   Documenting Business Case for your AI System

(3)   Testing your AI System

(4)   Transferring your first AI Project ("Manage emails") to production

This is the first part of your **fifth** milestone (***Develop and operate AI Systems***) of your AI Ecosystem Journey. The next chapter continues this exciting journey by describing how to operate AI Systems.

Annex 1: User/Business Needs for AI Project "Manage Emails"

Examples of the needs to be satisfied and the functions required to be performed by the "Manage emails" AI System are the following:

1. Check incoming email messages to ensure they are proper (not "spam," not "chain," ethical, not discriminatory, biased, or racist, etc.).

2. Prioritize incoming email messages.

3. Summarize email threads.

4. Proofread email messages.

5. Create quick and timely replies.

6. Recommend compelling subject lines.

7. Improve content of email replies.

8. Organize email replies.

9. Streamline email creation.

10. Check outgoing email messages to ensure they are proper (polite, courteous, ethical, not discriminatory, biased, or racist, comply with security and data privacy, etc.). If they commit the company, ensure the person who sends it is authorized and this message is kept in a special file, etc.

11. Personalize email replies.

12. Optimize email scheduling.

13. Categorize, organize, and save emails by function and individual.

14. Flag all rejected emails and ensure they are managed by an authorized person.

15. Maintain logs for incoming and outgoing emails.

16. Report all email activity to top management.

17. Label email messages for AI purposes and store in the Enterprise Data Repository.

18. Ensure an effective search capability for emails is established.

19. Back up and restore emails as per corporate backup controls.

20. Transfer emails to archive as per corporate retention policies.

21. Ensure email processing and storage use a dedicated server.

Annex 2: AI Systems Development and Operation Methodology

Phase 1: AI Needs Analysis

Step 1. Understand user problem and needs for an AI System/Solution.

Step 2. Define needs and requirements (business, data) of the AI System/Solution.

Step 3. Document needs and requirements (business, data) of AI System/Solution.

Step 4. Carry out feasibility study.

Step 5. Decide whether to develop system internally or purchase and use an external system/solution or model, or a combination of both, etc.

Step 6. Perform an Algorithmic Impact Assessment of the proposed AI system/solution.

Step 7. Perform a Privacy Impact Assessment of the proposed AI system/solution.

Step 8. Perform an initial assessment of potential risks associated with the use of the designed AI system/solution.

Step 9. Decide whether the use of AI is appropriate for your documented needs.

Step 10. Review and approval of feasibility study by end users.

Step 11. Craft AI Project Plan and AI Quality Plan.

Step 12. Review and approval by senior management for AI Project Plan, Budget, and Phase 2.

Phase 2: AI System Analysis, Design, and Development

Step 1. Carry out General AI System Analysis and Design.

Step 2. Execute Detailed AI System Analysis and Design.

Step 3. Develop computer programs (or use an external system/solution or model, etc.).

Step 4. Test the AI System.

Step 5. Train end users.

Step 6. Assess and address potential biases introduced by the dataset selection.

Step 7. Assess the level of interpretability needed and make design decisions accordingly.

Step 8. Document datasets and models used.

Step 9. Perform evaluation and validation, including retraining as needed.

Step 10. Build in mechanisms for human oversight and monitoring.

Step 11. Document appropriate use(s) and limitations.

Step 12. Keep documentation regarding how the requirements for design and development have been met.

Step 13. Provide appropriate documentation to users regarding datasets used, limitations, and appropriate uses.

Step 14. Perform a risk assessment regarding the way the system has been made available.

Step 15. Review and approval of system by end users.

Step 16. Craft a System Migration Plan.

Step 17. Review and approval by senior management.

Phase 3: AI System Deployment and Operation

Step 1. Install the system into the production environment.

Step 2. Implement a System Migration Plan and transfer or load data into the production system.

Step 3. Run the system as a pilot or in parallel, as needed.

Step 4. Initiate the production system.

Step 5. Log and monitor the output of the system as appropriate in the context,

Step 6. Ensure adequate monitoring and human oversight.

Step 7. Intervene as needed based on operational parameters.

Phase 4: AI System Maintenance

Step 1. Execute technical support procedures (backup/recovery and media control; security/access control administration for users; performance monitoring of application, network, etc.; data and document archival and deletion; etc.).

Step 2. Manage security issues and resolve problems.

Step 3. Manage changes.

Step 4. Carry out a post-implementation review (after first year of operation).

Annex 3: Human Aspects Improvement Guidelines

Plato provides us with the guiding principle: "Friendship, freedom, justice, wisdom, courage and moderation are the key values that define a good society."

Here are **ten guidelines** you should (or might) use to improve your professional and business emotional and mental health in this regard.

Action 1: Be sensitive. Show sensitivity to other professions and companies by avoiding derogatory comments and do not criticize, condemn, or complain to anyone about them.

Action 2: Collaborate. Make your professional and business goal the habit to work together with other professions and companies harmoniously.

Action 3: Patience. Show patience and maintain good relationships with everyone in business and economy (colleagues, supervisors, senior management, customers, authorities, etc.).

Action 4: Be honest. In a business environment, be interested in others (colleagues, supervisors, senior management, customers, etc.) with sincerity, always showing friendship, goodness, and love to all.

Action 5: Be polite. Address the other professional or businessperson always in plural terms, unless the other person allows you to speak in the singular.

Action 6: Use importance in associating with others. Make the other professional or businessperson feel important to you, and you do that with sincerity.

Action 7: Employ friendly rules of communication. Start a professional or business communication in a friendly and pleasant manner. When you are in error, accept it quickly and emphatically and apologize with honesty. Express your sympathy to the other person. Keep your humor within acceptable social boundaries while rejecting slander and vulgarities.

Action 8: Manage your business time with friendship. Examine your business activities in accordance with the values of love and friendship and your obligations. Spend 60% of your business time in critical non-emergency activities, 30% of your time in critical and emergency activities, and the remaining 10% of your time in uninteresting activities. Learn to say a friendly "no" when others attempt to load you with activities that are not aligned with your professional and business needs, vision, mission, and values.

Action 9: Use positive and friendly thinking and priority. Use positive and friendly thinking to manage all the events, issues, problems, and facts related to your business life and take preventive action when it is required on your part. Perform your activities based on the priorities set by you and the time requirements of your life and company, but also reinforcing the values of justice, goodness, fairness, love, and friendship in all business activities.

Action 10: Participate with friendship. Participate in social groups, professional societies, and corporate volunteering (unpaid) activities on the basis of love and friendship. Understand and know your personal limits and the limits of your business organization.

Annex 4: AI System Test Procedure

Step 1: Organize Test Project

Organizing the Test Project involves creating a System Test Plan and a Schedule and Test Approach and requesting and assigning resources.

Step 2: Review Testing Standards

Review the ISO Standard on Software Engineering for AI (ISO/IEC 25059:2023) and its testing principles,[7] such as user controllability, functional adaptability, functional correctness, robustness, transparency, and intervenability.

Consider their impact and use in your AI testing approach.

Step 3: Decide the Types of Testing

Decide the types of testing you will use in testing the specific AI system/solution. These are the six **types of testing**[8] **(TT)** that have proven valuable for AI-based products:

TT1. Functional Testing: This includes ensuring that the core AI algorithms and logic produce the expected outcomes in various scenarios.

TT2. Usability Testing: This includes evaluating the user-friendliness of the AI system and the ease and convenience of interacting with it and how errors are handled.

TT3. Integration Testing: This includes checking the correctness of the different integrated components of the specific AI system.

TT4. Performance Testing: This includes measuring overall AI model performance, response times, throughput, and other key performance metrics. See also Appendix 5 for examples of performance metrics.

TT5. API Testing: This includes verifying the functionality of AI application programming interfaces, including testing of individual methods and interactions between them.

TT6. Security Testing: This includes **testing to** prevent leakage of data processed by the AI model, as well as model configuration and system information. See also Appendix 30 for adding security controls to your AI systems.

Step 4: Design and Built System Tests

Designing and building system tests involves identifying Test Cycles, Test Cases, Entrance and Exit Criteria, Expected Results, etc. In general, test conditions and expected results will be identified by the Test Team in conjunction with the Project Business Analyst or Business Expert. The Test Team will then identify Test Cases and the Data required. The Test conditions are derived from the Business Design and the Transaction Requirements Documents.

Step 5: Design and Built Test Procedures

Designing and building test procedures includes setting up procedures such as error management systems and status reporting and setting up and loading the test database tables.

Step 6: Execute Tests

This involves executing unit, subsystem, operations acceptance, and integrated tests, as described in the Test Plan.

Step 7: Signoff

Signoff involves getting the approval of the users on the basis of the tests executed previously.

CHAPTER 12

Operate AI Systems

Narendra Modi:[1] "Technology transforms people's lives. From mitigating poverty to simplifying processes, ending corruption to providing better services, Technology is omnipresent. It has become the single-most important instrument of human progress."

Overview: This chapter describes how to develop effective AI Systems for your organization. It includes (a) **10 steps**, (b) over **51 actions**, (c) over **23 products** (outcomes, results, and outputs, such as organizational functions/HR resources; assessment reports; reference documentation; AI/ICT infrastructure; administrative support controls; AI governance, development, and operations support controls; and live AI systems/solutions/tools), and (d) **five assurance tasks** to enable you to support, achieve, and ensure the good and effective operation of AI Systems/Solutions. The goal, objectives, steps, actions, products, and assurance tasks presented below form Phase D (AI Systems Operation) of the AI Implementation Approach.

Phases of the AI Implementation Approach

The AI Implementation Approach (Component 3 of the AI Management System) includes five phases:

- AI Preparation (Phase A, Chapter 7)

- AI Management Framework (Phase B, Chapters 8–10)

- AI Systems Development (Phase C, previous chapter)

- AI Systems Operation (Phase D, *this chapter*)

- AI Infrastructure and Systems Assessment (Phase E)

© John Kyriazoglou 2025
J. Kyriazoglou, *AI Management Framework*, https://doi.org/10.1007/979-8-8688-1536-2_12

Goal and Objectives of Phase D (AI Systems Operation)

The goal of Phase D is to "Operate (deploy) AI Systems effectively."
The objectives of this goal are

Objective 1: Run and monitor the activities and results of AI Systems

Objective 2: Manage AI Incidents

Objective 3: Assess AI Systems after initial implementation

The above goal and the three objectives of Phase D will be achieved for all AI Systems through the steps and actions of these stages: Assurance, Deployment, and Review.

Steps of Phase D (AI Systems Operation)

Assurance Stage

Step D1. Review the IT Operational Aspects of AI Systems

Step D2. Review the quality of AI Systems

Step D3. Review the auditability of AI Systems

Step D4. Review application controls and logging of AI Systems

Deployment Stage

Step D5. Operate (deploy) the AI System

Step D6. Monitor performance of AI Systems

Step D7. Manage results and errors of AI Systems

Step D8. Manage user requests of AI Systems

Step D9. Manage AI Incidents

Review Stage

Step D10. Carry out Post-Implementation Review of AI Systems

Each step will contain one or more actions (and in some cases a questionnaire) to manage and resolve specific implementation issues. Also, each step will generate one or more products to achieve the specific step's purpose. These are listed in the section "Products of AI Systems Operation" later in this chapter.

Assurance Stage: Steps D1–D4

The assurance stage (Steps D1–D4) relates to understanding risks associated with IT and emerging technologies (like AI) and ensuring the IT environment is ready to enable the AI Systems of the company as well as the first system ("Manage emails") to run effectively.

During the actions of this stage, it is advisable to consider the AI Strategy and all aspects of ethics (e.g., AI Ethics Policy, the Harmony Mnemonic, the Seven Principles, etc.) of the company.

Also, improvement actions should be taken if any of the assessment steps of this stage are not successful and various gaps (e.g., there is no efficient AI Architecture, etc.) in the controls are evidenced.

Step D1: Review the IT Operational Aspects of AI Systems

Action 1. AI System Operations Support: Ensure you establish an AI Operations Support Team and an AI Incident Management Team. The staff included in these teams should have their duties documented in their specific employment agreements and should be trained effectively so that they can discharge their responsibilities as best as possible.

Action 2. AI System Production Configuration: Ensure your AI Systems, and specifically your first AI System ("Manage emails"), consist of five interrelated parts (P):

> **P1. Input**: The email messages (data) flowing into the system from outside.

> **P2. Processing**: The use of computer software (and AI Models, Techniques, and Tools) in a well-defined set of step-by-step sequence of activities to produce the expected results and outcomes of this system ("Manage emails") for the company.

P3. Output: The email messages, management reports, and processed data stored in computerized files.

P4. Resources: The IT staff (programmers, analysts, AI staff, operators, user support, database administrators, etc.) and the end-user personnel feeding and running the system.

P5. Storage: The usual IT and Communications as well as the special AI hardware and database servers and storage facilities where raw and processed data (e.g., email messages) are maintained safely.

Action 3. AI Computer Infrastructure: Ensure all necessary AI computer infrastructure is installed and tested and functions effectively before the first AI Project (Manage emails) is put in a production status.

Ensure this AI computer infrastructure includes

(2.1)   Hardware Components (GPU (Graphics Processing Unit) Servers, AI Accelerators, TPUs (Tensor Processing Units), High-Performance Computing (HPC) Systems, etc.)

(2.2)   Software Components (Machine Learning Frameworks, Model, and Tools)

(2.3)   Data Processing Libraries that are used for handling and processing large datasets

(2.4)   Storage Solutions, such as cloud storage, data lakes, and distributed file systems

(2.5)   An Intrusion Detection and Prevention Software properly supported by a legible vendor

You may want to use an Enterprise Architecture Approach (framework and platform software tools) to document and manage all operations activities. Also, you may want to acquire and use, as needed, AI Governance Tools (specific software) to manage, detect, and mitigate bias (e.g., IBM AI Fairness 360), ensure "Explainability" (e.g., LIME, SHAP), assess risks (e.g., NIST Risk framework and tool), evaluate EU AI Act Compliance (e.g., EU AI Act Compliance Checker), etc.

Action 4. Critical IT Controls: Ensure your AI Systems, and specifically your first AI System ("Manage emails"), are fully supported by various IT controls, such as information security management policies and procedures, vulnerability and malware management, access controls, account provisioning procedure, access revocation procedure, password controls policy, segregation of IT duties, third-party access controls, IT Change Management, etc.

For more details,[2] see Chapter 10.

Action 5. AI System Human Supervisor: Ensure you assign a company, well-trained staff member, to act as a human supervisor in checking each or on a sample basis the specific system's outputs, outcomes, results, and impact.

Step D2: Review the Quality of AI Systems

Action 1. Quality Aspects of AI Systems: Ensure your AI Systems, and specifically your first AI System ("Manage emails"), comply fully with the following quality (Q) characteristics in all its production aspects:

> **Q1. Conformity**: Conform to the AI System's initial design specifications.

> **Q2. Efficiency**: The software (as well as the algorithms, model, and data) of the AI System should use resources in the best way.

> **Q3. Reliability**: The hardware and software (as well as the algorithms, model, and data) of the AI System should function without errors, defects, or other anomalies.

> **Q4. Portability**: The software (as well as the algorithms, model, and data) of the AI System should be developed in such a way that it makes it possible for it to be used in other installations (in case of disaster recovery situations).

> **Q5. Flexibility**: The software (as well as the algorithms, model, and data) of the AI System should cover new needs easily.

> **Q6. Maintainability**: The errors and defects related to the hardware and software (as well as the algorithms, model, and data) of the AI System should be easily researched and corrected.

Action 2. Quality Documentation: Ensure your AI Systems, and specifically your first AI System ("Manage emails"), contain full documentation on all quality aspects of hardware and software (as well as the algorithms, model, and data) of the specific solution implemented.

Step D3: Review the Auditability of AI Systems

Action 1. Auditability Strategy: Ensure your AI Systems, and specifically your first AI System ("Manage emails"), include an Auditability Strategy[3] to ensure data and algorithms used for generating AI results and decisions, including data used for system learning, are stored securely and can be retrieved in a timely manner and in accordance with regulations (e.g., data privacy), so provenance of decisions can be provided.

Action 2. Validation: Ensure AI Solution results, decisions, and outcomes of your first AI System ("Manage emails") can be independently validated.

Action 3. Vault Principle: Apply the "Vault Principle," that is, an automated solution that securely stores any decision made by the AI solution (specifically your first AI System ("Manage emails"), as well as the data the decision was based on, and the latest version of the algorithm. Ensure you have a valid support agreement for the "Vault Principle" software you are using from an external vendor.

Action 4. Audit Trail Specification: Ensure the audit trails (manual or electronic) for your AI Systems, and specifically your first AI System ("Manage emails"), record chronologically in a special audit trail file transactions, changes, events, or procedures to provide support documentation and history that is used to authenticate security and operational actions or mitigate challenges.

Action 5. Audit Trail Testing: Ensure each AI System's audit trail is tested fully.

Step D4: Review Application Controls and Logging of AI Systems

Action 1. Ensure your AI Systems, and specifically your first AI System ("Manage emails"), include a set of application processing controls, such as Input, Output, Processing, Access, and Integrity.

Action 2. Ensure all AI ethical principles are either accessed from a specific independent file and used or are hard-coded within the AI solution.

Action 3. Ensure AI's input datasets are configured securely against human or machine intervention. Where relevant, completeness and accuracy checks are automatically performed on the data input.

Action 4. Ensure each AI Application System uses an audit trail to record all activities and actions.

Action 5. Ensure AI Application internal controls are fully tested for each AI Application.

Action 6. Ensure your AI Systems, and specifically your first AI System ("Manage emails"), include logging of activities.

Action 7. Ensure the AI System's activities can be traced back to a unique Bot or program via an end-to-end audit trail to log and monitor AI System activities.

Action 8. Ensure AI Application controls are fully documented for each AI Application.

Deployment Stage

The deployment stage (Steps D5–D9) relates to taking actions associated with operating (deploying) the AI Systems of the company, as well as the first system ("Manage emails") so that they run effectively and produce correct results.

During the actions of this stage, it is advisable to consider the AI Strategy and all aspects of ethics (e.g., AI Ethics Policy, the Harmony Mnemonic, the Seven Principles, etc., as per Chapters 2, 4–6) of the company.

Step D5: Operate (Deploy) the AI System

Action 1. AI System Compliance Assessment: Ensure the AI System Owner supports the legal and IT functions, under the oversight and with the support of the AI Steering Committee and the AI Ethics and Data Governance Committees, in conducting and documenting a compliance assessment (see Appendix 27, the EU AI Act Compliance Checker,[4] "Annex 1," and "Annex 2"), for this purpose, before transferring the AI System to production.

This assessment may also include an AI Ethics assessment and a Data Governance assessment.

Action 2. DPIA: Ensure the AI System Owner supports the Data Protection or Privacy Officer and IT to carry out a Data Protection Impact Assessment, as required, before each AI system (as well as the first AI Project ("Manage emails")) is approved for operational use or a materially new version is deployed.

Action 3. Transfer AI System ("Manage emails") to production status and inform all interested parties.

This includes the following tasks (T):

> T1. Load data onto the AI production system ("Manage emails") or transfer it from the Enterprise Data Repository.
>
> T2. Deploy the model into the intended infrastructure, such as the cloud or on-premises environment, and run the system to produce the intended results.
>
> T3. Inform all interested stakeholders (senior management, AI committees, etc.) and external parties.
>
> T4. Govern Model. This involves monitoring and managing all AI models to ensure their performance aligns well with business, ethics, and regulatory goals.

Action 3. Ensure backup and recovery procedures are available and complete for all AI Systems.

Action 4. Ensure design and operating system documentation is complete for all AI Systems and for the first AI System ("Manage emails").

Action 5. Ensure staff are trained to run the specific AI System ("Manage emails").

Action 6. Ensure version control and configuration management are implemented for the productive AI System's code, data, and infrastructure, with backups and restore mechanisms in place.

Action 7. Ensure, in case the AI System ("Manage emails") becomes ineffective (i.e., a major incident occurs or the solution has inappropriately evolved), a rollback mechanism is in place and a process, algorithms, and cleansed data are available to get the solution to be implemented and (re)trained quickly to reflect new/changed requirements.

Action 8. Ensure you define measurable criteria for success and failure of your AI solution deployments ("Manage emails"), and monitor them closely during and after the process.

Action 9. Ensure you communicate the rollback process to your AI team and stakeholders.

Action 10. Ensure you monitor the rollback process and system status (of the "Manage emails" system) to verify that the desired state has been restored.

Action 11. Ensure you perform testing of the rollback process in different scenarios and environment, with documentation of the steps and outcomes.

Action 12. Ensure you analyze the root cause and impact of the AI deployment failure (and of the "Manage emails" system), and take corrective and preventive actions to avoid it in the future.

Step D6: Monitor Performance of AI Systems

Action 1. Ensure your AI Systems, and specifically your first AI System ("Manage emails"), include a performance monitoring process for the following: AI Business Outcomes, Data Sources (internal, external), AI Accuracy (correct results, no bias, algorithm errors), Data Quality, Privacy of Data, IT Security Policies and Procedures, Security and AI Incidents and Data Breaches, and AI System Performance Metrics.

Action 2. Ensure these performance metrics and events are reported to top management via the corporate management reporting process.

Action 3. Ensure management monitors each AI System's application audit trails and regularly reviews the solution outcomes against the business requirements from all aspects (i.e., ethical, technical, functional, etc.) and takes appropriate actions to resolve the situation or errors.

Action 4. Ensure AI System's outputs and results are aligned with its stated goals and ethical principles and do not harm people.

Action 5. Ensure detailed logs are maintained to obtain last execution status in case the AI System fails.

Step D7: Manage Results and Errors of AI Systems

Action 1. Ensure your AI Systems, and specifically your first AI System ("Manage emails"), include a process to review its processing results.

Action 2. Ensure this review process

- Checks that the results from the AI System are correct and appropriate by ensuring that the model accurately reflects the true underlying quantitative parameters, the logic makes accurate decisions, etc.

- Checks that controls are in place for monitoring data quality for solutions that are evolving over time

- Checks that controls are in place to consider sensitivities when dealing with different ethical/political/ethnic/race/gender/cultural and other groups

- Checks that controls are in place to prevent the AI System from processing the same data more than once, including file and data validation checks, etc.

- Checks that controls are in place to ensure human oversight of results of the AI System, as needed

For more details, see Appendix 32.

Action 3. Ensure you provide a capability and procedures for addressing, investigating, and correcting errors and making changes related to the data used, logic, processing flow, decisions, and outcomes of the AI Systems of your company. You should also do the same for the first AI System ("Manage emails").

Action 4. Ensure you maintain full documentation on all AI System errors and your management actions and replies.

For more details, see Appendix 33.

Step D8: Manage User Requests of AI Systems

Action 1. Ensure you provide a capability and procedures for addressing, investigating, and reporting all issues related to results, requests, and complaints by individuals about the data used, logic, processing flow, decisions, and outcomes of the AI Systems of your company. You should also do the same for the first AI System ("Manage emails").

Action 2. Ensure you maintain full documentation on all user requests and your management actions and replies.

For more details, see Appendix 34.

Step D9: Manage AI Incidents and Hazards

Action 1. Ensure your staff know how to identify AI Incidents and Hazards.

Action 2. Ensure staff are trained on handling AI incidents and hazards.

Action 3. Ensure your AI environment follows a consistent incident management approach with clear procedures and work instructions that are to ensure timely resolution of incidents with appropriate escalation where required.

Action 4. Ensure this approach applies to the first AI System ("Manage emails") and is integrated with the "regular" incident management approach to ensure a consistent approach across the AI and related environments.

Action 5. Ensure incident management is aligned with good practice standards (e.g., ITIL).

For more details, see Appendixes 36 and 37.

Review Stage

The review stage (Step D10) relates to actions associated with reviewing the performance of the AI Systems of the company, as well as the first AI system ("Manage emails"), so that they can be improved accordingly.

During the actions of this stage, it is advisable to consider the AI Strategy and all aspects of ethics (e.g., AI Ethics Policy, the Harmony Mnemonic, the Seven Principles, etc.) of the company.

Step D10: Carry Out Post-Implementation Review of AI Systems

Action 1. Review AI System's Needs Satisfaction

Q1. Did the AI System ("Manage emails") fully satisfy the requirements and needs of managing emails?

Q2. Did the AI System ("Manage emails") fully solve the problem that it was designed to address?

Q3. Can things go further so that the AI System ("Manage emails") can deliver even bigger and better benefits?

Q4. What lessons did we learn from implanting the AI System ("Manage emails") that we can apply to future projects?

For more details, see Appendix 38.

Action 2. Review AI System's Business Value

Q1. Accuracy: Is the AI System ("Manage emails") delivering results correctly?

Q2. Repeatability: Are the AI System's ("Manage emails") results repeatable?

Q3. Completeness: Is the AI System ("Manage emails") making correct use of all data sources?

Q4. Timeliness: Are modified or final email messages delivered to the point of need, at the time of need?

Q5. Volume: Will the AI System ("Manage emails") continue to function if data volumes or user numbers grow over time?

Q6. Compatibility: Is the AI System ("Manage emails") open to integration with third-party data sources and services, using standard protocols?

Q7. Flexibility: Is the AI System ("Manage emails") capable of adapting to changes (e.g., data, models, etc.)?

Q8. Bias: Have you made sure that the AI System ("Manage emails") does not have a biased view of the world?

Q9. Fairness: Have you made sure that the AI System's ("Manage emails") results are fair?

Q10. Transparency: Are the AI System ("Manage emails") actions explained in terms the user can understand?

Action 3. Review AI System's Benefits Management

Q1. Does the company ensure that the estimated "benefits" are systematically managed and measured during the AI System's ("Manage emails") lifetime?

Q2. Does the company measure the total cost of ownership of the AI System ("Manage emails"), including development, operating, and maintenance costs for data acquisition, technology infrastructure, personnel, software licenses, and third-party services?

Q3. Are ongoing costs of the AI System ("Manage emails") for model maintenance, updates, and monitoring measured?

Q4. Is the realization of expected benefits of the AI System ("Manage emails") calculated (e.g., speed and accuracy of processes, people savings, confidence in quality of decision-making, cost savings, increased revenue, improved operational efficiency, enhanced customer experience, improved decision-making, increased innovation, etc.)?

Action 4. Review AI System's/Solution's Exit Strategy

Q1. Has the company crafted an AI solution exit strategy for the AI System ("Manage emails")?

Q2. Are there escrow and portability arrangements in place for the AI System ("Manage emails") in vendor agreement(s) of the AI technical solution(s) used in case the organization desires to change to a new technological structure or transfer data and outcome (results) of logic and processing to a new AI solution?

Q3. Has the portability capability for the AI System ("Manage emails") in the AI technical solution(s) used been tested to make certain they work properly in case the company desires to change to one or more new AI solutions?

Products of AI Systems Operation

The products (outcomes, results, and outputs) define (a) what's required (i.e., organizational functions, HR resources, ICT hardware and software, policies, etc.) to establish, develop, operate, implement, and assess AI infrastructure and systems/solutions and (b) what outputs and results (i.e., reference documentation, assessment reports, decisions of live AI systems, AI data, etc.) are produced, managed, used, and maintained by AI systems/solutions and their developmental, implementation, operational, and assessment aspects.

The main outcomes, results, and outputs of this chapter include the following types of products:

> **Type 1. Organizational Functions/HR Resources**: These include (a) establishing an AI Operations Support Team and an AI Incident Management Team and (b) appointing an AI System Human Supervisor for each AI System.

> **Type 2. Assessment Reports**: These include carrying out the necessary assessment and review actions and issuing the following analyses and reports: AI System Compliance Assessment Report, AI System Data Protection Impact Assessment Report, AI System's Needs Satisfaction Evaluation Report, AI System's Business Value Evaluation Report, AI System's Benefits Management Evaluation Report, AI System's Post-Implementation Review Report.

Type 3. Reference Documentation: This includes crafting and issuing reference documentation, such as AI System Production Configuration Documentation, AI Computer Infrastructure Documentation, Critical IT Governance Controls Documentation, AI Systems Quality Documentation.

Type 4. AI/ICT Infrastructure: This includes the installation and operation of Intrusion Detection and Prevention Software, "Vault Principle" software, and Enterprise Architecture Approach (framework and platform software tools), and a set of AI Governance Tools (specific software) to manage, detect, and mitigate bias (e.g., IBM AI Fairness 360), to ensure "Explainability" (e.g., LIME, SHAP), assess risks (e.g., NIST Risk framework and tool), evaluate EU AI Act Compliance (e.g., EU AI Act Compliance Checker), etc.

Type 5. Administrative Support Controls: These include issuing, sharing, and retaining on file AI System Operations Support staff training notes, "Vault Principle" software vendor agreement, Intrusion Detection and Prevention Software agreement, AI Operations Support Team duties included in employee agreements, AI Incident Management Team duties included in employee agreements, AI System Production Transfer Staff Training Notes, AI System Operations Monitoring Management Review Notes, AI System Results Review Notes.

Type 6. AI Governance, Development, and Operations Support Controls: These include issuing, sharing, using, implementing, and keeping current policies and procedures, such as Auditability Strategy, Audit Trail Specification Documentation, Audit Trail Testing Documentation, AI Application Processing Controls Documentation, AI System Rollback Process Testing Documentation, AI System Operations performance metrics, AI System Errors Management Documentation, AI System User Requests Management Documentation, AI Incidents and Hazards Management Process Documentation, EU Act Assessment Questionnaire, UK Government AI Assurance and Governance

Standards, AI Results Verification Procedure, AI Error Correction Procedure, AI User Complaints Policy, AI Incident Reporting Policy, AI Incident Response Procedure, AI Solution Exit Strategy Documentation.

Type 7. Live AI Systems/Solutions/Tools: These include issuing, managing, using, sharing, and retaining on file AI System (in production), "Vault Principle" digital files, and AI System's input datasets.

All these may be used and implemented at the appropriate AI Implementation phase. Also, they may be used for awareness, reference, and training purposes by company board members, managers, and staff, as well as compliance and auditing purposes by internal corporate functions and external regulatory authorities and audit partners.

AI Systems Operation Recommended Assurance Actions

In order to have the best results and outcomes and achieve the **goal of AI Systems Operation** more effectively, the following assurance actions (RAA) are recommended:

RAA1. Assess Actions Taken: Assess the actions taken of the above seven steps of Phase A and improve the process of preparation, as required.

RAA2. Review Products: Review the *23 products* generated of this phase and consider their potential impact on your company's operations, production, and support processes, your employees and customers, and greater society, as needed.

More specifically, it is a good idea to review the operation of the first AI project ("Manage emails") to ensure that everything is done properly and in accordance with the AI ethics policy of your company.

RAA3. Implement Measures: Plan, improve, and implement any measures or controls identified during the above 12 steps (of Phase E) and by the review activities of RAA1 and RAA2 above, as required. It is critical to note that full documentation of the AI System ("Manage emails") is in place before you transfer the AI system in production.

Also, ensure data backups of all operational components are included in the IT Backup recovery process and the AI Budget is updated, as required.

RAA4. Report: Communicate results of your actions to the AI Steering Committee and Board, as required.

RAA5. Document: Document all activities carried out and retain full documentation in organized digital and paper files for transparency, accountability, and compliance purposes.

RAA6. Keep Products Current: Ensure you keep current the above products, by reviewing them and updating them every two to three years or as needs, expectations, and operating conditions and circumstances warrant.

Concluding Remarks

Executing the 12 steps and 51+ actions of this chapter supported you to better achieve your fifth goal (*Operate (Deploy) AI System*) and its three objectives (run and monitor the activities and results of AI Systems, manage AI Incidents, and assess AI Systems after initial implementation).

The most crucial tasks you have achieved in this phase were the following:

(1) Operating (deploying) your first AI System ("Manage emails")

(2) Managing results, errors, and user requests for your AI System

(3) Managing AI Incidents

(4) Reviewing your first AI Project ("Manage emails") after one year of the system's initial implementation

This and the previous chapter supported you to achieve your **fifth** milestone (***Develop and operate AI Systems***) in your AI Ecosystem Journey.

Develop AI Systems (Chapter 11) and Operate AI Systems (this chapter) are deemed to be the first effective and useful set of outcomes of using AI systems/solutions to benefit your company and the intended users of the specific AI systems/solutions deployed in your AI ecosystem.

The next five chapters (Part VI) continue this exciting journey by describing how to assess your AI infrastructure and AI Systems in order to improve their composing elements.

Chapter 13 describes how to assess Corporate Governance and HR Management Issues, Chapter 14 describes how to assess AI Governance and AI Data Management Issues, Chapter 15 describes how to assess AI Models and AI System Development Issues, Chapter 16 describes how to assess AI System Operation Issues, and Chapter 17 describes how to assess IT Governance Issues.

Annex 1: Example of an EU Act Assessment Questionnaire

Is the company established in the EU (see Article 2 of the EU AI Act)?

Is the AI system that has been developed a machine-based system (see Article 3 of the EU AI Act)?

Is the AI system designed to operate with varying levels of autonomy (see Article 3 of the EU AI Act)?

Will the AI system be able to adapt itself after its implementation (see Article 3 of the EU AI Act)?

Does the AI system infer from an input how an output is to be generated (see Article 3 of the EU AI Act)?

Can the AI system's output have an influence outside the specific AI system (see Article 3 of the EU AI Act)?

Does the AI system bear the name or trademark of a natural or legal person established outside the EU (see Article 3 of the EU AI Act)?

Are measures taken by the company to ensure a sufficient level of AI literacy of their staff and other persons dealing with the operation and use of AI systems (see Article 4 of the EU AI Act)?

Does the AI system make use or provide any prohibited practices, such as subliminal techniques, manipulating vulnerable individuals, social scoring, and certain uses of biometric data (see Article 5 of the EU AI Act)?

Has the company established, implemented, documented, and maintained in relation to high-risk AI systems a risk management system (see Articles 6 and 9 of the EU AI Act)?

Is the AI system classified as a high-risk system (see Articles 6 and 25 of the EU AI Act)?

Is the company required to register in the EU database (see Articles 6, 49, and 71 of the EU AI Act)?

Has the company established, implemented, documented, and maintained in relation to high-risk AI systems data governance techniques involving the training of AI Models with data, on the basis of training, validation, and testing datasets that meet the relevant quality criteria (see Article 10 of the EU AI Act)?

Does the high-risk AI system contain documentation as required (see Article 10 of the EU AI Act)?

Is the AI system designed and developed with appropriate human-machine interface tools, so that it can be effectively overseen by natural persons during the period in which it is in use (see Article 10 of the EU AI Act)?

Is the AI system designed and developed to achieve an appropriate level of accuracy, robustness, and cybersecurity and to perform consistently in those respects throughout its life cycle (see Article 14 of the EU AI Act)?

Has the company established, implemented, documented, and maintained a quality management system to ensure compliance with the AI Act (Articles 16 and 17)?

Is the AI system designed and developed in such a way that the natural persons concerned are informed that they are interacting with an AI system (see Article 50 of the EU AI Act)?

Is the information of the AI system provided to the natural persons concerned in a clear and distinguishable manner at the latest at the time of the first interaction or exposure (see Article 50 of the EU AI Act)?

Annex 2: UK Government AI Assurance and Governance Standards

Safety, Security, and Robustness: AI systems should function in a robust, secure, and safe way, and risks should be continually identified, assessed, and managed.

Appropriate Transparency and Explainability: AI systems should be appropriately transparent and explainable.

Fairness: AI systems should not undermine the legal rights of individuals or organizations, discriminate unfairly against individuals, or create unfair market outcomes.

Accountability and Governance: Governance measures should be in place to ensure effective oversight of the supply of AI systems, with clear lines of accountability across the AI life cycle.

Contestability and Redress: Where appropriate, users, affected third parties, and actors in the AI life cycle should be able to contest an AI decision or outcome that is harmful or creates material risk of harm.

PART VI

AI Infrastructure and Systems Assessment

An AI Audit Process (see Chapter 13) with the relevant tools (audit programs, audit plan, assessment questionnaires, audit report, etc.) is required to carry out all these assessment tasks. To support you in crafting your own AI Audit Process, in addition to the Audit Process detailed in Chapter 13, you may use the material and tools included in my Audit books in "Additional Resources."

More details related to assessing the eight AI Audit Areas by using specific assessment questionnaires are contained in Chapters 14–18. An example of an AI Audit Report is presented in Appendix 39.

Managing the process of assessing AI infrastructure and systems supports you to achieve the **sixth** milestone (*Improve AI infrastructure and systems*) of your AI Ecosystem Journey.

All these (actions of Chapters 13–18) compose the **third and final constituent** element of the **third** component (**AI Implementation Approach**) of your **AI Management System**.

The overall purpose of these six chapters is to find potential gaps and errors in the process of developing and operating AI infrastructure and systems, so that they could be improved accordingly and make your whole AI Ecosystem more stable and robust.

The products (outcomes, results, and outputs) define (a) what's required (i.e., organizational functions, HR resources, ICT hardware and software, policies, etc.) to establish, develop, operate, implement, and assess AI infrastructure and systems/ solutions and (b) what outputs and results (i.e., reference documentation, assessment reports, decisions of live AI systems, AI data, etc.) are produced, managed, used, and maintained by AI systems/solutions and their developmental, implementation, operational, and assessment aspects.

The main outcomes, results, and outputs of this part include the following types of products:

Type 1. Organizational Functions/HR Resources: These include (a) establishing an AI Auditing Team and (b) adding relevant audit staff.

Type 2. Assessment Reports: These include carrying out the necessary assessment and review actions and issuing the following analyses and reports – AI Audit Report.

Type 3. Reference Documentation: This includes crafting and issuing reference documentation, such as AI Audit management plan, Completed Assessment Questionnaires, AI Audit Working Notes, and AI Audit Test Results.

Type 4. AI/ICT Infrastructure: This includes the installation and operation of audit software tools.

Type 5. Administrative Support Controls: This includes issuing, sharing, and retaining on file AI Auditing Team training notes.

Type 6. AI Governance, Development, and Operations Support Controls: These include issuing, sharing, using, implementing, and keeping current policies and procedures, such as AI Audit Process, AI Audit Program, AI Audit Checklist, and Assessment Questionnaires.

Type 7. Live AI Systems/Solutions/Tools: These include issuing, managing, using, sharing, and retaining on file AI Audit Test Environment and AI Test Data for each AI System to be audited.

Develop AI Infrastructure and Systems Audit Process

Ralph Waldo Emerson:[1] "Plato says that the punishment which the wise suffer who refuse to take part in the government, is, to live under the government of worse men; and the like regret is suggested to all the auditors, as the penalty of abstaining to speak, --that they shall hear worse orators than themselves."

Overview: This chapter describes how to audit AI Infrastructure and Systems in order to improve the AI ecosystem of your organization. It includes an AI Audit Process of five stages (AI Audit planning and preparation, AI Audit execution, AI Audit reporting, AI Audit follow-up, and AI Audit Project management) with 29 steps (e.g., Define objective and scope, Review Company characteristics, Determine processes and personnel to be covered, Collect relevant Corporate Compliance Documentation, etc.).

This is part 1 of Phase E (AI Infrastructure and Systems Assessment) of the AI Implementation Approach.

Phases of the AI Implementation Approach

The AI Implementation Approach (Component 3 of the AI Management System) includes five phases:

- AI Preparation (Phase A, Chapter 7)

- AI Management Framework (Phase B, Chapters 8–10)

- AI Systems Development (Phase C, Chapter 11)

© John Kyriazoglou 2025
J. Kyriazoglou, *AI Management Framework*, https://doi.org/10.1007/979-8-8688-1536-2_13

- AI Systems Operation (Phase D, Chapter 12)
- AI Infrastructure and Systems Assessment (Phase E, *this and the following five chapters*)

Goal and Objectives of Phase E (AI Infrastructure and Systems Assessment)

The goal of Phase E is "To improve AI Infrastructure and Systems."
The objectives of this goal are

Objective 1: Audit, review, and assess governance issues

Objective 2: Audit, review, and assess development and operation of AI systems

Steps of AI Infrastructure and Systems Assessment

The eight steps to support the achievement of the goal and objectives of Phase E are

Step E1. Assess Corporate Governance

Step E2. Assess HR Management

Step E3. Assess AI Governance

Step E4. Assess AI Data Management

Step E5. Assess AI Model and Hypotheses Management

Step E6. Assess AI System Development

Step E7. Assess AI System Operation

Step E8. Assess IT Governance

These eight assessment steps are supported by the five-stage audit process detailed in this chapter.

Steps E1–E8 are described in other chapters (Chapters 14–18).

Introduction to AI Audit

AI audits largely involve a systematic independent review and examination of a company's existing level of compliance with AI ethics, AI regulations, data protection regimes (e.g., GDPR, e-PRIVACY, etc.), rules and corporate ethics, AI, IT, and data protection policies.

AI auditing also involves thoroughly reviewing AI infrastructure and AI systems, focusing on data, algorithms, and outcomes. The purpose is to verify that AI operates as intended, adheres to legal and ethical standards, and produces accurate and fair results. This process encompasses many AI technologies, including deep learning, natural language processing, and advanced machine learning models.

AI Auditing Challenges, Opportunities, and Risks

From a technological perspective, AI systems introduce new kinds of complexity not found in more traditional IT systems that you may be used to using. Depending on the circumstances, your use of AI systems is also likely to rely heavily on third-party code and/or relationships with AI suppliers. Also, your existing systems need to be integrated with several other new and existing IT components, which are also intricately connected. This complexity may make it more difficult to identify and manage some security risks and may increase others, such as the risk of outages. From a human perspective, the people involved in building and deploying AI systems are likely to have a wider range of backgrounds than usual, including traditional software engineering, systems administration, data scientists, statisticians, as well as domain experts. Security practices and expectations may vary significantly, and for some there may be less understanding of broader security compliance requirements, as well as those of data protection law more specifically.[2]

From the point of view of auditors, there are several challenges, opportunities, and risks that do not occur in audits in other fields (e.g., IT auditing), but that are specific for auditing AI infrastructure and AI systems.

AI Challenges

A high level of expert knowledge is necessary: AI is a complex topic, and the field is developing at an enormous pace. Auditing an AI system requires specialized knowledge and skills, including expertise in machine learning, data analysis, and programming. It is unfeasible to expect that auditors will have in-depth knowledge in all these areas, considering there is currently a shortage of experts in these areas.

Rapidly evolving technology: AI is a rapidly evolving field, and new techniques and algorithms are being developed continuously. This means that auditors may need to stay up to date with the latest developments in the field and adapt their evaluation methods accordingly.

Reliance of the used system/model on potentially large amounts of data: an AI model is the result of the combination of a training algorithm (known) and data used to train it. For a trustworthy application, therefore, the data needs to be (1) trustworthy and (2) suited for the task at hand. Both issues are complicated questions in practice.

Data availability: Auditing an AI system often requires access to large amounts of data, including training data, test data, and real-world data. However, this data may not always be available or may be difficult to obtain, particularly in cases where the data is sensitive or proprietary.

Lack of transparency: Many AI models use thousands to millions of parameters and thus are impossible to interpret, even by experts. While the advent of explainable AI techniques (XAI) has started to address this issue, most models remain hard up to impossible to interpret.

Constantly changing systems: Many AI systems are regularly updated with new data ("retrained"). From a conservative viewpoint, this would mean that we have a new AI system that consequently would need to be tested from the start.

Supply chain complexity: Usually, AI developers rely on tools and systems provided by various suppliers. For a full understanding of the AI system, input from these suppliers is also required but often hard to get.

Lack of standards: There are currently no widely accepted standards or metrics for evaluating the trustworthiness of AI systems. This means that auditors may need to develop their own evaluation frameworks or rely on subjective judgments, which can lead to inconsistencies.[3]

AI Opportunities

Examples of AI opportunities include

- The ability to compress the data processing cycle

- The ability to reduce errors by replacing human actions with perfectly repeatable machine actions

- The ability to replace time-intensive activities with time-efficient activities (process automation), reducing labor time and costs

- The ability to have robots or drones replace humans in potentially dangerous situations, etc.[4]

AI Risks

Examples of AI risks include

- The risk that unidentified human biases will be imbedded in the AI technology

- The risk that human logic errors will be imbedded in the AI technology

- The risk that inadequate testing and oversight of AI results in ethically questionable results

- The risk that AI products and services will cause harm, resulting in financial and/or reputational damage, etc.[5]

AI Audit Objectives

The objectives of an AI Audit are to

1. Assist and support Management and staff to perform all required AI implementation tasks in the right and effective way, within a creative, entrepreneurial, and ethical framework

2. Encourage the use and exploitation of the most efficient and cost-effective AI control systems, methods, and practices for the most accurate, well-protected, and timely outcomes and outputs of AI systems/solutions

3. Promote AI, IT, and data protection good governance and complete all AI functions and activities of all AI systems/solutions and the business or organization in a proper and effective way

4. Improve the profitability of the company and its review by all stakeholders (social and institutional partners, regulators, social and other audit committees, etc.)

AI Audit Process

Several AI auditing frameworks have been published by a mix of international organizations and governments that can aid the internal audit function. These are

1. Control Objectives for Information and Related Technologies (COBIT) Framework

2. Committee of Sponsoring Organizations (COSO) Enterprise Risk Management Framework

3. US Government Accountability Office (GAO) AI Framework

4. Institute of Internal Auditors (IIA) Artificial Intelligence Auditing Framework

5. Singapore Personal Data Protection Commission (PDPC) Model AI Governance Framework[6]

The **AI Audit process** I am proposing consists of 5 stages and 29 steps following, in general terms, the ISO 19011 Auditing Standard:[7]

- **Stage 1. AI Audit planning and preparation**
- **Stage 2. AI Audit execution**
- **Stage 3. AI Audit reporting**

- **Stage 4. AI Audit follow-up**

- **Stage 5. AI Audit Project management**

During each stage and step of the AI Audit process, the involvement of the company's personnel is critical and will consist in setting up a technical test environment for audit testing, answering questions, participating in interviews, preparing documents for testing, as well as designing and overseeing the implementation of AI and other IT and privacy controls following management's response to previous AI Audit reports.

The AI Auditor will establish the timing of the audit and the scheduling of the staff in conjunction with the senior management of the company taking into consideration the busy periods of different departments and units trying to minimize disruption.

These 5 stages and the most important 29 steps, according to my audit and consulting experience in various sectors and industries, are detailed next.

Stage 1: AI Audit Planning and Preparation

This stage consists of planning everything that is to be done in advance by interested parties, such as the auditor, the client, and the audit stakeholders (company board, senior management, functional managers, compliance manager, IT staff, AI and data science staff, DPO (Data Protection Officer), etc.) to ensure that the audit complies with the client's AI audit objectives. This stage of an AI audit begins with the decision to conduct the audit and ends when the audit itself begins.

This stage is important for determining the required resources which are to be dedicated to the AI audit. The more time and energy spent planning an AI audit, the more accurate and expedient the specific AI audit will be. All these are achieved by the following eight steps:

Step 1. Define Objective and Scope

The crucial first step of any audit is to define the objective and scope. It must be decided whether the audit should cover

- All business units that use AI systems/solutions or only specific AI systems

- All issues included in all AI audit areas or a specific audit area (e.g., AI Data Management)

- All issues related to AI models and algorithms, etc.

Two examples follow:

> **Audit Objective #1**: Evaluate the physical security and environmental aspects of the facilities (physical, technical, etc.) that house the AI infrastructure in the main data center.

> **Audit Objective #2**: Determine if the processing operations and transactions of the specific AI system/solution are performed in accordance with the company's procedures, as well as the relevant ethics principles, privacy laws, and AI regulations.

An AI audit may become time-consuming, as it usually involves meeting and interviewing various key company people, management, and line staff. It is therefore essential that each AI audit be carried out in a strict time schedule to ensure consistent and effective results. Over a longer period, the functional and legal position of an organization may have changed.

Step 2. Review Company Characteristics

Any AI audit needs to take the structure of the company into consideration by asking the following questions (Q):

Q1. Is the audited company a single legal business entity or does it belong to a group of companies?

Q2. What business departments or units exist and what functions do they have?

Q3. Does the audited company have an operational matrix structure?

Q4. How are the AI systems/solutions and their activities organized?

Q5. How are the IT processing activities organized?

Q6. Have certain functions been centralized or are they carried out locally or by outsourcing entities?

Q7. Are databases shared among business units or legal entities?

Q8. Are AI models developed within the company or are external models used?

Q9. How are the data required for the AI system/solution obtained?

Q10. How many AI vendors are providing services for the company?

Each AI audit will be different and should be tailored to suit the particular needs of the individual company. In general, an audit will consist of the following steps described next.

Step 3. Determine Processes and Personnel to Be Covered

The next and equally crucial step of this stage is to determine the processes and personnel to be covered by the AI audit:

1. A member of the company's internal audit personnel should be delegated the task of managing the AI audit, to ensure that the process runs smoothly.

2. It is essential to determine which departments and personnel will be involved in the AI audit process, in which order and within what time frame.

3. It is also very important at this phase to inform personnel in advance about the AI audit and to obtain the support of senior management and staff members involved in managing the AI audit and providing the AI audit responses.

Step 4. Collect and Review Relevant Corporate Compliance Documentation

This step entails what background information and data should be first collected to support the whole audit process. These include AI Plans, Policies, and Procedures; AI data sources; IT Plans, Policies, and Procedures; Corporate Plans, Policies, and Procedures; Data Management Policies and Procedures; and Data Protection (Privacy) Plans, Policies, and Procedures. See Annex 1 for a detailed list.

AI auditors should review all these documents as well as take into consideration the ethics, privacy, security, and human oversight principles defined in the "Seven Ancient Greek Wisdom Principles handbook," the "Corporate Philosophy Statements and Policies," the "AI Global Standards and Guidelines handbook," the "Major Data Protection Laws and Privacy by Design handbook," and the "Digital and Secure AI System Development Guidelines handbook" in Chapters 2–6.

Information, data, and other details in these sources will help and enable the AI auditor to navigate the landscape of data assets, information systems, and the processing of personal, AI, and other corporate data carried out by the specific functions or departments of the specific company. It should be noted that internal documents must often be treated with extremer caution and should be taken for granted, because they may be out of date, incomplete, or representative of an official viewpoint that has little relation with actual everyday business practice.

Step 5. Obtain Management, User, and IT Commitment

AI Auditors must review what they will audit with the management of the particular area or AI system they will be auditing to ensure (a) their role is accepted and (b) that management, users, AI staff, DPO, IT managers, and line personnel commit and make available both end-user personnel as well as qualified AI staff and IT personnel to support and collaborate in the upcoming AI audit.

Step 6. Finalize List of Issues to Audit

Based on this study and the audit objectives, AI Auditors will compile a list of issues that are critical to shaping their audit opinion.

For example, the audit issues for Audit Area 4 (**AI Data Management**) include the following:

- AI Data governance roles and responsibilities

- Data governance policies and procedures

- Data quality

- Completeness and accuracy of data

- Big data management

- Processing Records Documentation

- Data Privacy and Protection Controls

Step 7. Design Audit Samples

AI Auditors will design the audit sample to achieve the audit objectives based on

1. The number of data/documents/transactions

2. The size of the system

3. Whether it is objective and representative of the total population

4. The expected errors

5. With the help of methods such as statistical random sampling, statistical systematic sampling, haphazard sampling, and judgmental sampling

Step 8. Prepare an AI Audit Program

To review, assess, and measure a specific company's compliance with AI ethics, AI regulations including data protection law (e.g., GDPR), IT policies and procedures, cyber resilience, and Information Security Controls, it is necessary to develop a benchmark against which the AI audit can be assessed.

Benchmarking, in business terms, is the practice of comparing business processes and performance metrics to industry best practices from other companies.

The benchmark, in AI auditing terms, may be the applicable AI regulations, global digital guidelines, the relevant data protection law (e.g., GDPR), or the company's internal AI strategy and ethics, privacy policies, information security standards, or a combination of all these, etc.

This benchmark for auditing a company's AI infrastructure and AI systems/solutions and within the terms of this book is an **AI Audit Program**. Two examples of AI Audit Programs are included in Appendix 40.

This AI Audit Program is structured in eight AI Audit Areas as detailed in Annex 2.

Each issue is assessed on the basis of a specific questionnaire (see examples in Chapters 14–18), a checklist (see example in Annex 4), and other relevant audit actions, explained in Chapters 14–18.

Questionnaires. An AI Audit can be carried out on the basis of face-to-face interviews conducted with the relevant staff members or the use of written questionnaires or both.

Written questions have the advantage of ensuring that the AI audit is conducted in a standardized way across the whole company.

Questionnaires should be tailored to take account of the scope of the AI Audit and the structure of the company, but will typically seek information on the following:

1. The legal entity or business unit or the AI specifics being audited

2. Existing policies, procedures, AI vendor contracts, and AI Governance and AI Data Management compliance measures as regards the company's AI Ecosystem

3. AI systems/solutions, AI models, databases, and software applications containing AI data, corporate and personal data, as well as the relevant AI processing activities

4. Categories of personal data (including sensitive data) being processed and used for AI

5. Categories of data subjects whose personal data is being processed and used for AI

6. Controllers, processors, and any other stakeholders or external entities that provide AI services

7. Data flows within and outside the audited company and inside and outside of the EU or others relevant to the company region, country, or area

8. Technical and organizational security and AI measures, etc.

Carrying out an AI Infrastructure and systems audit consists largely of completing questionnaires and providing supporting documents such as internal guidelines and procedures. It may also include testing an AI System's/Solution's outcomes, decisions, outputs, and results.

It is important to ensure that the right questions are asked of the right people. Relevant personnel should be given sufficient time to provide a comprehensive response.

After reviewing the responses, it may be necessary to seek further clarifications, if responses are found to contain contradictions or if they are not sufficiently concise.

Interviews with key personnel are a good way to ensure that the questionnaires are completed in an efficient and accurate manner.

It is important that the relevant staff members know in advance what is expected of them.

Stage 2: AI Audit Execution

The execution stage of an audit is often called the fieldwork. It is the data-gathering portion of the AI audit and covers the time period from arrival at the audit location up to the exit meeting. It consists of multiple activities, including on-site AI audit management, meeting with the auditees, interviewing various staff, understanding the AI ecosystem and its system controls and verifying that these AI controls work, testing specific AI systems/solutions, communicating among team members, and communicating with the auditees, etc. All these are achieved by the following five steps:

Step 1. Create a Test Environment and Select Audit Techniques

Ensure IT sets up a test environment with dedicated resources and test data for each AI system/solution audited.

Review the data and the test cases as well as the whole testing process of each AI system/solution audited to ensure you know what goes on in each system. It is good practice to also add your own test data and test cases.

Ensure your AI staff resources are adequately supported by other relevant company personnel (e.g., IT, data science, DPO, etc.).

Review the user requests and complaints to get a good idea of any system shortfalls or errors.

Review the documentation of the AI vendor for each AI system/solution using their model for your purposes.

Employ an external or internal subject expert to support you in effectively testing each AI system/solution.

Based on the above and the AI Audit Program for each specific audit (Step 8 of Stage 1), AI Auditors will also select the types of audit testing and the types of control techniques that will be followed during the execution of the audit.

Audit tests include compliance tests, weakness tests, and substantive tests.

Testing techniques include interviews, questionnaires, numerical operations on transactions, walk-throughs, flowcharts, data capture and analysis, confirmation of movements/documents (vouching), observation, sampling checks (spot checks), analytical review, and use of special software (audit software).

IT prepares and creates the computerized test environment with specific dedicated resources and data for carrying out tests by AI Auditors on the specific AI system/solution.

Step 2. Execute Audit Tests

AI Auditors will carry out the following sets of tests according to the AI Audit Program, etc.

Set 1. Weakness Testing: AI Auditors may, in many cases, conduct a preliminary assessment of IT Controls in the system or the area under audit to derive an understanding of assurance that existing IT controls (General IT Controls and Application Controls) are reliable and operate under a suitable IT Governance framework. The assessment of controls at this level would include the assessment of effective and suitable IT Governance mechanisms, development of application systems, procuring of IT solutions, operation of computerized application systems, information security, business continuity, IT disaster recovery, etc.

235

Next, the AI Audit Area to be audited is reviewed and evaluated.

Examples of weakness tests are lack of physical and logical security, inadequate documentation/records, inexistent security policy, ineffective or informal password policy and controls, lack of proper oversight for making application changes, etc.

Set 2. Compliance Testing: A detailed examination and evaluation of AI controls is carried out, through the review of AI policies, procedures, and AI systems documentation. The AI auditor performs tests in order to verify that the AI control policies, practices, and procedures set by AI and IT management work as planned. The auditor also examines documents such as descriptions, diagrams, and source program code. In the case of *desk checking*, the auditor processes false or true data through the logic of the program.

Examples of compliance tests include

1. To verify configuration of all routers for controls

2. To verify change management steps to ensure controls are effective for all application systems (including AI systems/ solutions)

3. Review of system access rights for all AI systems

4. Review of firewall settings

5. Review compliance with password policy for all personnel

For a detailed example, see also Annex 3.

It should be noted that Chapters 14–18 include the assessment steps for all eight AI Audit Areas.

See Annex 2 for more details.

Set 3. Substantive Testing: In substantive testing, the AI auditor gathers evidence to evaluate the integrity of data, transactions, or other controls. Substantive testing checks the integrity of contents.

Examples of substantive tests include

1. Set up a test database with fictitious test data and test an AI application system (e.g., payroll processing) or the encryption process and results of the personal data stored.

2. Use of the actual AI system/solution production environment with fictitious (test) transactions.

3. Integrate special code specified by AI Auditors (Embedded Audit Routines) in the production programs and recording of the processing in special files (audit files).

4. Use of special software (Audit Software) that collects the transactions and movements, examines the results in the production files, and analyzes the possible wrong processing or events by the given AI system/solution.

5. Test the backup policy and procedures to ensure that all applications and software (including all AI components) are recovered as per policy.

All tests, findings, results, etc., shall be documented in the AI audit working notes.

Step 3. Evaluate and Document Findings

AI Auditors will evaluate, based on the evaluation criteria (low, medium, and high priority), and will summarize all findings, results, and suggestions in the working notes and in a report. The report is usually discussed with the specific executives of the company before its final version, as described below.

Step 4. Review of Initial Findings with the Auditees

Initial AI audit findings are discussed (except in proven fraud cases), and test results are reviewed with all stakeholders for the purpose of understanding the tests, designing additional tests and controls, and cross-checking the audit evidence and findings.

Step 5. Perform Additional Tests

Depending on the findings of the AI audit, additional tests may need to be performed in the area under audit, for example, to do more tests on the AI systems used in the specific business operation for which the AI audit is performed, etc.

Stage 3: AI Audit Reporting

This stage is where the principal product from the audit occurs. It expresses the AI Auditor's opinion, presents AI Audit findings, and discusses recommendations for improvements.

The purpose of the AI Audit report is to communicate the results of the investigation. The report should provide correct and clear data that will be effective as a management aid in addressing important AI organizational issues. The AI Audit process may end when the report is issued by the lead auditor or Audit Manager or after follow-up actions are completed, depending on the specifics of the particular AI audit assignment or company. All these are achieved by the following five steps:

Step 1. Issue Draft AI Audit Report: Once the areas and issues of non-compliance have been identified, they should be described in detail and then given priority according to their seriousness. At this stage, it is usually a good idea for the AI Auditor to also compile a list of potential remedies for the issues that have been identified. This information can be contained in an audit report (see example in Appendix 39). Audit reports are also a useful tool in seeking the support of senior management for implementing the necessary improvements.

Step 2. Overview Initial "Draft" AI Audit Report with the Auditees: The initial "draft" AI audit report is reviewed with all those directly audited, and their comments and observations are recorded.

Step 3. Review Initial "Draft" AI Audit Report with Management: The initial "draft" AI audit report is reviewed with all levels of management of the auditees, and their relevant comments and remarks are recorded.

Step 4. Improve Initial "Draft" AI Audit Report: The initial "draft" AI audit report is improved with all the relevant comments and remarks collected by the directly audited and the management of the audited unit, and its final version is being prepared.

Step 5. Issue "Final" AI Audit Report: The final "official" AI audit report is prepared and issued. This includes the initial findings of the AI audit, with all relevant comments and observations collected from those directly audited and the management of the audited entity, and a set of AI Audit recommendations to improve the errors, gaps, and omissions found in the areas and systems audited by the AI Auditors. This final version is transmitted to all the competent and approved levels of management of the audited unit as well as to senior management levels (e.g., CEO, audit committee, AI Committee, chairman, managing director, etc.).

Stage 4: AI Audit Follow-Up

The chief audit executive must establish a follow-up process to monitor and ensure that management actions have been effectively implemented or that senior management has accepted the risk of not taking action. A follow-up is also needed because one important measure of the effectiveness of the internal audit function is its success in achieving a high implementation rate of recommendations made in audit reports. All these are achieved by the following three steps:

Step 1. Follow-Up Review: The AI Auditor will keep an updated log of issues to be followed up (within a predetermined time period) from the previous AI Audits, including the deadline for the implementation of the proposed and agreed-upon recommendations.

Step 2. Review with Management: The AI Auditor will contact the department manager responsible for AI (usually IT for AI infrastructure and systems) as well as the AI System Owner to follow up on the implementation of the recommendation as the deadlines approach. They will discuss and understand the process that is implemented, asking for different documents supporting the implementation.

Step 3. Issue Follow-Up Report: A follow-up report will be issued to the management and a copy sent to the audit committee, describing the AI issues followed up on, the management's control implementation, the assessment of the appropriateness of the AI control, and a listing of unresolved findings, including their deadlines.

Stage 5: AI Audit Project Management

To avoid the potential failure and mismanagement of corporate and other resources and to achieve the success of an endeavor, a project, a series of activities, etc., a scientific approach, effective organization, and resources are needed, such as "project management."

The goal of AI Audit Project Management is to motivate all stakeholders to achieve the agreed and approved project objectives within the time and budget boundaries and on a basis of a better overall cost-total beneficial impact and results. This is achieved by the following eight steps:

Step 1. Manage and Organize AI Audit Project

Action 1. Establish an AI Auditing Team and ensure it is trained very well on all AI aspects (ethics, technology, etc.).

Action 2. Identify the AI Audit management plan, organizational chart, milestones, phases, tasks, and activities of the AI Audit Project.

Action 3. Manage the Project's human resources.

Action 4. Complete the implementation of the Audit Project.

Step 2. Monitor and Control Project: Monitor, audit, report, and evaluate progress and results of the AI Audit Project.

Step 3. Support Project: Provide technical support and troubleshooting of the AI Audit Project and its activities.

Step 4. Manage Risks: Carry out Risk Classification, Risk Assessment, Risk Resolution through Prevention Actions, and Risk Monitoring of the AI Audit Project.

Step 5. Manage Changes and Problems: Determine how changes to the AI Audit Project will be managed (individuals, degree of readiness, approach setting, support, communication, collaboration, participation, etc.).

Step 6. Manage Quality: Define a quality assurance framework, quality control, and quality improvement actions of the AI Audit Project.

Step 7. Document AI Audit Work Notes: To ensure that the company's AI audit personnel can continue to develop further the processes and controls required to maintain the highest possible level of AI audit functionality, the AI Audit Project team will document in detail all project phases, with their corresponding working notes, findings, and results.

Step 8. Close Project: Project closure is the last step of the AI Audit Project. It's when the project manager verifies that the company stakeholders have accepted the AI Audit Project deliverables.

The AI Audit Project manager may also prepare and issue a Project Closure Report. This summarizes the outcomes of the AI Audit Project after it has been completed. The Project Closure Report should contain the following elements: Project Goals and Objectives, Key Project Deliverables, Realized Benefits, Lessons Learned, and a Financial Summary.[8]

Recommendations

As regards the better use of the above-described five-stage AI Audit Process, the following recommendations (REC) are proposed:

REC 1. Ensure you review, adopt to your needs, and use the above AI Audit Process with the relevant tools (audit programs, audit plan, assessment questionnaires, audit report, etc.) to carry out all assessment tasks. To support you in crafting your own AI Audit Process, you may use the material and tools included in my Audit books in "Additional Resources."

REC 2. Review all of the above steps and consider how they may impact your AI systems/solutions in your operating landscape and how you may utilize them.

REC 3. Customize them, if required, to your purposes, by making the necessary changes to satisfy your needs and expectations.

REC 4. Ensure all your AI staff and relevant managers and board members are fully aware of the AI audit process and how it may support your corporate needs and requirements in improving all aspects of your AI Ecosystem.

REC 5. Ensure you keep current the above products (IT Audit Process, IT Audit Programs, etc.), by reviewing them and updating them every two to three years or as needs, expectations, and operating conditions and circumstances warrant.

Conclusion

This is the first part of your **sixth** milestone (***Improve AI infrastructure and systems***) of your AI Ecosystem Journey. The next chapter continues this exciting journey by describing how to assess your Corporate Governance and HR Management Issues.

Annex 1: AI Compliance Documentation

AI Plans, Policies, and Procedures

AI asset list

AI systems/solutions list

AI data sources

AI vendor list

AI Glossary

AI Readiness Assessment Questionnaire

Privacy Readiness Assessment Questionnaire

AI Awareness Action Plan

AI Performance Metrics

AI Risk Assessment Procedure

AI Strategy Questionnaire

AI Strategy

AI Acceptable Use Policy

AI Third-Party Controls

AI Staff Education and Training Policy

AI Data Governance Job Descriptions

AI Trustworthiness Assessment Questionnaire

AI Algorithmic Impact Assessment Questionnaire

AI Application Controls

AI Model Development Procedure

AI Results Verification Procedure

AI Error Correction Procedure

AI User Support Procedure

AI Incident Reporting Policy

AI Incident Response Procedure

AI System Post-Implementation Review Questionnaire

AI Audit Findings Report

IT Plans, Policies, and Procedures

Lists and registers of IT systems and information systems

Documents describing the IT technical architecture in place

IT system documentation

Disaster recovery plans for IT systems

IT Acceptable Use Policy

Minimum IT Security Controls

Minimum Data Center Physical and Environmental Controls

IT Policies and Procedures Compliance Statement

Antimalware Protection Policy

User Access Authorization Policy

Configuration Management Policy

IT Procurement Procedure

Security and Privacy Methodology in IT Systems Development

Information Systems Development Security Integration Plan

Training on Security and Breach Awareness and Management

Data Loss Prevention (DLP) solution

Intrusion Detection and Prevention System

Vulnerability assessment

Data Breach Management System (Policy, procedures, form, notification to authority and data subjects, breach register, management responsibilities for responding, etc.)

IT Change Management Procedure

Corporate Plans, Policies, and Procedures

Annual company reports

Strategic planning documents

Employee confidentiality agreements

Internal (Employee) Threat Response Plan

A recent organizational chart

Relevant legislation and regulations

Disaster plan or contingency plan

Procedural manuals and system workflows

Results of any other relevant audits, departmental assessments, or self-assessments

Vital records lists

Corporate Policies and Procedures Manual

Corporate Records Retention and Destruction Policy and Procedures

IT Assets Inventory

Data Quality Policy and Procedures

Corporate Risk Management Process

Corporate Risk Register

Staff Training Plan

Corporate Education Policy

Corporate Personnel Hiring Procedures

Corporate Personnel Performance Review Procedures

Business Records Management System (policy, procedures, access register, destruction register, etc.)

Business Records Manager

Business Records Inventory

Data Management Policies and Procedures

Data Governance Policy

Data Quality Policy

Data Quality Improvement Procedure

Data Classification Policy

Corporate Information and Business Intelligence Policy

Intellectual Property Rights Protection Policy

Basic Personal Data Management Instructions

Data Protection (Privacy) Plans, Policies, and Procedures

Documentation of Personal Data (PD) Processing environment

PD Minimization Policy

PD Disposal Register

PD Inventory

Documentation of the legal bases recorded in the PD Inventory

Website Privacy Policy

Employee Privacy Policy

Privacy Laws and Standards Manual

GDPR Gap Analysis Report

Business Records and Data Management Guidelines

Updated (with privacy) Corporate HR policies

Consent System (Policy, Procedures, Forms, Register, Software)

Cookies Policy (with consent options)

DS Rights Satisfaction System (Policy, Procedures, Forms, Register, Software)

GDPR Compliance Plan

Announcement of GDPR Compliance to staff

Documentation for Controller Duties

Documentation (Job Description or Contract) for DPO

Announcement of DPO to Data Protection Authority

Documentation for EU Controller Representative

Privacy and Security Awareness and Training Plan

Privacy and Security Seminar Presentation

PD Management Guidelines for Employees

Transfer Agreements and BCRs

EU Standard Contractual Clauses (Controller to Controller)

EU Standard Contractual Clauses (Controller to Processor)

Third-Party Disclosure Agreements

Controller-Processor Agreements

Third-Party Monitoring Procedure

DP Monitoring System (Monitoring Procedure, Privacy Changes, DPO Monitoring Role, DP Audit Review Report, etc.)

DP Controls Testing Report

DPIA Methodology

DPIA Assessment Template

DP by Design/Default Policy

DP by Design/Default Techniques

DP by Design/Default Software (encryption, pseudonymization, masking, etc.)

Fictitious Test Data

Clean Desk and Screen Policy

Data Classification Policy

Privacy and Security Controls (data protection policy, backup policy, password policy, email policy, etc.)

Minimum Privacy Compliance Controls

PD Access Register

Annex 2: AI Audit Areas

AI Audit Area 1 (**Corporate Governance**) with 8 issues (AI requirements, standards, and rules compliance; AI Ethics; AI Audit Process; corporate strategy; corporate ethical rules and values; AI Guidelines; IP protection; and corporate knowledge retention management), 7 questionnaires, and over 57 questions.

The assessment of these issues is carried out in Step E1 (Assess Corporate Governance), in Chapter 14.

Audit Area 2 (**HR Management)** with 8 issues (AI management roles and responsibilities, human resource requirements management, human culture, AI awareness and training, Personnel Responsibilities and Skills, Basic or Minimum IT and Digital Required Skills, Intermediate or Second-Level IT and Digital Skills, and Advanced or Third-Level IT and Digital Skills), 8 questionnaires, and over 72 questions.

The assessment of these issues is carried out in Step E2 (Assess HR Management), in Chapter 14.

Audit Area 3 (**AI Governance)** with 13 issues (AI governance framework, AI strategy, AI program management, AI risk and control framework, human oversight, AI benefits management, AI language and concept definitions, AI expectation management, AI Operating Model, AI solution exit strategy, AI awareness and training, AI third-party controls, and AI incident management), 13 questionnaires, and over 72 questions. The assessment of these issues is carried out in Step E3 (Assess AI Governance), in Chapter 15.

Audit Area 4 (**AI Data Management)** with 7 issues (AI data governance roles and responsibilities, data governance policies and procedures, data quality, completeness and accuracy of data, big data management, Processing Records Documentation, and Data Privacy and Protection Controls), 7 questionnaires, and over 45 questions. The assessment of these issues is carried out in Step E4 (Assess AI Data Management), in Chapter 15.

Audit Area 5 (**AI Model and Hypotheses Management**) with 4 issues (AI Hypotheses governance, AI Algorithms governance, AI Model governance, and AI Model validation), 4 questionnaires, and over 30 questions. The assessment of these issues is carried out in Step E5 (Assess AI Model and Hypotheses Management), in Chapter 16.

Audit Area 6 (**AI System Development**) with 10 issues (AI architecture and development, business case documentation for AI systems/solutions, business process documentation, AI Application controls, AI system/solution testing methodology, "Explainability by design" in AI systems/solutions, "Security by design" in AI systems/ solutions, "Privacy by design and by default" in AI systems/solutions, AI system/solution ownership, and AI system/solution regulatory risk analysis), 10 questionnaires, and over 75 questions. The assessment of these issues is carried out in Step E6 (Assess AI System Development), in Chapter 16.

Audit Area 7 (**AI System Operation**) with 16 issues (Critical IT Controls, AI Computer Infrastructure, IT Operational Aspects of AI systems/solutions, quality of AI systems/solutions, auditability of AI systems/solutions, application processing controls and logging of AI systems/solutions, AI systems/solutions operation (deployment), AI systems/solutions operation monitoring, AI systems/solutions results review, AI systems/solutions error management, AI systems/solutions user requests management, AI incidents and hazards management, Post-Implementation Review of AI systems/solutions, business value of AI systems/solutions evaluation, AI systems'/solutions' benefits management evaluation, and AI systems'/solutions' exit strategy evaluation), 16 questionnaires, and over 103 questions. The assessment of these issues is carried out in Step E7 (Assess AI System Operation), in Chapter 17.

Audit Area 8 (**IT Governance**) with 16 issues (AI computer infrastructure management, information security and privacy policies and procedures management, vulnerabilities and malware management, robotic accounts management, human accounts management, account provisioning and revocation management, password controls management, segregation of IT duties implementation, third-party access controls implementation, IT change management, AI systems/solutions inventory management, IT resource management, IT knowledge retention management, IT configuration management, system software, and backup and recovery process management), 16 questionnaires, and over 120 questions. The assessment of these issues is carried out in Step E8 (Assess IT Governance), in Chapter 18.

Annex 3: Example of Auditing Issue 7 (Data Privacy and Protection Controls) in AI Audit Area 5 (AI Data Management)

Audit Action 1. Collect evidence. Collect the relevant evidence (documentation, controls, etc.) related to this issue, such as

- Information Security Policy
- Cookie Policy
- Website Privacy Policy
- Employees Privacy Policy
- Data Retention/Removal Policy
- Data Quality Policy
- Backup/Recovery Policy

- Malware Protection Policy

- Encryption Policy

- Pseudonymization/Anonymization/Data Aggregation Policy

- Consent Management System

- Subject Rights Satisfaction System

- Security Incident Management System

- Data Breach Management System

- Privacy Education and Training Policy

- DPIA Methodology

- Data Protection Audit Methodology

- Security and Privacy Controls in Information Systems Plan

- Personal Data (PD) Inventory

- IT Assets Inventory

- PD Minimization Policy

- Corporate Records Retention and Destruction Policy and Procedures

- PD Disposal Register

- Data Quality Policy and Procedures

- Website Privacy Policy

- Employee Privacy Policy

Audit Action 2. Review Controls and Documentation. Review the evidence (documentation, controls, etc., as per audit action 1) on the basis of the relevant questionnaire and specifically how the company operates in the **Data Privacy and Protection** controls environment in order to safeguard and protect the personal data used for AI purposes of the persons involved.

Audit Action 3. Document Audit Findings (AF). Note down the findings of these review and assessment actions, such as

AF1. The company collects PD on the basis of a PD Minimization Policy.

AF2. The company does not have a Corporate Records Retention and Destruction Policy and Procedures.

AF3. The company does not use a PD Disposal Register.

AF4. The company does not use Data Quality Policy and Procedures for PD.

Audit Action 4. Evaluate Findings. Analyze the answers obtained by using the relevant questionnaire and assessing the audit evidence in terms of various specific criteria (see example below).

Audit Action 5. Make Recommendations. Make specific recommendations to improve the protection of the privacy aspects of the PD processed by the company and address the lack of measures and controls identified in the findings and evaluation actions.

Example: Issue 7 Audit Recommendations (AR)

AR2.1. Ensure the company implements a Corporate Records Retention and Destruction Policy and Procedures and a PD Disposal Register.

AR2.2. Ensure the company implements a process (Data Quality Policy and Procedures) that includes the PD processed by the company.

Annex 4: Physical and Environmental Security Checklist

Section A: Exterior Building Perimeter

A1. Protective barriers: Yes: _____ or No: _____

A2. Security Guards

A2.1. Building entrance: Yes: _____ or No: _____

A2.2. Parking entrance: Yes: _____ or No: _____

A2.3. Visiting floors at night: Yes: _____ or No: _____

A3. Guest register: Yes: _____ or No: _____

A4. Accompanying guests: Yes: _____ or No: _____

A5. Entrance to underground parking: Yes: _____ or No: _____

A6. External fencing: Yes: _____ or No: _____

A7. Checking cars with special equipment (for bombs, etc.): Yes: _____ or No: _____

A8. CCTV system (television, etc.): Yes: _____ or No: _____

A9. Dogs: Yes: _____ or No: _____

A10. Alarm system: Yes: _____ or No: _____

A11. Choice of data center space (safe location: away from rivers, highways, trains, etc.; not in the basement of a building, etc.): Yes: _____ or No: _____

Section B: Interior Building Space and Offices

B1. System with access cards: Yes: _____ or No: _____

B2. Recording (automatic) of workers in the building (entry, exit, visit to which areas of the building, etc.): Yes: _____ or No: _____

B3. Alarm system: Yes: _____ or No: _____

B4. Entry Control

B4.1. People (airport procedures): Yes: _____ or No: _____

B4.2. Mail (scanner for bombs, etc.): Yes: _____ or No: _____

B5. Double doors (bank entry system): Yes: _____ or No: _____

B6. Lock mechanism: Yes: _____ or No: _____

B7. Biometric access control systems: Yes: _____ or No: _____

B8. Closed-circuit television: Yes: _____ or No: _____

B9. Building evacuation instructions (manual, tests): Yes: _____ or No: _____

B10. Generator and UPS (Backup Power System)

B10.1. Building: Yes: _____ or No: _____

B10.2. Data center: Yes: _____ or No: _____

B11. Structural collapse of building (seismic protection): Yes: _____ or No: _____

B12. Building management system (air-conditioning, water, etc.): Yes: _____ or No: _____

B13. Fire detection system: Yes: _____ or No: _____

B14. Building fire extinguishing system: Yes: _____ or No: _____

B15. Safe storage of building cleaning materials: Yes: _____ or No: _____

B16. Maintenance Approval Process

B16.1. Action log: Yes: _____ or No: _____

B16.2. Escort, etc.: Yes: _____ or No: _____

Section C: Computer Room and PBX Room

C1. Security cameras: Yes: _____ or No: _____

C2. Locks: Yes: _____ or No: _____

C3. Badge Systems: Yes: _____ or No: _____

C4. Alarm system: Yes: _____ or No: _____

C5. Fire detection – fire fighting (system, tests): Yes: _____ or No: _____

C6. Moisture, ionization detectors: Yes: _____ or No: _____

C7. Fire extinguishers (inspection, training): Yes: _____ or No: _____

C8. Fire-safety vault: Yes: _____ or No: _____

C8.1. On-site: Yes: _____ or No: _____

C8.2. Outside building: Yes: _____ or No: _____

C9. Electromagnetic shielding of servers: Yes: _____ or No: _____

C10. Infrastructure control procedure (cables, plumbing, etc.): Yes: _____ or No: _____

C11. Location of servers and cabling in protected areas: Yes: _____ or No: _____

CHAPTER 14

Assess Corporate Governance and HR Management Issues

Carol Ann Tomlinson:[1] "Assessment is today's means of modifying tomorrow's instruction."

Overview: This chapter describes how to assess Corporate Governance and HR Management issues in order to improve the AI ecosystem of your organization. It includes over 110 audit review and evaluation questions for 14 issues related to Corporate Governance (Audit Area 1) and HR Management (Audit Area 2), such as AI requirements, standards, and rules compliance, AI Audit Process, Corporate Strategy, AI management roles and responsibilities, human resource requirements management, AI awareness and training, etc.

This is part 2 of Phase E (AI Infrastructure and Systems Assessment) of the AI Implementation Approach.

Phases of the AI Implementation Approach

The AI Implementation Approach (Component 3 of the AI Management System) includes five phases:

- AI Preparation (Phase A, Chapter 7)

- AI Management Framework (Phase B, Chapters 8–10)

- AI Systems Development (Phase C, Chapter 11)

253

© John Kyriazoglou 2025
J. Kyriazoglou, *AI Management Framework*, https://doi.org/10.1007/979-8-8688-1536-2_14

- AI Systems Operation (Phase D, Chapter 12)

- AI Infrastructure and Systems Assessment (Phase E, *this and the following four chapters*)

Goal and Objectives of Phase E (AI Infrastructure and Systems Assessment)

The goal of Phase E is "to improve AI Infrastructure and Systems."
    The objectives of this goal are

> Objective 1: Audit, review, and assess governance issues

> Objective 2: Audit, review, and assess development and operation of AI systems

Steps of AI Infrastructure and Systems Assessment

The eight steps to support the achievement of the goal and objectives of Phase E are

> Step E1. *Assess Corporate Governance*

> Step E2. *Assess HR Management*

> Step E3. Assess AI Governance

> Step E4. Assess AI Data Management

> Step E5. Assess AI Model and Hypotheses Management

> Step E6. Assess AI System Development

> Step E7. Assess AI System Operation

> Step E8. Assess IT Governance

Steps E1 (Assess Corporate Governance) and E2 (Assess HR Management) are described in the following paragraphs (later in this chapter). Steps E3–E8 are described in other chapters (Chapters 15–18).

The assessment actions of this chapter are carried out on the basis of the AI Audit Process (see Chapter 13), the available compliance documentation, the corresponding AI Audit Program (example in Appendix 40, in Part VII) of each Audit Area, and the assessment questions (and their replies) of this chapter. Auditing AI systems/solutions requires a relevant independent test environment with a model, test data, and other audit tools (test cases, transactions, queries, etc.). The assessment results with the recommendations for each audit finding are documented in an AI Audit Report (example in Appendix 39, in Part VII).

Please note that you should add the text "Answer: Yes: ____ or No: ____" with a reply after each question as well as the text "Auditor comments: _____" after each question in the questionnaires in this chapter.

Step E1: Assess Corporate Governance

Summary: This part includes over 57 audit review and evaluation questions for eight issues related to Corporate Governance (Audit Area 1), such as AI requirements, standards, and rules compliance, AI Ethics, AI Audit Process, Corporate Strategy, corporate ethical rules and values, AI Guidelines, IP protection, and corporate knowledge retention management.

Issue 1: AI Requirements, Standards, and Rules Compliance

Q1. Has the company implemented a compliance policy and related compliance procedures in all AI systems/solutions (as well as the first AI System ("Manage e-mails")?

Q2. Has the company implemented controls to ensure AI systems/solutions comply with all relevant legal, regulatory, and state requirements, the organization's own corporate standards, as well as security and business continuity policies and requirements?

Q3. Is each AI system/solution reviewed on a periodic basis to assure continuous compliance with all rules and standards?

Q4. Has the company implemented controls to ensure, for data captured, processed, and/or created through/by the AI system/solution, the full protection and monitoring of their confidentiality, integrity, and availability?

Q5. Are the data privacy requirements of the European General Data Protection Regulation (GDPR) embedded within existing risk management methodologies and policies?

Q6. Are data flows mapped and privacy considerations identified, including requirements for the secure storage and timely disposal of privacy-related data?

Q7. Are privacy-related data inventories maintained effectively?

Q8. Is compliance with privacy requirements monitored, privacy notices and consent forms and their tracking issued and managed, breach incidents resolved and reported, etc.?

Q9. Have appropriate software licenses been obtained for all components of the AI solution and a mechanism is in place to renew these in a timely manner?

Q10. Are AI software licenses recorded in the IT assets inventory of the company?

Issue 2: AI Ethics

Q1. Do you ensure that the final decision-making through algorithms and data processing carried out by your AI systems/solutions preserve the autonomy of the person and the supervision of the process by the human?

Q2. Does your use of Artificial Intelligence aim at the common good, the benefit, and progress of man?

Q3. Do you ensure that privacy and personal data are protected and no harm is caused, especially in the processing of sensitive data, which concern the health and medical history of the person?

Q4. Are there transparency, social justice, and respect for human diversity in the use of Artificial Intelligence by your AI systems/solutions?

Q5. Do you ensure that your people are fully aware of ethical AI principles and practices, understanding bias types and their impact on your business operations and systems?

Q6. Have you implemented measures to ensure effective AI governance, data, and delivery processes such as fairness measures, identifying advantaged and disadvantaged groups, and data sampling to check bias and fairness?

Q7. Have you implemented technology-based ethical AI practices ensuring end-to-end traceability, flagging bias-related issues, human intervention at the right time, and the right choice of tools?

Q8. Are company staff aware and do they take into consideration of the ethics and human oversight principles defined in the relevant documents (e.g., "Seven Ancient Greek Wisdom Principles handbook," "Corporate Philosophy Statements and Policies," "AI Global Standards and Guidelines handbook," "Major Data Protection Laws and Privacy by Design handbook," and "Digital and Secure AI System Development Guidelines handbook" in Chapters 2-6)?

Issue 3: AI Audit Process

Q1. Has the company developed and implemented an AI Audit Process?

Q2. Does this process include auditing all AI components (e.g., data sources, data quality, model validation, hosting models (e.g., cloud), AI explainability, AI supply chain, AI model outputs, social feedback, etc.)?

Q3. Are auditors proficient in AI and aware of the relevant AI regulations and security and privacy guidelines?

Q4. Are AI experts used to assist AI auditors?

Q5. Are large amounts of data (e.g., training data, test data, and real-world data) available for effective AI systems auditing?

Q6. Is a separate and dedicated test environment used for auditing AI systems?

Q7. Has this process been applied to all AI Systems on a periodic basis?

Issue 4: Corporate Strategy

Q1. Are there vision, mission, and values statements and an overall business strategy of the company?

Q2. Is there a vision, mission, and overall security strategy of the company?

Q3. Have these been formally issued and communicated to all staff of the company?

Q4. Have these been made aware to all interested stakeholders and approved third parties?

Q5. Is there an Artificial Intelligence (AI) culture in the company?

Q6. Is there a register of the company's information assets?

Q7. Do staff know what the company's information assets are?

Q8. Do staff know the risks and threats of the company's information assets?

Q9. Is there a Security System with IT security policies and procedures in the company?

Q10. Is there anything that scares staff about the implementation of AI?

Q11. Do senior managers think the company is ready for such a big undertaking (AI)?

Q12. Does the company's staff have the skills and qualifications for AI?

Issue 5: Corporate Ethical Rules and Values

Q1. Has the company implemented and communicated a set of corporate ethical rules and values?

Q2. Is AI aligned well with the organization's cultural and ethical values?

Q3. Are corporate ethical rules and values coded into the AI algorithms?

Q4. Are controls in place to review the output of AI systems/solutions?

Q5. Does, during the AI system/solution design phase, a multidisciplinary team brainstorm about the potential ways the AI solution or its outcomes could be misused?

Q6. Are data reviewed to ensure they are complete, accurate, and free from bias?

Q7. Is AI logic reviewed and tested to verify that it remains valid, with specific testing to ensure there are no unintended biases?

Issue 6: AI Guidelines

Q1. Are relevant managers aware of the EU AI Act and its clear transparency and reporting obligations for any company placing an AI system on the EU market?

Q2. Are relevant managers aware of the Universal Guidelines for Artificial Intelligence (Right to Transparency, Right to Human Determination, Identification Obligation, Fairness Obligation, Assessment and Accountability Obligation, etc.) and their potential impact on company operations?

Q3. Are relevant managers aware of the OECD AI Principles that establish international standards for AI use (inclusive growth, sustainable development, and well-being; human-centered values and fairness; transparency and explainability; robustness, security, and safety; and accountability) and their potential impact on company operations?

Issue 7: IP Protection

Q1. Has the company implemented an Intellectual Property (IP) protection policy?

Q2. Are AI-related IP assets protected by this policy?

Q3. Is there a repository of all corporate IP assets related to an AI system/solution (i.e., data, code, models, and "learning data") set up and accessible in-house, secured, and protected?

Q4. Are these included in the company's backup and recovery policy and procedures?

Issue 8: Corporate Knowledge Retention Management

Q1. Has the company implemented corporate knowledge retention management controls?

Q2. Has the company implemented a strategy for managing knowledge related to decisions to be made – or supported – by the AI system/solution?

Q3. Is sufficient business knowledge retained and developed to train new effective AI systems/solutions?

Q4. Is subject matter expertise, thought leadership, and traditional business knowledge retained to support the organization in developing new AI capabilities effectively?

Q5. Are functional and business processes well documented and maintained for the end-to-end process for each AI system/solution?

Q6. Are detail process narratives and flowcharts (including data flows) available, incorporating all use cases and process variations, as well possible exceptions?

Q7. Are current internal controls documented as an integrated part of the overall process documentation?

Q8. During the specific AI system/solution design and development stages, is sufficient documentation built in the AI system/solution to enable the required knowledge to be retained and maintained that supports decision-making?

Step E2: Assess HR Management

Summary: This part includes over 72 audit review and evaluation questions for 8 issues related to HR Management (Audit Area 2), such as AI management roles and responsibilities, human resource requirements management, Human Culture, AI awareness and training, Personnel Responsibilities and Skills, Basic or Minimum IT and Digital Required Skills, Intermediate or Second-Level IT and Digital Skills, and Advanced or Third-Level IT and Digital Skills.

Issue 1: AI Management Roles and Responsibilities

Q1. Has the company established clear AI management roles and responsibilities of all AI systems/solutions?

Q2. Are these roles and responsibilities defined in organizational charts and job descriptions for all company functions?

Consider: AI developers, data scientists, business process owners, technical AI owners, application owners, operations, Service Desk, security teams, etc.

Q3. Has the company established a Human Resource Management System?

Consider: Employee handbook, benefits and awards policy, human resource policy and procedures, training budget, etc.

Q4. Are AI human resource aspects considered in this system?

Q5. Have all employees received conflict of interest/ethics training?

Q6. Have all employees received IT and AI training?

Issue 2: Human Resource Requirements Management

Q1. Has the company crafted a human resource requirements management plan for AI resources?

Q2. Does this include recruiting excellent employees, orientating and training, managing wages and salaries, evaluating performance, resolving disputes, and communicating with employees at all levels?

Q3. Are the requirements for human resources for AI well defined (e.g., recruitment, role profiles, retention strategy, third-party involvement, etc.)?

Q4. Are these requirements well aligned with the AI strategy and implementation plan?

Issue 3: Human Culture

Q1. Does the company maintain up-to-date corporate human resources policies and procedures and an employee handbook, along with the relevant personnel files for all functions (IT, Production, etc.) and their supporting documentation?

Q2. Does the company conduct reviews, or have an ongoing reporting system for awarding benefits and pay increases (to all personnel, including IT), to ensure that they are operated in a fair and equitable manner?

Q3. Does the company have a positive and supportive attitude toward integrity and ethics education and training, and does this include all personnel, including IT?

Q4. Does the company conduct periodic reviews on ethics issues for all personnel and have an ongoing system to report on outside activities, financial disclosure, and other components of the ethics program?

Q5. Have all company employees received conflict of interest/ethics training?

Q6. Does the company conduct merit promotion case file reviews for all personnel and have an ongoing reporting system that is used to assure that these programs are operating in a fair and equitable manner?

Q7. Does the company ensure that there is equity of treatment and opportunity within the employee relations and training programs, and does this include all personnel?

Q8. Does the company periodically review, or have an ongoing system to report, the time and attendance of all employees?

Q9. Does the company ensure that there is equity of treatment and opportunity within the equal employment opportunity and affirmative employment program, and does this include all personnel?

Q10. Does the company have an employee handbook outlining the code of conduct and policies and procedures for vacation, leave of absence, sick leave, bereavement, personal leave, military leave, holidays, drugs, alcohol, smoking, medical support, life insurance, travel expenses, training, complaints handling, racial or other abuses, etc., and does this apply to all personnel as well?

Q11. Do all personnel who leave the company go through an exit review process whereby all entrusted items, passwords, keys, etc., are properly returned, and all feedback from the personnel who leave are recorded for action to be taken, as needed?

Q12. Does the company segregate personnel in all critical functions, including finance and IT?

Q13. Are company staff aware of and do they take into consideration the ethics and human oversight principles defined in the relevant documents (e.g., "Seven Ancient Greek Wisdom Principles handbook," "Corporate Philosophy Statements and Policies," "AI Global Standards and Guidelines handbook," "Major Data Protection Laws and Privacy by Design handbook," and "Digital and Secure AI System Development Guidelines handbook" in Chapters 2–6)?

Issue 4: AI Awareness and Training

Q1. Has the company crafted and executed an AI Awareness and Training Policy?

Q2. Are senior managers informed and aware of all aspects of AI?

Q3 Are all relevant company staff developed and continuously trained on AI aspects to the required level of capability and capacity?

Q4. Do company human resources include both AI-skilled people, for example, to develop AI solutions, and non-AI-skilled resources, for example, to retain business knowledge?

Q5. Do all relevant company staff have the necessary skills to develop and maintain AI systems?

Consider: General knowledge of AI, specific knowledge of AI models and tools, AI security, data privacy, data science skills, digital skills, programming language skills (in particular, Python), big data analysis, data visualization, cloud computing, cognitive skills (creative problem-solving, analytical skills, problem-solving, critical thinking, judgment, etc.).

Issue 5: Personnel Responsibilities and Skills

Q1. Do all personnel have the required attitude, know-how, and skills in executing their business tasks (including AI)?

Consider: Hiring and training policies for board members, executives, middle management, and employees.

Q2. Do all personnel have the required skills in the design, implementation and monitoring process of performance measurement?

Consider: Board members, executives, middle management, employees, and stakeholders.

Q3. Do all personnel have a clear understanding of their role in performance measurement (including AI performance)?

Consider: Board, executives, middle management, employees, stakeholders.

Q4. Are individual accountabilities for performance activities (including AI) well prescribed, instituted, and executed?

Q5. Are all personnel heavily involved (on a clear and concise basis) in performance measurement (including AI)?

Consider: Board/executives, middle management, employees, and stakeholders.

Q6. Have performance process leaders been assigned and trained to drive and implement performance measurement?

Q7. Does management (board, senior management) review, improve, and change (at least every 6-12 months) both the business model and the strategic aspects of the organization?

Q8. Do staff have the relevant IT and digital skills (including AI), as required for their role and job (basic, intermediate, advanced)?

Issue 6: Basic or Minimum IT and Digital Required Skills

Q1. Do staff have the necessary skills to handle basic hardware matters?

Consider: Using a keyboard and operating touch-screen technology, turning on the device and entering any account information as required, using settings in menus to change device display to make content easier to read, keeping login information for a device and any websites secure, not shared with anyone or written down and left prominently near your device, etc.

Q2. Do staff have the necessary skills to handle standard office software and tools?

Consider: Microsoft Word, Excel, and PowerPoint, managing files on laptops, managing privacy settings on mobile phones, etc.

Q3. Do staff have the necessary skills to execute basic online operations?

Consider: Email, search, completing an online form, etc.

Q4. Do staff know how to access and navigate the company's network, web content, and application systems?

Q5. Do staff understand and comply with the company's IT (password, access control, disaster recovery, etc.) and social media policies, procedures, and practices?

Q6. Do staff know how to apply rules of conduct when using digital technologies and when interacting in digital environments?

Q7. Do staff understand the risks and threats in digital environments and know how to protect ICT devices and digital content?

Q8. Do staff understand the company's privacy policy and controls and know how to apply them in order to protect personal data and privacy in digital environments?

Q9. Do staff understand the Application and Validity of Copyright and Licensing of Data, Information, and Digital Content?

Q10. Do staff know how to identify technical problems during the operation of devices, teleworking tasks, and the use of digital environments and obtain support from the company's IT function or other authorized parties to solve them effectively?

Issue 7: Intermediate or Second-Level IT and Digital Skills

Q1. Do staff know how to explore, search, and filter data, information, and digital content?

Q2. Do staff know how to access and navigate digital environments?

Q3. Do staff have the skills to analyze and evaluate data, information, and digital content in a critical way?

Q4. Do staff know how to organize, manage, store, and retrieve data, information, and digital content?

Q5. Do staff know how to communicate and interact through various digital technologies and understand the appropriate means of digital communication?

Q6. Do staff know how to share data, information, and digital content with third parties through appropriate digital technologies?

Q7. Do staff know how to use public and private digital services to participate in public discussions?

Q8. Do staff know how to use digital tools and technologies for collaborative processes?

Q9. Do staff know how to synchronize and share information across different devices including computers, tablets, and mobile phones?

Q10. Do staff know how to use the Internet to find sources of help for a range of activities?

Q11. Do staff know how to use chat facilities (where available) on websites to help you solve problems?

Q12. Do staff know how to use online tutorials, FAQs, and advice forums to solve problems and improve your skills in using devices, software, and applications?

Q13. Do staff know how to use appropriate software to present information and manipulate and analyze data to help solve problems at work?

Q14. Do staff understand how the different digital tools can improve your own and the company's productivity?

Q15. Do staff know how to create and manage your digital identity and protect your personal reputation?

Q16. Do staff know how to protect their health and well-being while working with digital technologies and avoid health risks and threats to their physical and mental well-being when using digital technologies?

Issue 8: Advanced or Third-Level IT and Digital Skills

Q1. Do staff know how to create and edit digital content in different formats?

Q2. Do staff know how to modify, improve, and integrate information into existing content to create new, original, and relevant digital content?

Q3. Do staff know how to use Digital Design and Data Visualization tools to analyze complex data to help management make vital business decisions?

Q4. Do staff know how to use the tools of desktop publishing, digital graphic design, and digital marketing?

Q5. Do staff have the necessary skills for advanced data literacy functions?

Consider: Knowing what data or information is appropriate or relevant for a particular purpose; interpreting data visualizations, such as graphs and charts; thinking critically about information yielded by data analysis; understanding data analytic tools and methods and when and where to use them; etc.

Q6. Do staff know programming languages and have the skills to develop advanced online, web, mobile, and other related applications?

Q7. Do staff know and understand the environmental impacts of digital technologies and their use?

Q8. Do staff know how to carry out an assessment of needs and identify, evaluate, select, and use digital tools to meet them?

Q9. Do staff know how to use digital tools and technologies to create knowledge as well as innovative processes and products?

Q10. Do staff understand how to solve conceptual problems in digital environments?

Q11. Do staff know how to identify the areas where digital skills need to be improved as well as enable third parties to support the development of their digital skills?

Q12. Do staff know how to search for opportunities for self-improvement and information on digital evolution?

Recommendations

As regards the better use of the above-described 14 assessment questionnaires of over 110 questions for the audit areas of Corporate Governance and HR Management, the following recommendations (REC) are proposed:

> REC 1. Ensure you use an effective AI Audit Methodology with the relevant tools (audit programs, audit plan, assessment questionnaires, audit report, etc.) to carry out all assessment tasks. To support you in crafting your own AI Audit Methodology, you may use the material and tools included in my Audit books in "Additional Resources."

> REC 2. Review all of the above issues, assessment questionnaires, and questions and consider how they may impact your AI systems/solutions in your operating landscape and how you may utilize them.

> REC 3. Customize them, if required, to your purposes, by making the necessary changes to satisfy your needs and expectations.

> REC 4. Ensure all your AI staff and relevant managers and board members are fully aware of the AI audit findings and have reviewed them and contributed to resolving the gaps included in the audit report (see example of an audit findings report in Appendix 39).

REC 5. Ensure you keep current the above products (IT Audit
Questionnaires), by reviewing them and updating them every two
to three years or as needs, expectations, and operating conditions
and circumstances warrant.

Conclusion

This is the second part of the **sixth** milestone (***Improve AI infrastructure and systems***)
of your AI Ecosystem Journey. The next chapter continues this exciting journey by
describing how to assess your AI Governance and AI Data Management Issues.

CHAPTER 15

Assess AI Governance and AI Data Management Issues

Charles Babbage:[1] "Errors using inadequate data are much less than those using no data at all."

Overview: This chapter describes how to assess **AI Governance** and **AI Data Management issues** in order to improve the AI ecosystem of your organization. It includes over 115 audit review and evaluation questions for 19 issues related to AI Governance (Audit Area 3) and AI Data Management (Audit Area 4), such as AI governance framework, AI strategy, AI program management, AI data governance roles and responsibilities, data governance policies and procedures, etc.

*This is part 3 of Phase E (**AI Infrastructure and Systems Assessment**) of the AI Implementation Approach.*

Phases of the AI Implementation Approach

The AI Implementation Approach (Component 3 of the AI Management System) includes five phases:

- AI Preparation (Phase A, Chapter 7)

- AI Management Framework (Phase B, Chapters 8–10)

- AI Systems Development (Phase C, Chapter 11)

© John Kyriazoglou 2025
J. Kyriazoglou, *AI Management Framework*, https://doi.org/10.1007/979-8-8688-1536-2_15

- AI Systems Operation (Phase D, Chapter 12)

- AI Infrastructure and Systems Assessment (Phase E, Chapters 13 and 14, *this chapter and the following three chapters*)

Goal and Objectives of Phase E (AI Infrastructure and Systems Assessment)

The goal of Phase E is "to improve AI Infrastructure and Systems."
    The objectives of this goal are

> Objective 1: Audit, review, and assess governance issues

> Objective 2: Audit, review, and assess development and operation of AI systems

Steps of AI Infrastructure and Systems Assessment

The eight steps to support the achievement of the goal and objectives of Phase E are

> Step E1. Assess Corporate Governance

> Step E2. Assess HR Management

> *Step E3. Assess AI Governance*

> *Step E4. Assess AI Data Management*

> Step E5. Assess AI Model and Hypotheses Management

> Step E6. Assess AI System Development

> Step E7. Assess AI System Operation

> Step E8. Assess IT Governance

Steps E3 (Assess AI Governance) and E4 (Assess AI Data Management) are described in the following paragraphs (later in this chapter).
    Steps E1, E2, and E5–E8 are described in other chapters (Chapters 14, 15, 16, and 18).

The assessment actions of this chapter are carried out on the basis of the AI Audit Process (see Chapter 13), the available compliance documentation, the corresponding AI Audit Program (example in Appendix 40, in Part VII) of each Audit Area, and the assessment questions (and their replies) of this chapter. Auditing AI systems/solutions requires a relevant independent test environment with a model, test data, and other audit tools (test cases, transactions, queries, etc.). The assessment results with the recommendations for each audit finding are documented in an AI Audit Report (example in Appendix 39, in Part VII).

Please note that you should add the text "Answer: Yes: _____ or No: _____" with a reply after each question as well as the text "Auditor comments: _____" after each question in the questionnaires in this chapter.

Step E3: Assess AI Governance

Summary: This part includes over 79 audit review and evaluation questions for 13 issues related to AI Governance (Audit Area 3), such as AI governance framework, AI strategy, AI program management, AI risks and controls framework, human oversight, AI benefits management, AI language and concept definitions, AI expectation management, AI operating model, AI solution exit strategy, AI awareness and training, AI third-party controls, and AI incident management.

Issue 1: AI Governance Framework

Q1. Has the company established an AI governance framework for AI systems/solutions?

Q2. Does the governance framework for the use of AI provide consistent governance over the overall AI program?

Q3. Does the AI program include representation from relevant business functions (e.g., IT, Ethics, Data, Human Resources, Risk, and other impacted divisions)?

Q4. Does the AI governance body oversee the implementation of existing AI policies and review and amend them where necessary?

Q5. Has an AI policy been crafted and formally issued?

Q6. Has the AI policy been communicated to all staff, stakeholders, and third parties?

Issue 2: AI Strategy

Q1. Has an AI strategy been crafted and formally issued?

Q2. Has the AI strategy been communicated to all staff, stakeholders, and relevant third parties?

Q3. Does the AI strategy support the development and use of AI, providing direction to apply AI to deliver business value as well as achieve benefits for the organization itself and the people involved?

Q4. Is the AI strategy aligned with other corporate strategies (e.g., business, sales, data protection, IT, etc.)?

Q5. Is our strategy still current in this world of smarter products and services?

Q6. Do we know how AI can help us deliver our strategic goals?

Q7. Do we have the right sort of data and enough data to achieve our AI priorities?

Q8. Do we have measures to avoid invading people's privacy?

Q9. Are there any legal implications of using AI in the way we plan?

Q10. What sort of consent do we need from customers/users/employees?

Q11. Do we know how to ensure our AI is free of bias and discrimination?

Q12. What technology is required to achieve our AI priorities (e.g., machine learning, deep learning, reinforcement learning, etc.)?

Q13. Do we know our AI skills gaps?

Q14. Do we know which employees and business functions will be most impacted by AI?

Q15. Do we know how AI will change our company culture and how we will manage that culture change?

Issue 3: AI Program Management

Q1. Has an AI program management framework/methodology been crafted and formally issued?

Q2. Has the AI program management framework/methodology been communicated to all staff, stakeholders, and relevant third parties?

Q3. Does the AI program management framework/methodology manage well the development of the AI systems/solutions to achieve successful outcomes and to meet strategic and business requirements?

Q4. Does the AI program management framework/methodology include an organizational structure, staff, and resources to develop, design, and deploy the specific AI systems/solutions?

Issue 4: AI Risks and Controls Framework

Q1. Has an AI risks and controls framework been crafted and formally issued?

Q2. Does this framework ensure overviews of AI risks and controls for all key areas, including the AI systems/solutions, self-learning capabilities, interfaces, management processes, KPIs, etc.?

Q3. Does this framework ensure a structured risk assessment process with involvement of all stakeholders?

Q4. Are remedial measures in place to effectively and efficiently address the identified risks in a sustainable manner?

Q5. Is an assessment of the post-deployment process, incorporating the AI system/solution, completed to validate that the system/solution will operate in compliance with the organization's policies and procedures and any applicable regulation and standards?

Issue 5: Human Oversight

Q1. Do you train your people adequately to ensure they provide meaningful oversight, including the ability to challenge the AI system/solution decision and provide an independent review?

Q2. Do you ensure your AI system developers have understood the skills, experience, and ability of human users and overseers when designing AI systems?

Q3. Do you include in pre-implementation testing an assessment of human oversight to ensure it is meaningful?

Q4. Do you set and document levels of approval authority for the development/use of AI systems, particularly in relation to model complexity, to ensure human reviewers can interpret and challenge the system?

Q5. Do you monitor the decisions made by AI systems/solutions and compare them to human decisions and document any action taken as a result of performance which goes outside of defined tolerances?

Q6. Do you monitor data subjects' rights requests and complaints from individuals?

Q7. Do you re-review or overturn decisions made by AI systems/solutions?

Q8. Are company staff aware of and do they take into consideration the ethics and human oversight principles defined in the relevant documents (e.g., "Seven Ancient Greek Wisdom Principles handbook," "Corporate Philosophy Statements and Policies," "AI Global Standards and Guidelines handbook," "Major Data Protection Laws and Privacy by Design handbook," and "Digital and Secure AI System Development Guidelines handbook" in Chapters 2–6)?

Issue 6: AI Benefits Management

Q1. Does the company ensure that the estimated "benefits" are systematically managed and measured during the AI system's/solution's lifetime?

Q2. Does the company measure the total cost of AI ownership (including development, operating, and maintenance costs for data acquisition, technology infrastructure, personnel, software licenses, and third-party services)?

Q3. Are ongoing costs for model maintenance, updates, and monitoring measured?

Q4. Is the realization of expected benefits calculated?

Consider: Speed and accuracy of processes, people savings, confidence in quality of decision-making, cost savings, increased revenue, improved operational efficiency, enhanced customer experience, improved decision-making, increased innovation, etc.

Issue 7: AI Language and Concept Definitions

Q1. Has the company crafted a common AI language, terms, and definitions plan?

Q2. Are definitions of different concepts, terms, and types of AI documented in a glossary?

Q3. Are these shared to provide a common language across all staff of the organization?

Q4. Is the AI Glossary maintained effectively?

Issue 8: AI Expectations Management

Q1. Has the company crafted an AI expectations management plan?

Q2. Does this plan describe the limitations of AI technologies, the human elements in AI, as well as the AI state of maturity to avoid unreal high expectations and overconfidence in the implementation effort of the AI solutions deployed within the specific company?

Q3. Is the CEO educated on the risks, costs, and potential benefits of AI systems/solutions?

Q4. Does this plan specify a budget, resources, and pilot projects before full AI implementation?

Q5. Has the company requested and used the advice and support of an external AI consultant to manage its AI expectations effectively?

Issue 9: AI Operating Model

Q1. Has the company established an AI operating model?

Q2. Does the AI operating model specify all that are required?

Consider: Business-critical data, IT operations, central databases, dedicated IT personnel, data science and AI-skilled resources, AI service delivery management options, etc.

Q3. Does the AI operating model ensure that the AI governance mechanisms and AI policies and procedures are clearly defined?

Q4. Is the AI operating model aligned effectively with the business operating model of the company?

Q5. Does the AI operating model ensure that the AI system's/solution's human owner needs are clearly defined?

Q6. Does the AI operating model ensure roles and responsibilities are defined in organizational charts and job descriptions for all company functions?

Consider: AI developers, data scientists, business process owners, technical AI owners, application owners, operations, service desk, security teams, etc.

Issue 10: AI Solution Exit Strategy

Q1. Has the company crafted an AI solution exit strategy?

Q2. Are there escrow and portability arrangements in place in vendor agreement(s) of the AI technical solution(s) used in case the organization desires to change to a new technological structure or transfer data and outcome (results) of logic and processing to a new AI system/solution?

Q3. Has the portability capability in the AI technical solution(s) used been tested to make certain they work properly in case the organization desires to change to one or more new AI solutions?

Issue 11: AI Awareness and Training

Q1. Has the company crafted and executed an AI Awareness and Training Policy?

Q2. Are senior managers informed and aware of all aspects of AI?

Q3. Are all relevant company staff developed and continuously trained on AI aspects to the required level of capability and capacity?

Q4. Do company human resources include both AI-skilled people, for example, to develop AI solutions, and non-AI-skilled resources, for example, to retain business knowledge?

Q5. Do all relevant company staff have the necessary skills to develop and maintain AI systems?

Consider: General knowledge of AI, specific knowledge of AI models and tools, AI security, data privacy, data science skills, digital skills, programming language skills (in particular, Python), big data analysis, data visualization, cloud computing, cognitive skills (creative problem-solving, analytical skills, problem-solving, critical thinking, judgment, etc.).

Issue 12: AI Third-Party Controls

Q1. Has the company implemented AI third-party controls?

Q2. Has the company implemented actions to ensure the organization's risk exposure or performance is not negatively impacted by AI third-party systems/solutions that operate at a lower level of control maturity and/or security standards?

Q3. Are AI supplier relations formalized in contracts, with clear SLAs, relevant clauses, etc.?

Q4. Is the performance of third parties, both on the solution's performance and risk, frequently monitored, and where necessary, is action taken in a timely manner?

Q5. Is an inventory of all third-party providers and sub-providers maintained, including their roles?

Q6. Is an assessment performed periodically on the end-to-end "supply chain" of third-party providers and sub-providers to validate the accuracy of the AI supplier inventory?

Q7. Does the company ensure the logic within the AI solution is fully understood and is not "a black box solution"?

Q8. Do the agreements, for third-party solutions or parts thereof, include clauses for ownership of IP, data, code, models, "learning," etc.?

Q9. Are clauses in agreements in place to ensure the organization can have access to the code, if need be, the right to audit, and the specification of clear supplier/customer roles and responsibilities?

Q10. Does the company ensure that each AI vendor solution is not a black box solution by adding clauses in the relevant support agreement to train corporate staff and provide adequate training with real examples, having full documentation, having a user query capability, etc.?

Q11. Have formal advanced support and "warranty" arrangements been made with the AI vendors, also during the post-go-live/stabilization phase, to maintain sufficiently available and effective solutions to adequately support relevant business processes?

Q12. Do the agreements include clear and tangible service levels?

Q13. Is a responsible manager appointed to manage, monitor, and resolve all aspects of the vendor agreements?

Issue 13: AI Incident Management

Q1. Has the company implemented AI incident management controls?

Q2. Does the company ensure the AI environment follows a consistent incident management approach with clear procedures and work instructions that enable timely resolution of incidents with appropriate escalation where required?

Q3. Is the AI incident management approach integrated with the "regular" incident management approach (e.g., IT security, etc.) to ensure a consistent approach across the AI and related environments?

Q4. Is AI incident management aligned with good practice standards (e.g., ISO 27001, ITIL, etc.)?

Q5. Has the company developed and implemented an error correction procedure for operational errors of AI systems/solutions?

Step E4: Assess AI Data Management

Summary: This part includes over 45 audit review and evaluation questions for seven issues related to AI Data Management (Audit Area 4), such as AI data governance roles and responsibilities, data governance policies and procedures, data quality, completeness and accuracy of data, big data management, processing records documentation, and Issue 7 (Data Privacy and Protection Controls).

Issue 1: AI Data Governance Roles and Responsibilities

Q1. Has the company defined and implemented clear AI data governance roles and responsibilities?

Q2. Are roles to manage data and its ownership defined effectively in AI (e.g., data owner, data steward, learning data owner, algorithm owner, AI engineer, AI software developer, data scientist, machine learning engineer, etc.)?

Q3. Are roles and responsibilities implemented effectively in employment or consulting agreements and job descriptions?

Q4. Have all AI staff signed a confidentiality statement?

Issue 2: Data Governance Policies and Procedures

Q1. Has the company developed and implemented data governance policies and procedures?

Q2. Do the data governance policies, standards, and processes ensure that high-quality data exists throughout the complete life cycle covering all relevant quality aspects (i.e., availability, usability, integrity, and security)?

Q3. Do the data governance controls include all aspects of managing data, such as data collection, data labeling, data storage and security, and data management?

Q4. Are relevant parts of the "learning data" "held back" to be used during testing and quality control, and are (different) parts retained for future verification and/or audit purposes?

Q5. Are company staff trained in all aspects of data governance controls (e.g., data collection, data labeling, data storage and security, and data management).

Q6. Are AI test data and AI "learning data" effectively protected (e.g., access controls, encryption, separate servers, backup and restore controls, etc.)?

Issue 3: Data Quality

Q1. Has the company developed and implemented data quality controls?

Q2. Has the company developed and implemented best practices for ensuring data quality in AI?

Consider: Implement data governance policies, utilize data quality tools to ensure that AI models have access to high-quality data consistently, establish a dedicated team responsible for data quality, etc.

Q3. Are employees aware of the importance of data quality and trained in managing data quality issues?

Q4. Is there a process established to measure and continuously monitor data quality metrics and address potential issues before they impact AI performance?

Q5. Is there a process established to ensure identification and monitoring of data transfer between AI systems of entities to detect indications of compromised issues and take appropriate action if such a compromise is detected?

Q6. Is there a process established to ensure, where the AI systems are in a cloud environment, that the service provider has appropriate controls in operation and that compromises are reported promptly and fully?

Q7. Are data cleaned, as needed?

Q8. Are content filter solutions implemented to check data corrupted?

Q9. Are all AI (changes to) data sources – internally or externally – which interacts with the AI solution, monitored and documented?

Q10. Do all changes require human approval in advance, which includes a risk assessment and an assessment to validate data quality?

Issue 4: Completeness and Accuracy of Data

Q1. Has the company developed and implemented controls to ensure completeness and accuracy of data?

Q2. Are controls in place to check and verify the completeness and accuracy of the datasets used by the AI solution according to its stated objectives?

Q3. Are controls in place to have reasonable assurance that sufficient data (e.g., covering a time period or sufficient variations in the population) was provided to enable the model to generate accurate results?

Q4. Are completeness and accuracy of data controls reviewed and improved on a periodic basis?

Issue 5: Big Data Management

Q1. Has the company established controls to manage big data (i.e., large volumes of data)?

Q2. Has the company assessed the potential risks of managing big data (e.g., data breaches, unauthorized access, data loss, and regulatory non-compliance) and developed adequate remedial measures (e.g., encrypting sensitive data, using access controls, and conducting regular audits)?

Q3. Has a secure data infrastructure been implemented?

Q4. Are staff aware of data security issues and trained to handle them?

Q5. Are the big data controls compliant with regulations like GDPR?

Answer: Yes: _____ or No: _____

Issue 6: Processing Records Documentation

Q1. Is there documentation for personal data flows, personal data per company operation (function), and IT infrastructure (systems, equipment, devices, etc.)?

Q2. Does this documentation (PD, IT) include all the flows and all the personal data that exist in all business functions, locations, systems, equipment, and devices?

Q3. Is this documentation (PD, IT) maintained in the required formats (in paper, in electronic form)?

Q4. Does this documentation (PD, IT) contain all the information required under EU GDPR?

Q5. Is this documentation (PD, IT) updated regularly taking into account changes to various details such as representatives, processing activities, security measures, etc.?

Q6. Does this documentation include information for all the organizational and technical measures required by the relevant EU GDPR articles?

Issue 7: Data Privacy and Protection Controls

Q1. Are effective data privacy and protection controls implemented?

Q2. Do these include the following?

1. Information Security Policy

2. Cookie Policy

3. Website Privacy Policy

4. Employees Privacy Policy

5. Data Retention/Removal Policy

6. Data Quality Policy

7. Backup/Recovery Policy

8. Malware Protection Policy

9. Encryption Policy

10. Pseudonymization/Anonymization/Data Aggregation Policy

11. Consent Management System

12. Subject Rights Satisfaction System

13. Security Incident Management System

14. Data Breach Management System

15. Privacy Education and Training Policy

16. DPIA Methodology

17. Data Protection Audit Methodology

18. Security and Privacy Controls in Information Systems Plan

19. PD Inventory

20. IT Assets Inventory

Recommendations

As regards the better use of the above-described 19 assessment questionnaires of over 115 questions for the audit areas of AI Governance and AI Data Management, the following recommendations (REC) are proposed:

REC 1. Ensure you use an effective AI Audit Methodology with the relevant tools (audit programs, audit plan, assessment questionnaires, audit report, etc.) to carry out all assessment tasks. To support you in crafting your own AI Audit Methodology, you may use the material and tools included in my Audit books in "Additional Resources."

REC 2. Review all of the above issues, assessment questionnaires, and questions and consider how they may impact your AI systems/solutions in your operating landscape and how you may utilize them.

REC 3. Customize them, if required, to your purposes, by making the necessary changes to satisfy your needs and expectations.

REC 4. Ensure all your AI staff and relevant managers and board members are fully aware of the AI audit findings and have reviewed them and contributed to resolving the gaps included in the audit report (see example of an audit findings report in Appendix 39).

REC 5. Ensure you keep current the above products (IT Audit Questionnaires), by reviewing them and updating them every two to three years or as needs, expectations, and operating conditions and circumstances warrant.

Conclusion

This is the third part of the **sixth** milestone (***Improve AI infrastructure and systems***) of your AI Ecosystem Journey.

The next chapter continues this exciting journey by describing how to assess your AI Models and AI System Development Issues.

CHAPTER 16

Assess AI Models and AI System Development Issues

W. Edwards Deming:[1] "Manage the cause, not the result."

Overview: This chapter describes how to assess **AI Models** and **AI System Development issues** in order to improve the AI ecosystem of your organization in developing and deploying AI Systems/Solutions. It includes over 104 audit review and evaluation questions for 14 issues related to AI Model and Hypotheses Management (Audit Area 5) and AI Systems Development (Audit Area 6), such as AI Hypotheses governance, AI Algorithms governance, AI Model governance, AI Architecture and Development, AI Application controls, AI system/solution testing methodology, "Explainability by Design" in AI systems/solutions, etc.

*This is part 4 of Phase E (**AI Infrastructure and Systems Assessment**) of the AI Implementation Approach.*

Phases of the AI Implementation Approach

The AI Implementation Approach (Component 3 of the AI Management System) includes five phases:

- AI Preparation (Phase A, Chapter 7)

- AI Management Framework (Phase B, Chapters 8–10)

- AI Systems Development (Phase C, Chapter 11)

© John Kyriazoglou 2025
J. Kyriazoglou, *AI Management Framework*, https://doi.org/10.1007/979-8-8688-1536-2_16

- AI Systems Operation (Phase D, Chapter 12)

- AI Infrastructure and Systems Assessment (Phase E, Chapters 13–15, *this and the following two chapters*)

Goal and Objectives of Phase E (AI Infrastructure and Systems Assessment)

The goal of Phase E is "to improve AI Infrastructure and Systems."
    The objectives of this goal are

> Objective 1: Audit, review, and assess governance issues

> Objective 2: Audit, review, and assess development and operation of AI systems

Steps of AI Infrastructure and Systems Assessment

The eight steps to support the achievement of the goal and objectives of Phase E are

> Step E1. Assess Corporate Governance

> Step E2. Assess HR Management

> Step E3. Assess AI Governance

> Step E4. Assess AI Data Management

> *Step E5. Assess AI Model and Hypotheses Management*

> *Step E6. Assess AI System Development*

> Step E7. Assess AI System Operation

> Step E8. Assess IT Governance.

Steps E5 (Assess AI Model and Hypotheses Management) and E6 (Assess AI System Development) are described in the following paragraphs (later in this chapter).
    Steps E1–E4, E7, and E8 are described in other chapters (Chapters 13, 14, 16, and 17).
    The assessment actions of this chapter are carried out on the basis of the AI Audit Process (see Chapter 13), the available compliance documentation, the corresponding AI Audit Program (example in Appendix 40, in Part VII) of each Audit Area, and the

assessment questions (and their replies) of this chapter. Auditing AI systems/solutions requires a relevant independent test environment with a model, test data, and other audit tools (test cases, transactions, queries, etc.). The assessment results with the recommendations for each audit finding are documented in an AI Audit Report (example in Appendix 39, in Part VII).

Please note that you should add the text "Answer: Yes: ____ or No: ____" with a reply after each question as well as the text "Auditor comments: _____" after each question in the questionnaires in this chapter.

Step E5: Assess AI Model and Hypotheses Management

Summary: This part includes over 30 audit review and evaluation questions for four issues related to AI Model and Hypotheses Management (Audit Area 5), such as AI Hypotheses governance, AI Algorithms governance, AI Model governance, and AI Model validation.

Issue 1: AI Hypotheses Governance

Q1. Are staff trained on generating AI Hypotheses?

Q2. Have AI hypotheses governance policies, standards, and processes been established to ensure that AI hypotheses remain relevant and appropriate throughout the complete life cycle?

Consider: Problem Definition, Data Acquisition and Preparation, Model Development and Training, Model Evaluation and Refinement, Model Deployment, and Model Maintenance and Improvement of an AI system/solution.

Q3. Is a software tool used to craft effective AI Hypotheses, and is this tool effectively supported by a specific vendor agreement?

Q4. Does your hypothesis generation involve making informed guesses about various aspects of the issue or problem you are trying to resolve with AI?

Q5. Are AI hypotheses documented properly, and is this documentation kept current by a responsible officer?

Issue 2: AI Algorithms Governance

Q1. Are AI algorithms process data that contain all aspects of data quality, such as Accuracy, Consistency, Completeness, Timeliness, and Relevance?

Q2. Is data quality managed and improved by a relevant data quality program and organizational structure?

Q3. Are relevant techniques used to analyze the use and impact of the AI algorithms used?

Consider: Relevant techniques are SWOT (Strengths, Weaknesses, Opportunities, and Threats), PEST (Political, Economic, Social, and Technological), and STOPES (Social, Technological, Operational, Political, Economic, and Sustainability factors).

Q4. Are AI algorithms documented properly, and is this documentation kept current by a responsible officer?

Q5. Are staff trained on using SWOT, PEST, and STOPES effectively?

Issue 3: AI Model Governance

Q1. Is your AI Model Quality based across four key categories: model performance, societal impact, operational compatibility, and data quality?

Consider: Four key categories, including model performance (model accuracy, stability, conceptual soundness, and robustness), societal impact (fairness, transparency, privacy, and security), operational compatibility (AI system effectiveness, model function, documentation, and collaborative capabilities), and data quality (capability to build and test models that impact model fitness, including missing data and data representativeness, as well as the quality of production data).

Q2. Are roles and responsibilities for model developers, users, and validators and other control functions clearly articulated to achieve ownership and accountability for risks?

Q3. Is the intended use of the AI models aligned with real-world applications?

Q4. Are measures taken to avoid model poisoning that may compromise the learning process of an AI model by injecting the training dataset with false and misleading data, leading to erroneous conclusions?

Q5. Are measures (e.g., encryption, anonymization, access controls, etc.) taken to protect sensitive data when these data are used as part of a training dataset?

Q6. Are measures taken to avoid data leakage?

Q7. Are measures taken to avoid bias and hallucination in AI models?

Q8. Are measures taken to ensure that data can be trusted before training an AI model?

Q9. Are relevant techniques (e.g., SWOT (Strengths, Weaknesses, Opportunities, and Threats), PEST (Political, Economic, Social, and Technological), STOPES (Social, Technological, Operational, Political, Economic, and Sustainability factors)) used to analyze the use and impact of the AI models used?

Q10. Are AI Model Quality components fully documented?

Issue 4: AI Model Validation

Q1. Is there a list of trusted data sources kept and updated?

Q2. Does management approve collecting untrusted data on a case-by-case basis?

Q3. Are collected data for an AI system reviewed prior to use or storage?

Q4. Are collected data cleaned of undesirable entries?

Q5. Are data sources documented and kept with the data?

Q6. Are collected data assigned to an owner who is responsible for its adherence to documented policies?

Q7. Has a process been implemented to monitor AI model drift (i.e., concept drift, prediction drift, input data drift, operational data drift, the model been tested on unseen data?)

Q8. Has the AI model been tested on unseen data?

Q9. Has the AI model's parameters, architecture, or data been adjusted when its performance is not satisfactory?

Q10. Has the AI model been deployed to a production environment successfully?

Q11. Is the AI model maintained and updated with new data and on the basis of user feedback?

Step E6: Assess AI System Development

Summary: This part includes over 75 audit review and evaluation questions for 11 issues related to AI System Development (Audit Area 6), such as AI Architecture and Development, business case documentation for AI systems/solutions, business process documentation, AI application controls, AI system/solution testing methodology, "explainability by design" in AI systems/solutions, "security by design" in AI systems/solutions, "privacy by design and by default" in AI systems/solutions, AI system/solution ownership, and AI system/solution regulatory risk analysis.

Issue 1: AI Architecture and Development

Q1. Is an AI architecture and development methodology defined and used?

Q2. Does the enterprise AI architecture and methodology offer multiple models for different types of solutions, covering preferred technologies, design concepts such as logging, security controls, and monitoring requirements, and "portability"?

Q3. Does the enterprise AI architecture contain all relevant components (e.g., organizational, information, business, application, and technological)?

Q4. Are staff aware and trained on using this methodology?

Q5. Is this methodology well documented and maintained by a responsible officer?

Issue 2: Business Case Documentation for AI Systems/Solutions

Q1. Has a clear business case for the AI system/solution been established and formally approved by relevant stakeholders?

Q2. Are all data related to the business case for the AI system/solution being kept up to date to reflect any changes in expected total cost of AI ownership and/or AI benefits?

Q3. Are individual AI systems/solutions assessed in the context of the organization's strategy?

Q4. Are expected costs and benefits of the AI systems/solutions clearly articulated and tracked during the course of implementing the AI program?

Q5. Is the business case for the AI system/solution well documented and maintained by a responsible officer?

Issue 3: AI Design and Development Methodology

Q1. Has an AI development standard (AI design and development methodology) been established and is this integrated with the broader development of IT standards?

Q2. Is this AI standard followed for all AI developments?

Q3. Does the AI design and development methodology include all required steps?

Consider: Risk Management, Problem Definition, Data Acquisition and Preparation, Model Development and Training, Model Evaluation and Refinement, Model Deployment, and Model Maintenance and Improvement.

Q4. Are AI Ethics, AI Strategy, and the EU Act taken into consideration in developing AI systems/solutions?

Q5. Does each AI system/solution developed include the classical system development documentation?

Consider: Feasibility Study, User/Business Needs, Systems Analysis and Design Document, Software Code (source listing, source code, object code), and Application Documentation.

Q6. Does each AI system/solution developed include, in addition to the classical system development documentation, the relevant AI system development documentation?

Consider: Learning model, model data, machine learning algorithms, and hypotheses used.

Q7. Are the two sets of documentation of each AI system/solution retained and maintained by a responsible officer?

Issue 4: Business Process Documentation

Q1. Do the relevant staff fully understand the "As-Is" and "To-Be" business processes and their impact on AI systems/solutions development and deployment?

Q2. Are your company's "As-Is" process narratives and flowcharts well documented and available?

Q3. Is the impact of automation on current processes and internal controls been assessed?

Q4. Do documented business processes portray accurately the organization's transactions and data flows?

Q5. Are "To-Be" process narratives and flowcharts complete and accurate?

Q6. Have all "As-Is" and To-Be' process narratives and flowcharts been approved by the appropriate management level?

Q7. Are techniques or tools, such as SIPOC or COPIS, used to document processes and flows?

Consider: SIPOC is an acronym that stands for Suppliers, Inputs, Process, Outputs, and Customers. In practical terms, SIPOC is a process mapping and improvement method that summarizes the inputs and outputs of one or more processes using a SIPOC diagram. Some organizations use the opposite acronym COPIS, which puts the customer requirements first and illustrates the value of the customer to the organization.

Q8. Are staff aware and trained on using these techniques/tools (SIPOC or COPIS)?

Q9. Are the two sets of documentation (the "As-Is" and "To-Be") effectively retained and maintained by a responsible officer?

Issue 5: AI Application Controls

Q1. Has your AI system/solution development process been set up to ensure that processes and internal controls are developed in line with the AI system/solution design?

Q2. Does each AI Application include the relevant internal controls (Input, Output, Processing, Access, and Integrity) as well as ethical principles which are either configured or hard-coded within the AI system/solution?

Q3. Are AI system's/solution's input datasets configured securely against human or machine intervention?

Q4. Are completeness and accuracy checks automatically performed on the data input?

Q5. Does each AI system/solution use an audit trail to record all activities and actions?

Q6. Are AI Application internal controls fully tested and documented for each AI system/solution?

Issue 6: AI System/Solution Testing Methodology

Q1. Is adequate testing carried out for each AI system/solution, resulting in an application that meets business requirements and corporate strategic objectives?

Q2. Are automated test cases, test scripts, and test data in place, so that they may be used when major changes or data sources are introduced to each AI system/solution?

Q3. Are separate environments available and used for development, test, and production to allow for testing being performed with a due diligence in the environment identical to production?

Q4. Are testing and production strategy and approach defined and followed, including data migration between environments and contingency planning?

Q5. Is appropriate User Acceptance Testing (UAT) for the system/solution performed with appropriate consideration of business input for design, execution, and approval testing and signed off prior to being accepted?

Q6. Is documentation of test cases and approvals for each AI system/solution retained and maintained by a responsible person?

Q7. Is the AI model that will solve the defined problem for each AI system/solution trained well with the prepared data?

Q8. Are training data separate from the production data of each AI system/solution to reduce the risk of compromising the training data?

Q9. Are the training data of each AI system/solution thoroughly validated and verified before it is used to train the model?

Q10. Are the training data of each AI system/solution stored in a secure manner, such as using encryption, secure data transfer protocols, and firewalls?

Issue 7: "Explainability by Design" in AI Systems/Solutions

Q1. Do AI systems/solutions developed and deployed by the company consider, as a strategy, the four principles of explainable AI, as per NIST 8312 Standard (Explanation, Meaningfulness, Accuracy, and Knowledge Limits)?

Q2. Is the Principle of Explanation fully satisfied?

Consider: Each AI system/solution delivers or contains accompanying evidence or reason(s) for outputs and/or processes.

Q3. Is the Principle of Meaningfulness fully satisfied?

Consider: Each AI system/solution provides explanations that are understandable to the intended consumer(s).

Q4. Is the Principle of Accuracy fully satisfied?

Consider: An explanation correctly reflects the reason for generating the output and/or accurately reflects the AI system's/solution's process.

Q5. Is the Principle of Knowledge Limits fully satisfied?

Consider: Each AI system/solution only operates under conditions for which it was designed and when it reaches sufficient confidence in its output.

Q6. Do AI systems/solutions developed and deployed by the company include a query capability that is able to answer how each outcome and decision is reached by the specific AI system/solution?

Q7. Is each AI system/solution fully tested to ensure that it generates the correct decision on the basis of the input, data, and process executed?

Q8. Is the query capability of each AI system/solution fully documented and maintained effectively by a responsible person?

Issue 8: "Security by Design" in AI Systems/Solutions

Q1. Are "Security by Design" principles embedded in the AI architecture, approach, and development methodology to ensure appropriate and sustainable level of security?

Q2. Are security needs defined in the initial software considerations?

Q3. Is threat modeling used?

Q4. Are security aspects reviewed, tested, and updated in all phases of AI systems/solution development?

Q5. Are secure coding practices used?

Q6. Are access controls (especially for sensitive data) implemented?

Q7. Are controls applied to ensure secure communication?

Q8. Is security monitored on a continuous basis?

Q9. Are security needs and requirements for each AI system/solution fully documented and maintained effectively by a responsible person?

Issue 9: "Privacy by Design and by Default" in AI Systems/Solutions

Q1. Are "Privacy by Design and by Default" (PDD) principles embedded in the AI architecture, approach, and development methodology to ensure appropriate and sustainable level of privacy of personal data?

Q2. Are "pseudonymizing" techniques on personal data implemented?

Consider: Redaction, encryption, and other measures to ensure the information cannot be attributed to a specific individual without further steps being taken.

Q3. Are transparency and monitoring controls on personal data implemented?

Consider: Being clear about why and how data is being processed and enabling the data subject to monitor processing.

Q4. Are technological safeguards used to limit access to data?

Q5. Are staff trained and educated on how to avoid behaviors that increase the vulnerability of personal data?

Q6. Are minimizing techniques in personal data processing implemented?

Consider: The amount of data collected, the extent of processing activities, the length of time for which data is stored, and the number of people able to access the data.

Q7. Are Data Protection Impact Assessments executed, when necessary?

Q8. Are privacy needs and requirements for each AI system/solution fully documented and maintained effectively by a responsible person?

Issue 10: AI System/Solution Ownership

Q1. Has an AI system/solution owner been appointed for each AI system/solution?

Q2. Have overseeing responsibilities been established for each AI system/solution?

Consider: To oversee AI system development, AI Algorithm use, AI data use, and AI system deployment, operations, and retirement decisions, as needed.

Q3. Are these AI system/solution owner responsibilities of each AI system/solution owner included in a job description and in a formal employment agreement?

Q4. Are these responsibilities and role of the System/Solution Owner of each AI system/solution communicated to all the relevant management positions (e.g., Data Privacy or Data Protection Officer) and staff?

Q5. Are the AI system/solution owner overseeing responsibilities for each AI system/solution approved by senior management and ratified by the board?

Issue 11: AI System/Solution Regulatory Risk Analysis

Q1. Has the AI system/solution owner, with the full support of the company's legal function and IT (as needed), conducted an in-depth analysis of the system/solution and its regulatory environment to identify key regulatory risks, constraints, and design parameters?

Q2. Is the in-depth analysis of the system/solution and its regulatory environment aspects fully documented and maintained effectively by a responsible person?

Q3. Are the results of this risk assessment taken into full consideration in developing AI system/solution?

Q4. Are your AI systems/solutions trustworthy in terms of the three AI components (i.e., comply with all applicable laws and regulations, adhere to ethical principles and values, and be robust both from a technical and social perspective)?

Recommendations

As regards the better use of the above-described 14 assessment questionnaires of over 104 questions for the audit areas of AI Models and AI System Development, the following recommendations (REC) are proposed:

REC 1. Ensure you use an effective AI Audit Methodology with the relevant tools (audit programs, audit plan, assessment questionnaires, audit report, etc.) to carry out all assessment tasks. To support you in crafting your own AI Audit Methodology, you may use the material and tools included in my Audit books in "Additional Resources."

REC 2. Review all the above issues, assessment questionnaires, and questions and consider how they may impact your AI systems/solutions in your operating landscape and how you may utilize them.

REC 3. Customize them, if required, to your purposes, by making the necessary changes to satisfy your needs and expectations.

REC 4. Ensure all your AI staff and relevant managers and board members are fully aware of the AI audit findings and have reviewed them and contributed to resolving the gaps included in the audit report (see example of an audit findings report in Appendix 39).

REC 5. Ensure you keep current the above products (IT Audit Questionnaires), by reviewing them and updating them every two to three years or as needs, expectations, and operating conditions and circumstances warrant.

Conclusion

This is the fourth part of the **sixth** milestone (***Improve AI infrastructure and systems***) of your AI Ecosystem Journey. The next chapter continues this exciting journey by describing how to assess your AI System Operation Issues.

CHAPTER 17

Assess AI System Operation Issues

W. Edwards Deming:[1] "A bad system will beat a good person every time."

Overview: This chapter describes how to assess **AI System Operation issues** in order to improve the AI ecosystem of your organization in deploying AI Systems/Solutions. It includes over 103 audit review and evaluation questions for 16 issues related to AI System Operation (Audit Area 7), such as Critical IT Controls, AI Computer Infrastructure, IT Operational Aspects of AI systems/solutions, quality of AI systems/solutions, auditability of AI systems/solutions, application processing controls and logging of AI systems/solutions, etc.

*This is part 5 of Phase E (**AI Infrastructure and Systems Assessment**) of the AI Implementation Approach.*

Phases of the AI Implementation Approach

The AI Implementation Approach (Component 3 of the AI Management System) includes five phases:

- AI Preparation (Phase A, Chapter 7)

- AI Management Framework (Phase B, Chapters 8–10)

- AI Systems Development (Phase C, Chapter 11)

- AI Systems Operation (Phase D, Chapter 12)

- AI Infrastructure and Systems Assessment (Phase E, Chapters 13–17, *this and the following chapter*)

© John Kyriazoglou 2025
J. Kyriazoglou, *AI Management Framework*, https://doi.org/10.1007/979-8-8688-1536-2_17

Goal and Objectives of Phase E (AI Infrastructure and Systems Assessment)

The goal of Phase E is "to improve AI Infrastructure and Systems."
  The objectives of this goal are

  Objective 1: Audit, review, and assess governance issues

  Objective 2: Audit, review, and assess development and operation of AI systems

Steps of AI Infrastructure and Systems Assessment

The eight steps to support the achievement of the goal and objectives of Phase E are

  Step E1. Assess Corporate Governance

  Step E2. Assess HR Management

  Step E3. Assess AI Governance

  Step E4. Assess AI Data Management

  Step E5. Assess AI Model and Hypotheses Management

  Step E6. Assess AI System Development

  Step E7. Assess AI System Operation

  Step E8. Assess IT Governance

Step E7 (Assess AI System Operation) is described in the following paragraphs (later in this chapter).

Steps E1–E6 and E8 are described in other chapters (Chapters 13–15 and 17).

The assessment actions of this chapter are carried out on the basis of the AI Audit Process (see Chapter 13), the available compliance documentation, the corresponding AI Audit Program (example in Appendix 40, in Part VII) of each Audit Area, and the assessment questions (and their replies) of this chapter. Auditing AI systems/solutions requires a relevant independent test environment with a model, test data, and other audit tools (test cases, transactions, queries, etc.). The assessment results with the recommendations for each audit finding are documented in an AI Audit Report (example in Appendix 39, in Part VII).

Please note that you should add the text "Answer: Yes: _____ or No: _____" with a reply after each question as well as the text "Auditor comments: _____" after each question in the questionnaires in this chapter.

Step E7: Assess AI System Operation

Summary: This part includes over 103 audit review and evaluation questions for 16 issues related to AI System Operation (Audit Area 7), such as

- Critical IT Controls

- AI Computer Infrastructure

- IT Operational Aspects of AI systems/solutions

- Quality of AI systems/solutions

- Auditability of AI systems/solutions

- Application processing controls and logging of AI systems/solutions

- AI systems/solutions operation (deployment)

- AI systems/solutions operation monitoring

- AI systems/solutions results review

- AI systems/solutions error management

- AI systems/solutions user requests management

- AI incidents and hazards management

- Post-Implementation Review of AI systems/solutions

- Business value of AI systems/solutions evaluation

- AI systems'/solutions' benefits management evaluation

- AI systems'/solutions' exit strategy evaluation

Issue 1: Critical IT Controls

Q1. Have information security management policies and procedures been implemented successfully?

Q2. Are vulnerability scans performed as required?

Q3. Are malware controls performed on all potential devices and network connection points effectively?

Q4. Are access controls operating, as required (according to IT security policy)?

Q5. Has an account provisioning procedure been implemented?

Q6. Has an access revocation procedure been implemented?

Q7. Are password controls operating, as required (according to IT security policy)?

Q8. Are IT duties segregated effectively?

Q9. Are third-party access controls operating, as required (according to IT security policy)?

Q10. Is an IT Change Management process established and performing as expected?

Issue 2: AI Computer Infrastructure

Q1. Is all necessary AI computer infrastructure installed, tested, and functioning effectively, before the first AI system/solution is put in a production status?

Q2. Do the AI computer hardware components include items, such as GPU (Graphics Processing Unit) Servers, AI Accelerators, TPUs (Tensor Processing Units), and High-Performance Computing (HPC) Systems?

Q3. Do the AI computer software components include items, such as Machine Learning Frameworks, Models, and Tools?

Q4. Does the AI computer infrastructure include data processing libraries for handling and processing large datasets?

Q5. Does the AI computer infrastructure include storage solutions, such as cloud storage, data lakes, and distributed file systems?

Q6. Are all necessary AI computer infrastructure items documented and managed properly, and is a file kept and upgraded as needed?

Issue 3: IT Operational Aspects of AI Systems/ Solutions

Q1. Does each AI system/solution consist of five interrelated parts (P), such as Input, Processing, Output, Resources, and Storage?

Q2. Are inputs flowing from outside the system/solution as specified and expected?

Q3. Is processing making use of computer software (and AI Models, Techniques, and Tools) in a well-defined set of step-by-step sequence of activities to produce the expected results and outcomes of each AI system/solution?

Q4. Are outputs and processed data stored in computerized files?

Q5. Are management reports on the operational aspects of each AI system/solution received and acted upon by proper management?

Q6. Are IT staff (programmers, analysts, AI staff, operators, user support, database administrators, etc.) and end-user personnel interacting, feeding, and running the system, in an effective way?

Q7. Are usual IT and Communications, as well as the special AI hardware and database servers and storage facilities where raw and processed data are stored, maintained safely?

Issue 4: Quality of AI Systems/Solutions

Q1. Do your AI systems/solutions comply fully, in all its production aspects, with the quality characteristic of conformity (i.e., the specific AI system/solution conforms to its initial design specifications)?

Q2. Do your AI systems/solutions comply fully, in all its production aspects, with the quality characteristic of efficiency (i.e., the software (as well as the algorithms, model, and data) of the specific AI system/solution uses resources in the best way)?

Q3. Do your AI systems/solutions comply fully, in all its production aspects, with the quality characteristic of reliability (i.e., the hardware and software (as well as the algorithms, model, and data) of the specific AI system/solution functions without errors, defects, or other anomalies)?

Q4. Do your AI systems/solutions comply fully, in all its production aspects, with the quality characteristic of portability (i.e., the software (as well as the algorithms, model, and data) of the specific AI system/solution is developed in such a way that it makes it possible for it to be used in other installations (in case of disaster recovery situations)?

Q5. Do your AI systems/solutions comply fully, in all its production aspects, with the quality characteristic of flexibility (i.e., the software (as well as the algorithms, model, and data) of the specific AI system/solution covers new needs easily)?

Q6. Do your AI systems/solutions comply fully, in all its production aspects, with the quality characteristic of maintainability (i.e., the errors and defects related to the hardware and software as well as the algorithms, model, and data of the specific AI system/solution are easily researched and corrected)?

Q7. Do your AI systems/solutions contain full documentation on all quality aspects of hardware and software (as well as the algorithms, model, and data) of the specific solution implemented?

Issue 5: Auditability of AI Systems/Solutions

Q1. Do your AI systems/solutions include an auditability strategy?

Q2. Does the auditability strategy ensure data and algorithms used for generating AI results and decisions, including data used for system learning, are stored securely and can be retrieved in a timely manner and in accordance with regulations (e.g., data privacy), so provenance of decisions can be provided?

Q3. Can the results, decisions, and outcomes of each specific AI system/solution be independently validated?

Q4. Is the "Vault Principle" (i.e., an automated solution that securely stores any decision made by the AI system/solution, as well as the data the decision was based on, and the latest version of the algorithm) applied to the operation of each AI system/solution?

Q5. Do your AI systems/solutions include an audit trail that record chronologically in a special audit trail file transactions, changes, events, or procedures to provide support documentation and history that is used to authenticate security and operational actions or mitigate challenges?

Q6. Is each AI system's/solution's audit trail tested fully?

Q7. Is documentation retained and maintained on all audit aspects?

Issue 6: Application Processing Controls and Logging of AI Systems/Solutions

Q1. Does each AI system/solution include a set of application processing controls, such as Input, Output, Processing, Access, and Integrity?

Q2. Are AI ethical principles either accessed from a specific independent file and used or are hard-coded within the specific AI system/solution?

Q3. Are each AI system's/solution's input datasets configured securely against human or machine intervention?

Q4. Are completeness and accuracy checks automatically performed on the data input for each AI system/solution?

Q5. Is each AI system/solution using an audit trail to record all activities and actions?

Q6. Are application processing controls fully tested for each AI system/solution?

Q7. Does each AI system/solution include logging of activities?

Q8. Can each AI system's/solution's activities be traced back to a unique Bot or program via an end-to-end audit trail to log and monitor AI system/solution activities?

Q9. Are AI system/solution application processing controls fully documented for each AI system/solution?

Issue 7: AI Systems/Solutions Operation (Deployment)

Q1. Has the AI system/solution owner carried out and documented a compliance of each specific AI system/solution going into production with the support of IT and legal functions?

Q2. Has the AI system/solution owner supported the Data Protection or Privacy Officer and IT to carry out a Data Protection Impact Assessment, as required, before each AI system/solution is approved for operational use?

Q3. Have staff been trained to run the specific AI system/solution before its production transfer?

Q4. Have data been loaded into AI production system/solution effectively?

Q5. Are backup and recovery procedures tested and available for each specific AI system/solution?

Q6. Are all AI systems/solution operating in a production status effectively?

Q7. Is design and operating system documentation complete for all productive AI systems/solutions?

Q8. Are version control and configuration management implemented for code, data, and infrastructure, with backups and restore mechanisms in place for all AI systems/solutions in production status?

Q9. Are rollback mechanisms in place and a process, algorithms, and cleansed data available to get the specific AI system/solution to be implemented and (re)trained quickly to reflect new/changed requirements?

Q10. Are measurable criteria for success and failure defined for each AI system/solution deployed?

Issue 8: AI Systems/Solutions Operation Monitoring

Q1. Do you monitor the performance of AI systems/solutions on the basis of a process (performance policy and procedures)?

Q2. Does this AI performance monitoring process include all elements?

Consider: AI Business Outcomes, Data Sources (internal, external), AI Accuracy (correct results, no bias, algorithm errors), Data Quality, Privacy of Data, IT Security Policies and Procedures, Security and AI Incidents and Data Breaches, and AI System Performance Metrics.

Q3. Are the AI performance metrics and events reported to top management via the corporate management reporting process?

Q4. Does management monitor each AI system's/solution's application audit trails?

Q5. Does management regularly review the system/solution outcomes against the business requirements from all aspects (i.e., ethical, technical, functional, etc.) and take appropriate actions to resolve the situation or errors, etc.?

Q6. Are each AI system's/solution's outputs and results aligned with its stated goals and ethical principles and do not harm people?

Q7. Are detailed logs maintained to obtain last execution status in case the given AI system/solution fails?

Issue 9: AI Systems/Solutions Results Review and Error Management

Q1. Does each AI system/solution include a process to review its processing results?

Q2. Does the review process check that the results from the AI system/solution are correct and appropriate by ensuring that the model accurately reflects the true underlying quantitative parameters and the logic makes accurate decisions, etc.?

Q3. Does the review process check that controls are in place for monitoring data quality for systems/solutions that are evolving over time?

Q4. Does the review process check that controls are in place to consider sensitivities when dealing with different ethical/political/ethnic/race/gender/cultural and other groups?

Q5. Does the review process check that controls are in place to prevent the AI system/solution from processing the same data more than once, including file and data validation checks, etc.?

Q6. Does the review process check that controls are in place to ensure human oversight of results of AI system/solution, as needed?

Issue 10: AI Systems/Solutions Error Management

Q1. Have you established a capability and procedures for addressing, investigating, and correcting errors?

Q1. Does error management include managing errors related to data used, logic, processing flow, decisions, and outcomes of the AI systems/solutions of your company?

Q3. Do you maintain full documentation on all AI system/solution errors and your management actions and replies?

Issue 11: AI Systems/Solutions User Requests Management

Q1. Have you established a capability and procedures for addressing, investigating, and responding on all user requests?

Q2. Does the user requests management process relate to results, requests, and complaints by individuals about the data used, logic, processing flow, decisions, and outcomes of the AI systems/solutions of your company?

Q3. Do you maintain full documentation on all AI system/solution user requests and your management actions and replies?

Issue 12: AI Incidents and Hazards Management

Q1. Do your staff know how to identify AI incidents and hazards?

Q2. Are your staff trained on handling AI incidents and hazards?

Q3. Does your AI environment follow a consistent AI incidents and hazards management approach with a policy and clear procedures that ensure timely resolution of AI incidents and hazards with appropriate escalation where required?

Q4. Is your AI incidents and hazards management approach integrated with the "regular" incident management approach to ensure a consistent approach across the AI and related environments?

Q5. Is your AI incidents and hazards management approach aligned with good practice standards (e.g., ITIL)?

Q6. Do you retain, maintain, and manage full documentation on all AI incidents and hazards?

Issue 13: Post-Implementation Review of AI Systems/Solutions

Note   Carry this out for each specific AI system/solution.

Q1. Did the AI system/solution ("<name of system/solution>") fully satisfy the requirements and needs as defined initially?

Q2. Did the AI system/solution ("<name of system/solution>") fully solve the problem that it was designed to address?

Q3. Can things go further so that the specific AI system/solution may deliver even bigger and better benefits?

Q4. Were lessons that we learned from implementing the specific AI system/solution documented so that we can apply to future projects?

Issue 14: Business Value of AI Systems/ Solutions Evaluation

Note   Carry this out for each specific AI system/solution.

Q1. Are the AI system's/solution's ("<name of system/solution>") results accurate?

Q2. Are the AI system's/solution's ("<name of system/solution>") results repeatable?

Q3. Is the AI system/solution ("<name of system/solution>") making correct use of all data sources?

Q4. Are the AI system's/solution's ("<name of system/solution>") outputs delivered on time?

Q5. Will the AI system/solution ("<name of system/solution>") continue to function if data volumes or user numbers grow over time?

Q6. Is the AI system/solution ("<name of system/solution>") open to integration with third-party data sources and services, using standard protocols?

Q7. Is the AI system/solution ("<name of system/solution>") capable of adapting to changes (e.g., data, models, etc.)?

Q8. Have you made sure that all AI systems/solutions do not have a biased view of the world?

Q9. Have you made sure that the results of all AI systems/solutions are fair?

Q10. Are the actions of all AI systems/solutions explained in terms the user can understand?

Issue 15: AI Systems'/Solutions' Benefits Management Evaluation

---

Note   Carry this out for each specific AI system/solution.

Q1. Does the company ensure that the estimated "benefits" are systematically managed and measured during the AI system's/solution's ("<name of system/solution>") lifetime?

Q2. Does the company measure the total cost of ownership of the AI system/solution ("<name of system/solution>"), including development, operating, and maintenance costs for data acquisition, technology infrastructure, personnel, software licenses, and third-party services?

Q3. Are ongoing costs of the AI system/solution ("<name of system/solution>") for model maintenance, updates, and monitoring measured?

Q4. Is the realization of expected benefits of the AI system/solution ("<name of system/solution>") calculated?

Consider: Example of expected benefits – speed and accuracy of processes, people savings, confidence in quality of decision-making, cost savings, increased revenue, improved operational efficiency, enhanced customer experience, improved decision-making, increased innovation, etc.

Q5. Are benefit evaluation results properly documented?

Q6. Are the benefit evaluation results effectively reported to senior management?

Issue 16: AI Systems'/Solutions' Exit Strategy Evaluation

Note   Carry this out for each specific AI system/solution.

Q1. Has the company crafted an AI solution exit strategy for the AI system/solution ("<name of system/solution>")?

Q2. Are there escrow and portability arrangements in place for the AI system/solution ("<name of system/solution>") in vendor agreement(s) of the AI technical solution(s) used in case the organization desires to change to a new technological structure or transfer data and outcome (results) of logic and processing to a new AI solution?

Q3. Has the portability capability for the AI system/solution ("<name of system/solution>") in the AI technical solution(s) used been tested to make certain they work properly in case the company desires to change to one or more new AI solutions?

Q4. Are the AI system's/solution's ("<name of system/solution>") exit strategy evaluation results properly documented?

Q5. Are the AI system's/solution's ("<name of system/solution>") exit strategy evaluation results effectively reported to senior management?

Recommendations

As regards the better use of the above-described 16 assessment questionnaires of over 103 questions for the audit areas of AI System Operation, the following recommendations (REC) are proposed:

> REC 1. Ensure you use an effective AI Audit Methodology with the relevant tools (audit programs, audit plan, assessment questionnaires, audit report, etc.) to carry out all assessment tasks. To support you in crafting your own AI Audit Methodology, you may use the material and tools included in my Audit books in "Additional Resources."

> REC 2. Review all of the above issues, assessment questionnaires, and questions and consider how they may impact your AI systems/solutions in your operating landscape and how you may utilize them.

> REC 3. Customize them, if required, to your purposes, by making the necessary changes to satisfy your needs and expectations.

> REC 4. Ensure all your AI staff and relevant managers and board members are fully aware of the AI audit findings and have reviewed them and contributed to resolving the gaps included in the audit report (see example of an audit findings report in Appendix 39).

REC 5. Ensure you keep current the above products (IT Audit Questionnaires), by reviewing them and updating them every two to three years or as needs, expectations, and operating conditions and circumstances warrant.

Conclusion

This is the fifth part of the **sixth** milestone (***Improve AI infrastructure and systems***) of your AI Ecosystem Journey. The next chapter continues this exciting journey by describing how to assess your IT Governance Issues.

CHAPTER 18

Assess IT Governance Issues

Bill Gates:[1] "Information technology and business are becoming inextricably interwoven. I don't think anybody can talk meaningfully about one without talking about the other."

Overview: This chapter describes how to assess IT Governance issues in order to improve the AI ecosystem of your organization in deploying AI Systems/Solutions. It includes over 120 audit review and evaluation questions for 16 issues related to IT Governance (Audit Area 8), such as AI computer infrastructure management, information security and privacy policies and procedures management, vulnerabilities and malware management, robotic accounts management, etc.

This is part 6 of Phase E (AI Infrastructure and Systems Assessment) of the AI Implementation Approach.

Phases of the AI Implementation Approach

The AI Implementation Approach (Component 3 of the AI Management System) includes five phases:

- AI Preparation (Phase A, Chapter 7)

- AI Management Framework (Phase B, Chapters 8–10)

- AI Systems Development (Phase C, Chapter 11)

- AI Systems Operation (Phase D, Chapter 12)

- AI Infrastructure and Systems Assessment (Phase E, Chapters 13–16 and *this chapter*).

© John Kyriazoglou 2025
J. Kyriazoglou, *AI Management Framework*, https://doi.org/10.1007/979-8-8688-1536-2_18

Goal and Objectives of Phase E (AI Infrastructure and Systems Assessment)

The goal of Phase E is "to improve AI Infrastructure and Systems."

The objectives of this goal are

Objective 1: Audit, review, and assess governance issues

Objective 2: Audit, review, and assess development and operation of AI systems

Steps of AI Infrastructure and Systems Assessment

The eight steps to support the achievement of the goal and objectives of Phase E are

- Step E1. Assess Corporate Governance

- Step E2. Assess HR Management

- Step E3. Assess AI Governance

- Step E4. Assess AI Data Management

- Step E5. Assess AI Model and Hypotheses Management

- Step E6. Assess AI System Development

- Step E7. Assess AI System Operation

- Step E8. Assess IT Governance

Step E8 (Assess IT Governance) is described in the following paragraphs (later in this chapter).

Steps E1–E7 are described in other chapters (Chapters 13–16).

The assessment actions of this chapter are carried out on the basis of the AI Audit Process (see Chapter 13), the available compliance documentation, the corresponding AI Audit Program (example in Appendix 40, in Part VII) of each Audit Area, and the assessment questions (and their replies) of this chapter. Auditing AI systems/solutions requires a relevant independent test environment with a model, test data, and other audit tools (test cases, transactions, queries, etc.). The assessment results with the recommendations for each audit finding are documented in an AI Audit Report (example in Appendix 39, in Part VII).

Please note that you should add the text "Answer: Yes: _____ or No: _____" with a reply after each question as well as the text "Auditor comments: _____" after each question in the questionnaires in this chapter.

Step E8: Assess IT Governance

Summary: This part includes over 120 audit review and evaluation questions for 16 issues related to IT Governance (Audit Area 8), such as

- AI computer infrastructure management
- Information security and privacy policies and procedures management
- Vulnerabilities and malware management
- Robotic accounts management
- Human accounts management
- Account provisioning and revocation management
- Password controls management
- Segregation of IT duties implementation
- Third-party access controls implementation
- IT change management
- AI systems/solutions inventory management
- IT resource management
- IT knowledge retention management
- IT configuration management
- System software
- Backup and recovery process management

Issue 1: AI Computer Infrastructure Management

Q1. Are all necessary AI computer infrastructure components (i.e., hardware, software, etc.) installed, tested, and operating effectively?

Q2. Do the AI computer infrastructure hardware components include Graphics Processing Unit Servers, AI Accelerators, Tensor Processing Units, High-Performance Computing Systems, etc.?

Q3. Do the AI computer infrastructure software components include Machine Learning Frameworks and Data Processing Libraries that are used for handling and processing large datasets, etc.?

Q4. Do the AI computer infrastructure hardware components include various storage solutions (e.g., cloud storage, data lakes, and distributed file systems)?

Q5. Does the AI computer infrastructure include an integrated development environment with proper AI tools for research, learning, training, and experimental purposes?

Q6. Is maintenance support provided for all these components via proper Services Agreements with the vendor(s) of these hardware and software components?

Q7. Have you implemented fully all the above before the first AI system/solution is developed and put in a production status?

Issue 2: Information Security and Privacy Policies and Procedures Management

Q1. Do your main information security and privacy management policies and procedures operate effectively and include all aspects of your AI environment?

Q2. Does your AI environment comply fully with your main information security and privacy policies, procedures, and daily practices?

Q3. Is your approach integrated with the "regular" security management controls to ensure a complete approach across the AI and related environments?

Consider: This must apply to code, algorithms, configuration, IT infrastructure, applications, data structures, data classification, and related management processes.

Q4. Is your information security management aligned with good practice standards (e.g., ISO 27001)?

Q5. Have you implemented measures to ensure code and data storage as well as network communications to/from/within the AI system/solution are adequately encrypted?

Q6. Are you carrying out penetration tests or "red team" reviews to assess the AI environment's exposure to vulnerabilities?

Q7. Is periodic security testing performed to ensure security controls, sensors, and monitoring are effective and operational?

Q8. Are you complying fully with privacy regulations for all your data?

Q9. Have you secured your data center by implementing relevant physical and environmental protection controls?

Q10. Have you implemented fully all the above before the first AI system/solution is developed and put in a production status?

Issue 3: Vulnerabilities and Malware Management

Q1. Have you implemented malware protection and ensured it includes all components and aspects of AI?

Q2. Are new patches tested before they are implemented to all software including AI components?

Q3. Is an impact assessment performed before the patch gets implemented in a timely manner?

Q4. Does malware protection apply to self-learning models and components, besides regular and AI hardware, AI application system software, and data?

Q5. Have you taken measures to ensure all the above are implemented fully before the first AI system/solution is developed and put in a production status?

Q6. Is effective documentation retained and maintained on all patch upgrades and impact assessments?

Q7. Do you report to senior management all malware protection issues and patch implementations?

Issue 4: Robotic Accounts Management

Q1. Have you obtained and are you using a bot (robotic) manager (e.g., software product) to manage bots, such as blocking undesired or malicious Internet bot traffic while still allowing useful bots to access web properties?

Q2. Are all bot accounts used by AI systems unique and have been assigned to a human with ultimate responsibility for these?

Q3. Do you ensure that for each Bot, usage of its account is tracked in between applications and services and all activities are recorded in logs?

Q4. Are each bot's access rights to relevant systems set up and assigned on a "need-to-have" basis?

Q5. Is bot access constrained to applications and data required for specific, intended transactions only?

Q6. Are the bot's access accounts and their system privileges reviewed periodically, the review results documented, and any inappropriate uses investigated and corrected?

Q7. Is access to all bot accounts monitored by proper management?

Q8. Are all the above implemented fully before the first AI system/solution is developed and put in a production status?

Issue 5: Human Accounts Management

Q1. Are human accounts to access the AI environment personal and unique?

Q2. Do the individuals have ultimate responsibility for these human accounts?

Q3. Is access to AI system logic and algorithms appropriately restricted to authorized individuals?

Q4. Is user access to the AI system/solution itself, additional (permanent or temporary) data storage facilities, log files, and other relevant components set up and assigned on a "need-to-have" basis?

Q5. Are user accounts and system privileges that have access to the AI solution itself, additional (permanent or temporary) data storage facilities, log files, and other relevant components reviewed periodically?

Q6. Are review results documented and any findings acted upon?

Q7. Is access to powerful user accounts (privileged accounts), which can be used to perform user access administration, change system configuration, or directly access interfaces or data, restricted to a defined set of system administration personnel?

Q8. Is access to all human accounts monitored by proper management?

Q9. Are all the above implemented fully before the first AI system/solution is developed and put in a production status?

Issue 6: Account Provisioning and Revocation Management

Q1. Is there an access provisioning procedure in place for the creation of (human) user and bot accounts and assigning user privileges to new or existing accounts?

Q2. Is formal approval required by appropriate management for the establishment of users and granting of access rights, both for human and robotic accounts?

Q3. Is an access revocation procedure in place for the timely deletion or locking of user accounts and their privileges when an employee leaves or when the employee or the bot no longer needs this access due to a change in role or decommissioning?

Q4. Are all account approvals and access revocations monitored by proper management?

Q5. Are all the above implemented fully before the first AI system/solution is developed and put in a production status?

Issue 7: Password Controls Management

Q1. Are effective authentication controls in place?

Consider: Password controls policy or biometrics, in line with the IT security policy for systems in scope across the IT environment (AI environment, network, OS, database, applications, and utilities).

Q2. Are these controls applicable to all user (robotic and human) accounts, including system administration accounts and automation authentication?

Q3. Are compensating controls implemented in case password controls are not implemented?

Consider: These may be required to mitigate the potential risk related to unauthorized individuals using accounts to access data or systems, in case certain accounts (e.g., system accounts or Bot accounts) do not have password controls in place or are required to use hard-coded passwords.

Q5. Have you taken measures to ensure that all the above are implemented fully before the first AI system/solution is developed and put in a production status?

Issue 8: Segregation of IT Duties Implementation

Q1. Has a segregation of IT duties policy been implemented that includes AI aspects?

Q2. Do you ensure that no single IT person can create user accounts (human, robotic) and assign access privileges to these accounts without approval by the IT manager?

Q3. Do you ensure that no single IT person can make changes to any IT components and the AI systems/solutions or their data directly in production?

Q4. Do you ensure that all changes to the AI environment are made in the development environment before these are applied to the AI production system/ solution?

Q5. Do you ensure that no single IT person can raise and approve the same change request?

Q6. Do you ensure all the above are implemented fully before the first AI System (Manage e-mails) is developed and put in a production status?

Issue 9: Third-Party Access Controls Implementation

Q1. Have you identified and mitigated any third-party vendor's access-related risks and ensured compliance with your internal policies and external regulations?

Q2. Have you assessed the third-party vendor's current control environment and cybersecurity posture?

Q3. Have you implemented measures to ensure access by third-party users to corporate data or data processing facilities or any AI part is subject to the same level of controls as "regular" users, data, and data processing facilities?

Q4. Have you implemented measures to ensure access by users to third-party data or data processing facilities is subject to the same level of controls as "regular" users, data, and data processing facilities?

Q5. Have you implemented measures to ensure effective third-party user provisioning and deprovisioning (i.e., creating, updating, and deleting user accounts and access permissions based on job roles and responsibilities)?

Q6. Are you using the Virtual Private Network (VPN) technology that creates a secure, encrypted connection between a user's device and a remote server over the public Internet to protect your data privacy and support secure sensitive data transmissions?

Q7. Have you implemented measures to ensure effective third-party user monitoring, logging, and reporting on third-party user access and activities to ensure compliance with internal policies and external regulations?

Q8. Have you implemented measures to ensure all the above are implemented fully before the first AI system/solution is developed and put in a production status?

Issue 10: IT Change Management

Q1. Do changes to the AI environment follow a consistent change management approach with clear procedures and work instructions around changes to IT infrastructure, AI models and algorithms, data, etc.?

Q2. Are AI changes integrated with the "regular" change management approach to enable a consistent approach across the AI and related environments?

Q3. Are data governance inventories, including data classification policy, AI inventory, data asset flagging, and data flow maps, maintained as part of the change management process?

Q4. Are changes to production not permitted, unless specific approval from the appropriate level of management is obtained?

Q5. Are changes caused by the dynamic nature of machine learning covered by additional measures, such as logging and review of any modifications and/or periodic comparison of the solutions at different time stamps to identify any changes made?

Q6. Is the impact of changes to AI processing and outputs on other IT services assessed and monitored?

Q7. Is change management aligned with good practice standards (e.g., ITIL), and is versioning in place for business processes, code, Bot configuration, applications, data structures, data classification, etc.?

Q8. Are all the above implemented fully before the first AI system/solution is developed and put in a production status?

Issue 11: AI Systems/Solutions Inventory Management

Q1. Has an inventory of all AI platforms, systems, tools, solutions, and use cases been established?

Q2. Is this inventory in a digital format and easy to manage?

Q3. Is this inventory complete and kept up to date?

Q4. Is a specific owner assigned for each AI system or solution in the inventory?

Q5. Is the AI inventory managed by a responsible IT person?

Q6. Are changes to the AI inventory reported to senior management?

Q7. Are all the above implemented fully before the first AI system/solution is developed and put in a production status?

Issue 12: IT Resource Management

Q1. Are controls in place to monitor IT resource demands, especially for AI?

Consider: Monitor all IT resource demands because AI systems might be more likely to be more unpredictable (need more resources on a dynamic basis, use of external systems or databases, etc.).

Q2. Does IT know or estimate the demand and use of IT resources by AI systems/solutions used?

Consider: Staff, processing time, capacity, processes with other systems, etc.

Q3. Do AI systems/solutions make decisions about the system resources they require taking into consideration that they may impact the cost and efficacy of the overall IT and AI environment?

Q4. Do you match your workloads to actual capacity and availability of your IT staff?

Q5. Do you guard your team's time from unnecessary interruptions?

Q6. Do you involve your team members in the IT and AI project planning process?

Q7. Are all the above implemented fully before the first AI system/solution is developed and put in a production status?

Issue 13: IT Knowledge Retention Management

Q1. Are AI system/solution and IT management processes, including business process, technology, and data requirements, well documented and maintained for the end-to-end process for each AI system/solution?

Q2. Is sufficient IT knowledge (staff and/or skills) retained and developed to effectively run and maintain the AI systems/solutions?

Q3. Are IT knowledge retention issues reported to the board/senior management and resolved accordingly?

Q4. Are there a development methodology, architectural standards, and other technical and data-related documentation available to sufficiently skilled resources to support the development of new AI systems/solutions or new parts of existing AI systems/solutions?

Q5. Is adequate knowledge transfer designed and executed to retain relevant knowledge within the organization when external vendors are used to develop AI systems/solutions?

Q6. Is documentation kept up to date through automated logging and reporting of changes (e.g., through an audit trail of changes to decision logic)?

Q7. Are all the above implemented fully before the first AI system/solution is developed and put in a production status?

Issue 14: IT Configuration Management

Q1. Has an IT Configuration Management Policy been developed and implemented?

Q2. Have all IT items been identified?

Q3. Have all AI items been identified?

Q4. Do you understand the IT and data components of the overall AI environment and systems as well as their aspects (security, software licenses, IT operations, business continuity, capacity, availability, etc.)?

Q5. Has a configuration management database been established and maintained to ensure a complete understanding of all IT, AI, and their data components and relationships?

Q6. Does the configuration management database include all AI-related IT and data components?

Q7. Are all the above implemented fully before the first AI System is developed and put in a production status?

Issue 15: System Software

Q1. Has the company implemented a policy to protect all systems software components (operating system, network management, database management system, AI software and tools, etc.) adequately?

Q2. Have adequate operational and access control procedures been implemented to restrict access to systems and AI-related software, such as change management, problem management and resolution, access control over specific AI and legacy databases, systems software upgrades, clear task assignments, authorizations by senior IT management, complete testing before putting into production, logging of all modifications, etc.?

Q3. Does a test environment exist for systems and AI software changes?

Q4. Does configuration control exist for systems and AI software?

Q5. Does documentation exist for systems software security administration?

Q6. Are effective procedures established for network management, such as configuration control, definition of access controls, network control function, network asset list, network performance monitoring, etc.?

Q7. Is access to the Internet, web applications, and AI platforms properly controlled (password, firewalls, intrusion prevention system, no access to critical data, etc.)?

Q8. Are backup revisions of the systems, AI, and database software taken (on-site, off-site)?

Q9. In a disaster recovery situation, is there a single systems and AI software pack in the original (bootstrap) version?

Q10. Are there fully documented restore procedures for the systems and AI software and database components?

Q11. Are the restore procedures regularly tested?

Q12. Are there written procedures informing AI users of what to do if the AI environment becomes unavailable?

Q13. Is transaction logging in use?

Q14. Are all backups and recoveries recorded in a register?

Issue 16: Backup and Recovery Process Management

Q1. Have effective business continuity plans (BCP) been developed and approved and are being maintained adequately?

Q2. Do these BCP plans include all AI systems/solutions and data (process, learning)?

Q3. Are BCP roles and responsibilities, including AI, third parties, and external suppliers, clearly defined?

Q4. Are relevant staff well trained in these BCP plans?

Q5. Are regular BCP simulations, including testing of alternative facilities, performed to ensure plans and facilities are effective for all processing, regular and AI?

Q6. Are resources (e.g., people, tools, process, technology, etc.) readily available when needed?

Q7. Have backup and recovery policy and procedures corresponding to BCP plans been developed, documented, and tested fully?

Q8. Do these (backup and recovery policy and procedures) include all AI systems and solutions and all their components (hardware, software, process and learning data, etc.)?

Q9. Do these (backup and recovery policy and procedures) cover IT infrastructure risks (i.e., not having core processing facilities available in time, access to data, etc.)?

Q10. Do these (backup and recovery policy and procedures) cover AI system/solution risks (i.e., not having an alternative AI system/solution in place in time that provides the same functionality, learnings, access to the same data, etc.)?

Q11. Do these (backup and recovery policy and procedures) cover business risks (i.e., not being able to manually – or otherwise – operate relevant business processes without an effective AI system/solution in place)?

Q12. Is, if needed, the "Vault Principle" applied, that is, an automated solution that securely stores any decision made by the AI system or solution, as well as the data the decision was based on, and the latest version of the algorithm(s) and code?

Q13. Are all the above implemented fully before the first AI system/solution is developed and put in a production status?

Recommendations

As regards the better use of the above-described 15 assessment questionnaires of over 112 questions for the audit areas of IT Governance, the following recommendations (REC) are proposed:

REC 1. Ensure you use an effective AI Audit Methodology with the relevant tools (audit programs, audit plan, assessment questionnaires, audit report, etc.) to carry out all assessment tasks. To support you in crafting your own AI Audit Methodology, you may use the material and tools included in my Audit books in "Additional Resources."

REC 2. Review all of the above issues, assessment questionnaires, and questions and consider how they may impact your AI systems/solutions in your operating landscape and how you may utilize them.

REC 3. Customize them, if required, to your purposes, by making the necessary changes to satisfy your needs and expectations.

REC 4. Ensure all your AI staff and relevant managers and board members are fully aware of the AI audit findings and have reviewed them and contributed to resolving the gaps included in the audit report (see example of an audit findings report in Appendix 39).

REC 5. Ensure you keep current the above products (IT Audit Questionnaires), by reviewing them and updating them every two to three years or as needs, expectations, and operating conditions and circumstances warrant.

Conclusion

This and the previous five chapters supported you to achieve the **sixth** milestone (*Improve AI infrastructure and systems*) of your AI Ecosystem Journey.

The AI Audit Process (Chapter 13) and the set of assessment questionnaires (Chapters 14–18) with their questions are deemed to be the most effective and useful tools to improve your AI infrastructure and systems/solutions.

The next part of the book (Part VII) continues this exciting journey by describing a set of AI support tools (see Appendixes 1–39) for your use. These are designed to enable, motivate, energize, and facilitate all establishment, development, and operational aspects of your AI ecosystem (AI principles and ethics, AI infrastructure, and AI systems/solutions).

Epilogue

Marvin Minsky: "If you understand something in only one way, then you really don't understand it at all. The secret of what anything means to us depends on how we've connected it to all the other things we know."[1]

According to recent research, most companies are still in the early stages of AI adoption.[2] While AI investment is rising and innovation is accelerating, too many leaders risk falling into the trap of complacency, satisfied with early wins rather than pursuing the transformative potential AI offers. The real challenge isn't just adopting AI as a differentiator – companies must ensure their AI strategies are actionable at every level of the business, turning bold visions into sustainable, transformative outcomes.

But what are the **Critical Success Factors (CSFs)** to ensure the effectiveness of AI transformations?

According to David Parsons and Chad Corneil of Slalom (an international business and technology consulting company), the CSFs likely to have the biggest impact on bridging the gap between the expected and the realized value of AI are as follows: put people first, anchor on value, challenge operating models, establish guardrails, align on a road map, and evolve services and information foundations for AI.[3]

Professor Victoria Uren of Aston University identified, in a recent research study, the following CSFs: address real, carefully scoped business problems, match the AI technology to the problem, build understanding of AI beyond the development team, invest to generate high-quality data, develop data capabilities, and embed AI expertise in the organization.[4]

The results of a Brunel University study indicate that technology readiness, security, privacy, customer satisfaction, perceived benefits, demand volatility, regulatory compliance, competitor pressure, and information sharing among partners are the most significant CSFs for adopting AI in the Food Supply Chains.[5]

© John Kyriazoglou 2025
J. Kyriazoglou, *AI Management Framework*, https://doi.org/10.1007/979-8-8688-1536-2

According to my international IT, Privacy, and AI experience, the **Critical Success Factors (CSFs)** to ensure the effectiveness of ethical and beneficial AI implementations, are as follows:

> **CSF 1. Leadership**: To envision the way forward, to commit to AI, to support and sponsor staff and AI projects, resolve issues, and oversee all AI activities. To improve the leadership qualities of your top managers in terms of AI, see Appendix 41.

> **CSF 2. Principles**: To establish ethical and other beneficial to society guidelines, inform all AI stakeholders and developers, and ensure their use in AI.

> **CSF 3. Regulations and Standards**: To ensure AI projects and AI systems outputs comply with AI, security, and privacy regulations.

> **CSF 4. AI Strategy**: To set realistic objectives and targets and ensure AI aligns well with other business objectives.

> **CSF 5. AI Technology**: To acquire, install, and use specialized IT hardware and software capable of running AI systems as best as possible.

> **CSF 6. Organization**: To establish organizational structures, appoint officers, and organize staff and teams to manage and drive AI implementations.

> **CSF 7. Data**: To locate, organize, manage, and use internal and external data in an efficient and moral way for AI projects.

> **CSF 8. Skills**: To develop the necessary skills and dexterities for corporate staff to enable the development and operation of viable and ethical AI systems.

> **CSF 9. Suppliers**: To locate, use services, and manage AI vendors for specialized AI equipment, software, platforms, data, algorithms, and models.

> **CSF 10. Support Tools**: To develop plans, policies, and procedures to support the development and operation of ethical and effective AI systems/solutions.

In conclusion, this book (*AI Management Framework: Practical Solutions for Ethical AI Deployment and Continuous Improvement*) provides you with all you require to establish, manage, and operate your whole AI Ecosystem and its particular elements (principles, organization, data, systems, tools, etc.).

Remember that to be successful and ethical in AI, it is best that you

Transcend the spiritual level and connect with the deep values of why you want to achieve with AI

Use ethical principles and a set of vision, mission, and values statements to permeate all your actions

Start your AI journey with a small pilot project so that you avoid major disasters and learn before you deploy AI across your complete organization

Get adequate resources and implement AI actions and hard controls (policies, procedures, etc.) with a soft hand and an open mind

I am ending this wonderful journey into AI with a poem I have written for your kind consideration:

Artificial Intelligence

Modern Artificial Intelligence
Fantasy without virtuous responsibility
With algorithmic logic without morality
Potentially awful, very destructive
It is in life, around us, everywhere
Not only in the world of the ideas.
It will threaten our existence in the future
If not tamed with humanism and ethics
Wake up all you humble users from your sleep of fate
Get out of the doom's end faster
Put human values, with feeling, into continuous action
And check her (AI) out before she sends you ingloriously to the bottom of the abyss.

In the end, as long as we humans retain and maintain control over our decisions and have the freedom to choose whether to embrace technological advancements (AI and others), we will always retain our humanity and preserve our physical world, as well as our psychosocial and mental worldview and mindset.

End Notes

Prologue: Can Computers Think?

1. For more Marshall McLuhan quotations, see

   `https://www.brainyquote.com/authors/marshall-mcluhan-quotes`

2. For more details, see

   `https://www.ibm.com/topics/artificial-intelligence`

3. *Homo sapiens* means "the wise man." *Homo sapiens sapiens* is the subspecies derived from *Homo sapiens*. They consist only of modern people. For more details, see Appendix 1.

4. For more details, see Odemakinde, Elisha (accessed: April 2, 2024): AI Software: 17 Most Popular Products for 2024.

   Also, see `https://viso.ai/deep-learning/ai-software/`

5. For more details, see

   (1) McCullogh, W. C., Pfeiffer, J. (1949): "Of digital computers called brains," Scientific Monthly 69: 368-376.

   (2) Von Neumann, J. (1964): The Computer and the Brain. Yale University Press.

   (3) Asimov, N. M. (1967): Modelling of Thinking and the Mind. New York: Spartan Books.

6. For more details, see
   Newell A., Simon, H. A. (1961). "Computer simulation of human thinking," Science 134: 2011-2017.

7. For more details, see Sagan, C. (1975): "Alien beings may share human understanding." Varsity 96:25, Nov. 7, 1975.

8. For more details, see

   https://www.cbsnews.com/news/neuralink-elon-musk-company-brain-chip-human-implant/

9. For more details, see Armer, P. (1962): Attitudes Toward Intelligent Machines. Santa Monica, Cal., USA, Rand Corporation.

10. For more quotations, see

    https://www.azquotes.com/author/36719-Thales

11. For more details, see Taube, M. (1961): Computers and common sense. McGraw Hill.

12. For more details, see

    https://www.oxfordlearnersdictionaries.com/definition/english/think_1?q=think

13. For more details, see Contestabile, B. (2020): The Socratic Way of Thinking

    https://www.socrethics.com/Folder1/Sokratisch.htm

14. For more details, see Green, A. K. (1931): Aristotle's psychology of conduct. London: Williams and Norgate.

15. For more details, see Drever, J. (1971): A dictionary of psychology. London: Penguin Books.

16. For more details, see Blanchard, B. (1939): The nature of thought. London: Allen and Unwin.

17. For more details, see Dimnet, E. (1944): The art of thinking. New York: Simon and Schuster.

18. For more details, see Caron, A. J. (1965): "Impact on motivational variables on knowledge seeking behaviour" in Aschner M. J. and Bish C. E. (Editors): Productive thinking in education. Washington, D.C.: The National Education Association.

19. For more details, see Hullfish, H. G., Smith, P. G. (1967): Reflective thinking: The method of education. New York: Dodd, Mead and Co.

20. For more details, see Bartlett, Sir Frederic (1958): Thinking. New York. Basic Books.

21. For more details, see Dewey, J. (1933): How we think. New York: D. C. Health and Co.

22. For more details, see Thompson, R. (1966): The psychology of thinking. London: Penguin Books.

23. For more details, see

    (1) Turing, A. M. (1950): "Computing machinery and intelligence." Mind, Oct. 1950, 59: 433-460.

    (2) Armer, P. (1962): Attitudes Toward Intelligent Machines. Santa Monica, Cal., USA, Rand Corporation.

24. For more details, see

    https://uwaterloo.ca/centre-for-teaching-excellence/catalogs/tip-sheets/blooms-taxonomy

    Source: Anderson, Lorin W., and David R. Krathwohl, eds. 2001. A Taxonomy for Learning, Teaching, and Assessing: A Revision of Bloom's Taxonomy of Educational Objectives. New York: Addison Wesley Longman, Inc.

25. For more details, see

    https://www.criticalthinking.org/pages/defining-critical-thinking/766

26. For more details, see

    Kahneman, Daniel (2012): Thinking, fast and slow. Penguin.

27. For more quotations, see

    https://www.azquotes.com/author/524-Aristotle

28. For more details, see

    https://www.criticalthinking.org/pages/defining-critical-thinking/766

    https://louisville.edu/ideastoaction/about/criticalthinking/what

Cottrell, Stella (2023): Critical thinking skills. Bloomsbury Academic.

Rutherford, Albert (2018): Models for critical thinking. Kindle Direct Publishing. USA.

Schuster, Steven (2023): The Critical Thinker. Available at `www.stevenschusterbooks.com`.

29. Types of problems. Simple problems, Complex problems and Wicked problems. For more details, see Appendix 1.

30. For more quotations, see

     `https://www.azquotes.com/author/4528-Epictetus`

31. For more details, see my book:

     Kyriazoglou, John: "Understanding Digital Age Effects"

     `https://bookboon.com/en/understanding-digital-age-effects-ebook`

32. For more details, see "The AI Index 2024 Annual Report," AI Index Steering Committee, Institute for Human-Centered AI, Stanford University, Stanford, CA, April 2024.

33. Dystopia (from the Greek dys- and topos: place, location, country (Greek "τόπος")). For more details, see Appendix 1.

34. Digitization is the process of converting elements or documents of information of all kinds to digital. For more details, see Appendix 1.

35. For more details, see my books:

     (1) Kyriazoglou, John: "Data Protection and Privacy Management System – Vol. 1"

         `https://bookboon.com/en/data-protection-and-privacy-management-system-ebook`

     (2) Kyriazoglou, John: "IT Management Controls"

         `https://bookboon.com/en/it-management-controls-ebook`

36. For more details, see Suller, John R. (2010): Psychology of the digital age. Cambridge University Press.

37. Artificial Intelligence Act of the European Union. It is a European regulation on artificial intelligence (AI). For more details, see Appendix 1.

Chapter 1: AI Management System

1. For more quotations by Peter Drucker, see

   https://www.goodreads.com/author/quotes/12008.
   Peter_F_Drucker

2. For more details, see

   https://www.microsoft.com/en-us/microsoft-cloud/
   blog/2024/04/03/the-ai-strategy-roadmap-navigating-the-
   stages-of-value-creation/

3. For more details, see

   https://www.ibm.com/think/insights/artificial-
   intelligence-strategy

4. For more details, see

   https://medium.com/@stahl950/ai-business-roadmap-a-
   strategic-necessity-214fb543f497

   https://www.techtarget.com/searchenterpriseai/tip/10-
   steps-to-achieve-AI-implementation-in-your-business

Chapter 2: The Seven Ancient Greek Wisdom Principles

1. Dr. Martha C. Beck, Professor of Philosophy, USA: `martha.beck@lyon.edu`

    Doctor of Philosophy, Professor of Philosophy at Lyon College

    Batesville, Arkansas United States

2. For examples of measures, see my "Duty of Care" books in "Additional Resources."

3. For more details, see

    `https://unsdg.un.org/2030-agenda/universal-values`

4. For examples of wellness and stress reduction policies, see my Wellness and Stress books in "Additional Resources."

Chapter 3: Corporate Philosophy Statements and Policies

1. For more quotations, see

    `https://www.quoteambition.com/ethics-quotes/?utm_content=cmp-true`

2. For more details, see

    `http://www.cipd.co.uk/hr-resources/factsheets/diversity-workplace-overview.aspx`

3. For more details, see

    `https://www.datacamp.com/blog/introduction-to-data-ethics`

    `https://dataethics.eu/data-ethics-principles/`

4. According to the independent European Data Ethics Think Tank (https://dataethics.eu/). For more details, see DATA ETHICS – Principles and Guidelines for Companies, Authorities & Organisations 1. Edition 2018 Copyright © 2018 The Authors.

   Authors: Pernille Tranberg, Gry Hasselbalch, Birgitte Kofod Olsen, and Catrine Søndergaard Byrne

   https://dataethics.eu/data-ethics-principles/

   https://dataethics.eu/data-ethics-principles/

   For other data cthics principles, see

   https://www.adp.com/spark/articles/2020/08/ai-and-data-ethics-5-principles-to-consider.aspx

   https://dataethics.eu/wp-content/uploads/Dataethics-uk.pdf

Chapter 4: AI Global Standards and Guidelines

1. For more quotations, see

   https://www.allgreatquotes.com/authors/gray-scott/

   https://www.allgreatquotes.com/quote-151556/

2. For more details, see

   https://www.iso.org/artificial-intelligence/ai-management-systems

3. For more details, see

   https://www.industry.gov.au/publications/australias-artificial-intelligence-ethics-framework/australias-ai-ethics-principles

4. For more details, see

   https://www.nist.gov/itl/ai-risk-management-framework

5. For more details, see

   https://thepublicvoice.org/ai-universal-guidelines/

   https://www.caidp.org/universal-guidelines-for-ai/

6. For more details, see

   https://www.oecd.org/en/topics/sub-issues/ai-
   principles.html

7. For more details, see

   https://artificialintelligenceact.eu/the-act/

8. For more details, see The EU AI Act, at

   https://eur-lex.europa.eu/eli/reg/2024/1689/oj

   https://eur-lex.europa.eu/legal-content/EN/TXT/
   PDF/?uri=OJ:L_202401689

   https://www.europarl.europa.eu/topics/en/article/
   20230601STO93804/eu-ai-act-first-regulation-on-
   artificial-intelligence

   https://artificialintelligenceact.eu/the-act/

9. For more details, see

   https://learn.microsoft.com/en-us/azure/machine-
   learning/concept-responsible-ai?view=azureml-api-2

   https://blogs.microsoft.com/wp-content/uploads/prod/
   sites/5/2022/06/Microsoft-Responsible-AI-Standard-v2-
   General-Requirements-3.pdf

10. For more details, see

    https://ai.google/responsibility/responsible-ai-
    practices/

11. For more details, see

    https://www.ibm.com/topics/responsible-ai

Chapter 5: Major Data Protection Laws and Privacy by Design Framework Principles

1. For more quotations, see

   https://www.azquotes.com/author/11530-Richard_Perle

2. For more details, see

   https://gdpr-info.eu/

3. For more details, see

   https://www2.senado.leg.br/bdsf/bitstream/handle/
   id/658231/Lei_geral_protecao_dados_pessoais_1ed.pdf

   https://gdpr.eu/gdpr-vs-lgpd/?cn-reloaded=1

4. For more details, see

   https://library.fiveable.me/key-terms/artificial-
   intelligence-and-ethics/privacy-by-design-principles

5. Source: Privacy by Design: Ann Cavoukian, Ph.D. Information and Privacy Commissioner, Ontario, Canada, December 2012, https://www.ipc.on.ca/

   http://www.privacybydesign.ca/content/uploads/2009/08/
   7foundationalprinciples.pdf

   https://www.sfu.ca/~palys/Cavoukian-2011-Privacy
   ByDesign-7FoundationalPrinciples.pdf

   https://privacy.ucsc.edu/resources/privacy-by-design---
   foundational-principles.pdf

Chapter 6: Digital and Secure AI System Development Guidelines

1. For more quotes, see

   https://www.brainyquote.com/authors/douglas-
   engelbart-quotes

2. For more details, see

    https://www.canada.ca/en/government/system/digital-government/improving-digital-services/digital-nations-charter.html

3. For more details, see

    https://digital-strategy.ec.europa.eu/en/policies/digital-principles#tab_1

4. For more details, see https://digitalprinciples.org/

5. For more details, see

    https://www.ncsc.gov.uk/files/Guidelines-for-secure-AI-system-development.pdf

Chapter 7: Prepare the Organization for AI

1. For more quotes, see https://www.azquotes.com/quote/176081

2. For more details, see

    https://www.techtarget.com/whatis/feature/Why-you-need-an-AI-ethics-committee

    https://hbr.org/2019/11/create-an-ethics-committee-to-keep-your-ai-initiative-in-check

3. For more details, see

    https://atlan.com/data-governance-committee/

    https://www.collibra.com/us/en/blog/data-governance-council-what-is-it-and-why-do-you-need-one

Chapter 8: Establish AI Governance Framework

1. For more quotes, see https://aidisruptor.ai/p/ai-industry-quotes

2. For more details, see "NIST Risk Implementation Approach."

   `https://www.nist.gov/itl/ai-risk-management-framework`

Chapter 9: Establish Data Governance Framework

1. For more quotes, see

   `https://careerfoundry.com/en/blog/data-analytics/`
   `inspirational-data-quotes/`

2. A Corporate Data Register or Data Dictionary, usually a computerized file, is used to record the attributes (data element description, type, format, validating and editing instructions, business processing rules, etc.) of the business data of all your corporate documents, records, and files used and maintained by the corporate filing systems, physical files, and databases of your company. For more details, see Appendix 1.

3. Data lakes can easily turn into "data swamps" without any constraints. That said, a key hurdle in managing a data lake is the unregulated accumulation of raw data.

   Studies show that a significant portion of data lake projects struggle to deliver expected value due to governance and data quality issues. This highlights the problem of uncontrolled data accumulation in data lakes that often leads to them becoming unusable data swamps.

   For more details, see

   `https://www.apica.io/blog/data-lakes-a-`
   `comprehensive-guide/`

4. For more details, see also my book *Data Governance Controls* available at `https://bookboon.com/en/data-governance-controls-ebook`

5. For more details, see also my book listed in note 4 above.

Chapter 10: Manage IT Governance and Privacy Controls

1. For more quotes, see

    `https://www.azquotes.com/author/26058-Narendra_Modi`

2. You may also want to review the following documents:

    2.1. NIST Special Publication 800-53 Revision 5, "Security and Privacy Controls for Information Systems and Organizations" available at

    `https://nvlpubs.nist.gov/nistpubs/`
    `SpecialPublications/NIST.SP.800-53r5.pdf`

    2.2. NIST Special Publication 800-53B, "Control Baselines for Information Systems and Organizations" available at

    `https://nvlpubs.nist.gov/nistpubs/`
    `SpecialPublications/NIST.SP.800-53B.pdf`

    2.3. A Guide to IT Controls: Oct 11, 2022, by Maya G, available at

    `https://www.itgov-docs.com/blogs/it-governance/a-`
    `guide-to-it-controls`

Chapter 11: Develop AI Systems

1. For more quotes, see

    `https://www.azquotes.com/quote/1304143?ref=information-`
    `technology`

2. These include as an example: Linear Regression, Logistic Regression, Decision Trees, Naive Bayes Classifiers, K-Nearest Neighbors, Support Vector Machines, Random Forest, K-Means Clustering, Principal Component Analysis, Gradient Boosting Algorithms, etc.

    Rosidi, Nathan: Top 10 Machine Learning Algorithms for Beginner Data Scientists, April 25, 2024.

For more details, see

https://nathanrosidi.medium.com/top-10-machine-learning-algorithms-for-beginner-data-scientists-aae78826712f

3. For more details, see

https://ai-governance.eu/ai-governance-framework/accountability-and-ownership/t55/

4. For more details, see

https://ai-governance.eu/ai-governance-framework/compliance/t61/

5. For more details, see

https://www.coe.int/en/web/artificial-intelligence/huderia-risk-and-impact-assessment-of-ai-systems

6. An example of different types of AI models: Machine learning, Supervised learning, Unsupervised learning, Deep learning, Reinforcement Learning, Generative AI, Hybrid AI, NLP AI, Computer Vision AI, etc. You may also consider a hybrid model. Hybrid models refer to integrating multiple AI techniques, such as machine learning, deep learning, rule-based systems, and symbolic reasoning, to leverage the strengths of each approach. For more details, see

https://techreport.com/artificial-intelligence/guide-to-ai-models/

https://machinelearningmastery.com/difference-between-a-parameter-and-a-hyperparameter/

https://www.mendix.com/blog/what-are-the-different-types-of-ai-models/

https://www.geeksforgeeks.org/common-ai-models-and-when-to-use-them/

https://www.snowflake.com/guides/ai-models-what-they-are-and-how-they-work

7. For more details, see INTERNATIONAL STANDARD ISO/
IEC 25059, Software engineering – Systems and Software
Quality Requirements and Evaluation (SQuaRE) – Quality
model for AI systems. Available at `https://www.iso.org/`
`standard/80655.html`

Testing Principles

5.2 User Controllability: User controllability is a property of an AI
system such that a human or another external agent can intervene
in its functioning in a timely manner. Enhanced controllability is
helpful if unexpected behavior cannot be completely avoided and
that can lead to negative consequences.

5.3 Functional Adaptability: Functional adaptability of an AI
system is the ability of the system to adapt itself to a changing
dynamic environment it is deployed in. AI systems can learn from
new training data, production data, and the results of previous
actions taken by the system.

5.4 Functional Correctness: The AI system product must be
functionally correct. It is necessary to measure correctness and
incorrectness carefully. Numerous measurements exist for these
purposes in the context of ML methods, and examples of these
as applicable to a classification model can be found in ISO/IEC
TS 4213.

5.5 Robustness: Robustness is used to describe the ability of
a system to maintain its level of functional correctness under
any circumstances including the presence of unseen, biased,
adversarial, or invalid data inputs, external interference,
environmental conditions, etc.

Information about functional safety in the context of AI systems
can be found in ISO/IEC TR 5469.

5.6 Transparency: Transparency relates to the degree to which
appropriate information about the AI system is communicated
to stakeholders. Transparency of AI systems can help potential
users of AI systems to choose a system to fit their requirements,

improving stakeholders' knowledge about the applicability and the limitations of an AI system and assisting with the explainability of AI systems.

Some aspects of transparency are discussed in ISO/IEC TR 24028:2020, 10.2.

5.7 Intervenability: The extent of intervenability can be determined depending on the scenarios where the AI system can be used. The key to intervenability is to enable state observation and transition from an unsafe state to a safe state. Operability is the degree to which an AI system has attributes that enable operation and control, which emphasizes the importance of an AI system's user interface. Compared to operability, intervenability is more fundamental from a quality perspective and is intended to prevent an AI system from doing harm or hazard. Intervenability is related to controllability, which is described in ISO/IEC 22989:2022.

8. For more details, see

    https://mobidev.biz/blog/how-to-test-ai-ml-applications-chatbots

    https://www.aitest.ai/aitest-guide

Chapter 12: Operate AI Systems

1. For more quotations, see

    https://www.azquotes.com/quote/1304143?ref=information-technology

2. For more details, also see my IT books listed in "Additional Resources."

3. You may also see my Audit books listed in "Additional Resources."

4. Available at https://artificialintelligenceact.eu/assessment/eu-ai-act-compliance-checker/)

5. Available at

    https://www.gov.uk/government/publications/introduction-
    to-ai-assurance/introduction-to-ai-assurance

Chapter 13: Develop AI Infrastructure and Systems Audit Process

1. For more details, see https://www.azquotes.com/quotes/
    topics/auditors.html

2. For more details, see Page 65, Guidance on the AI auditing
    framework, 20200214 103 Version 1.0, Published by ICO. UK,
    accessed December, 12, 2024.

3. For more details, see Towards AI Accountability Infrastructure:
    Gaps and Opportunities in AI Audit Tooling, by Victor Ojewale,
    Brown University Providence, Rhode Island, USA; Ryan Steed,
    Carnegie Mellon University Pittsburgh, Pennsylvania, USA;
    Briana Vecchione, Data & Society New York City, New York, USA;
    Abeba Birhane, Mozilla Foundation and Trinity College Dublin,
    Dublin, Ireland; Inioluwa Deborah Raji; Mozilla Foundation
    and University of California, Berkeley, Berkeley, California,
    USA, 2/2024.

    https://arxiv.org/pdf/2402.17861v1

    Auditing of AI: Legal, Ethical and Technical Approaches Jakob
    Mökander[1,2,3] Received: 28 August 2023 / Accepted: 25
    September 2023 / Published online: 8 November 2023 © The
    Author(s) 2023

    Digital Society (2023) 2:49 https://doi.org/10.1007/s44206-
    023-00074-y

4. For more details, see GLOBAL PERSPECTIVES AND INSIGHTS Artificial Intelligence – Considerations for the Profession of Internal Auditing Special Edition, Lake Mary, Fla., USA. For more information, visit www.globaliia.org

   Copyright © 2017 by The Institute of Internal Auditors, Inc. All rights reserved.

5. For more details, see GLOBAL PERSPECTIVES AND INSIGHTS Artificial Intelligence – Considerations for the Profession of Internal Auditing Special Edition, Lake Mary, Fla., USA. For more information, visit www.globaliia.org

   Copyright © 2017 by The Institute of Internal Auditors, Inc. All rights reserved.

6. For more details, see

   https://www.auditboard.com/blog/ai-auditing-frameworks/

7. For a description of the 13 steps of ISO 19011 Internal Audit Methodology, see

   ISO 19011:2018 Guidelines for auditing management systems

   https://www.iso.org/standard/70017.html

   These steps are Initiate the Audit, Review the Documents, Develop Audit Plan, Assign Work to Auditors per Plan, Prepare Working Papers, Determine the Audit Sequence, Conduct Opening Meeting, Review Documents and Communicate, Carry out the Audit, Generate Audit Findings, Present Findings and Conclusions, Formally Distribute Audit Report, and Follow Up on Actions/Corrective Actions.

8. For more details, see

   https://www.projectmanager.com/blog/project-closure

   https://www.projectmanager.com/templates/project-closure-template

Chapter 14: Assess Corporate Governance and HR Management Issues

1. For more quotations, see

   https://www.azquotes.com/author/38011-Carol_Ann_Tomlinson

Chapter 15: Assess AI Governance and AI Data Management Issues

1. For more quotations, see

   https://www.azquotes.com/author/725-Charles_Babbage

Chapter 16: Assess AI Models and AI System Development Issues

1. For more quotations, see

   https://www.azquotes.com/quote/1259658

Chapter 17: Assess AI System Operation Issues

1. For more quotations, see

   https://www.azquotes.com/author/3858-W_Edwards_Deming

Chapter 18: Assess IT Governance Issues

1. For more quotations, see

   https://www.azquotes.com/quote/107333?ref=information-technology

Appendix 1: AI Glossary

1. List of resources on AI concepts and terms

   https://digital-strategy.ec.europa.eu/en/policies/expert-group-ai

   https://www.britannica.com/technology/artificial-intelligence

   https://www.coursera.org/articles/data-lake-vs-data-warehouse

   https://www.geeksforgeeks.org/ml-understanding-hypothesis/

   https://www.ibm.com/topics/data-mart

   https://www.ibm.com/topics/ai-model

   https://www.semrush.com/blog/ai-models/

   https://oecd.ai/en/incidents-methodology

   https://www.britannica.com/topic/Homo-sapiens-sapiens

   Peter Cripps (Jan.1, 2021): Three types of problem, and how to solve them

   https://softwarearchitecturezen.blog/2021/01/01/three-types-of-problem-and-how-to-solve-them/

   https://artificialintelligenceact.eu/

   OECD, Recommendation of the Council on Artificial Intelligence, OECD/LEGAL/0449

   Managing Artificial Intelligence-Specific Cybersecurity Risks in the Financial Services Sector U.S. Department of the Treasury March 2024, U.S. Department of the Treasury: TREASURY.GOV

   Kyriazoglou, John: "IT Glossary," available at

   https://www.morebooks.de/shop-ui/shop/product/9786205523520

Appendix 6: AI Risk Assessment Procedure

1. For more details, see page 5: Artificial Intelligence Risk
    Management Framework (AI RMF 1.0). This publication is
    available free of charge from: `https://doi.org/10.6028/NIST.`
    `AI.100-1` January 2023

    `https://doi.org/10.6028/NIST.AI.100-1`

    Also, see Adding Structure to AI Harm: An Introduction to
    CSET's AI Harm Framework, Center for Security and Emerging
    Technology, July 2023. Available at `https://cset.georgetown.`
    `edu/contact-us/`

2. For a full list, see Chapter 1 (Annex 1).

    See also Page 38 NIST AI 100-1 AI RMF 1.0 Artificial Intelligence
    Risk Management Framework (AI RMF 1.0).

    This publication is available free of charge from: `https://doi.`
    `org/10.6028/NIST.AI.100-1` January 2023

    `https://doi.org/10.6028/NIST.AI.100-1`

Appendix 10: AI Third-Party Controls

1. For more details, see also Managing Artificial Intelligence-
    Specific Cybersecurity Risks in the Financial Services Sector.
    U.S. Department of the Treasury March 2024. Website:
    TREASURY.GOV.

Appendix 12: AI Data Governance Jobs

1. For more details, see also

    `https://www.techtarget.com/searchdatamanagement/`
    `definition/data-engineer`

2. For more details, see also

   https://www.datacamp.com/blog/how-to-become-a-data-architect

3. For more details, see also

   https://www.techtarget.com/searchenterpriseai/definition/knowledge-engineering

Appendix 27: AI Trustworthiness Assessment Questionnaire

1. This questionnaire is adopted from "THE ASSESSMENT LIST FOR TRUSTWORTHY ARTIFICIAL INTELLIGENCE (ALTAI) for self-assessment," available at

   https://digital-strategy.ec.europa.eu/en/policies/expert-group-ai

2. AI bias, also referred to as machine learning bias or algorithm bias, refers to AI systems that produce biased results that reflect and perpetuate human biases within a society, including historical and current social inequality. Bias can be found in the initial training data, the algorithm, or the predictions the algorithm produces. See

   https://www.ibm.com/think/topics/shedding-light-on-ai-bias-with-real-world-examples

3. In many ways, bias and fairness in AI are two sides of the same coin. While there is no universally agreed-upon definition for fairness, we can broadly define fairness as the absence of prejudice or preference for an individual or group based on their characteristics. For more details, see

   https://towardsdatascience.com/understanding-bias-and-fairness-in-ai-systems-6f7fbfe267f3

4. Diversity as a concept focuses on a broader set of qualities than race and gender. In the context of the workplace, valuing diversity means creating a workplace that respects and includes differences, recognizing the unique contributions that individuals with many types of differences can make, and creating a work environment that maximizes the potential of all employees. An example of a Diversity Policy is contained in Chapter 3 of this book.

   For more details, see also

   https://aiindex.stanford.edu/wp-content/ uploads/2021/03/2021-AI-Index-Report-_Chapter-6.pdf

   https://diversio.com/the-role-of-ai-in-diversity-equity- and-inclusion/

5. For more details, see https://universaldesign.ie/about- universal-design/the-7-principles

Appendix 28: AI Algorithmic Impact Assessment

1. For more details, see

   https://open.canada.ca/aia-eia-js/?lang=en

   https://www.nist.gov/itl/ai-risk-management-framework

Appendix 31: AI Model Development Procedure

1. You may also see other examples of model development procedures at the following links:

   https://keylabs.ai/blog/step-by-step-guide-to- developing-ai-models/

   https://machinelearningmastery.com/difference-between-a- parameter-and-a-hyperparameter/

2. In the context of machine learning, noise refers to random or unpredictable fluctuations in data or corrupt data that disrupt the ability of the model to identify target patterns or relationships. The result is decreased accuracy or reliability of a model's predictions or output.

    https://www.techtarget.com/searchbusinessanalytics/definition/noisy-data

    https://towardsdatascience.com/data-noise-and-label-noise-in-machine-learning-98c8a3c8322e

3. For more details, see

    https://www.akkio.com/post/data-transformation-in-machine-learning

    https://medium.com/data-empowerment-with-timextender/the-ultimate-guide-to-data-transformation-7402f330051f

4. For more details, see https://learn.g2.com/training-data

5. For more details, see

    https://www.datacamp.com/blog/ai-programming-languages

    https://www.datacamp.com/blog/top-ai-frameworks-and-libraries

6. A model parameter is a configuration variable that is internal to the model and whose value can be estimated from data. These parameters are required by the model when making predictions; their values define the skill of the model on your problem; they are estimated or learned from data; they are often not set manually by the practitioner; and they are often saved as part of the learned model.

7. For more details, see

    https://ourworldindata.org/grapher/artificial-intelligence-parameter-count

    https://www.datacamp.com/tutorial/parameter-optimization-machine-learning-models

8. We cannot know the best value for a model hyperparameter on a given problem. We may use rules of thumb, copy values used on other problems, or search for the best value by trial and error.

    For more details and examples, see

    https://machinelearningmastery.com/difference-between-a-parameter-and-a-hyperparameter/

    https://aimodels.org/training-ai-models-overview/model-training-model-selection/

    https://towardsdatascience.com/parameters-and-hyperparameters-aa609601a9ac

    https://www.datacamp.com/tutorial/parameter-optimization-machine-learning-models

9. For more details, see

    https://www.almabetter.com/bytes/articles/ai-algorithms

    https://aitrends.today/list-of-ai-algorithms/

10. For more details, also see

    https://www.tripo3d.ai/blog/how-to-train-an-ai-model

    https://research.aimultiple.com/ai-training/

11. For more details, see

    https://www.neurond.com/blog/how-to-train-ai

    https://aimodels.org/training-ai-models-overview/

    https://medium.com/@mailtodevens/ai-model-evaluation-and-testing-a-comprehensive-guide-3ff5cecd3953

    https://www.perfecto.io/blog/testing-ai

Appendix 32: AI Results Verification Procedure

1. You may also see other examples of verifying AI results at the following links:

   https://aicontentfy.com/en/blog/quality-control-how-to-verify-ai-generated-content

   https://www.longshot.ai/blog/ai-content-fact-check

Appendix 33: AI Error Correction Procedure

1. Another process for handling IT problems is contained in ITIL. For more details, see

   https://www.vivantio.com/blog/what-is-itil-problem-management-process-flow/

   https://www.atlassian.com/itsm/problem-management/process

2. For more details, see

   https://www.geeksforgeeks.org/software-testing-bug-vs-defect-vs-error-vs-fault-vs-failure/

3. For more details, see

   https://www.manageengine.com/products/service-desk/itsm/what-is-problem-management.html

4. For more details, see

   https://www.investopedia.com/terms/p/pareto-analysis.asp

   https://corporatefinanceinstitute.com/resources/management/pareto-analysis/

5. For more details, see

   https://www.geeksforgeeks.org/an-introduction-to-flowcharts/

https://www.programiz.com/article/flowchart-programming

https://www.codecademy.com/article/pseudocode-and-flowcharts

6. For more details, see

    https://classics.mit.edu/Aristotle/physics.html

    https://positivepsychology.com/socratic-questioning/

    https://medium.com/@Rahul_Nain/what-is-first-principles-thinking-a-comprehensive-guide-847886ae787a

7. For more details, see

    https://blog.minitab.com/en/the-basics-of-structured-problem-solving-methodologies-dmaic-8d

    https://www.learnleansigma.com/guides/a3-problem-solving/

Appendix 34: IT Change Management Procedure

1. Another process for handling IT problems is contained in ITIL. For more details, see

    https://www.vivantio.com/blog/what-is-itil-problem-management-process-flow/

    https://www.atlassian.com/itsm/problem-management/process

Appendix 35: AI User Support Procedure

1. For more details, see

    https://www.techtarget.com/whatis/definition/netizen

2. For more detailed examples, see

   `https://www.verywellmind.com/ten-rules-of-netiquette-22285`

   `https://www.kaspersky.com/resource-center/preemptive-safety/what-is-netiquette`

   `https://www.avast.com/c-netiquette`

   `https://www.britannica.com/topic/netiquette`

Appendix 36: AI Incident Reporting Policy

1. For more details, see OECD (2024), "Defining AI incidents and related terms," OECD Artificial Intelligence Papers, No. 16, OECD Publishing, Paris, `https://doi.org/10.1787/d1a8d965-en`

   `https://oecd.ai/en/wonk/defining-ai-incidents-and-hazards`

2. For more details, see

   `https://www.cio.com/article/190888/5-famous-analytics-and-ai-disasters.html`

   `https://tech.co/news/list-ai-failures-mistakes-errors`

   `https://www.evidentlyai.com/blog/ai-failures-examples`

3. For more details, see

   `https://www.zendata.dev/post/ai-incident-response-101-handling-ai-failures-and-unintended-consequences`

4. There are four major types of attacks, according to NIST: evasion, poisoning, privacy, and abuse attacks. NIST classifies them according to multiple criteria such as the attacker's goals and objectives, capabilities, and knowledge. For more details, see

   `https://www.nist.gov/news-events/news/2024/01/nist-identifies-types-cyberattacks-manipulate-behavior-ai-systems`

Appendix 37: AI Incident Response Procedure

1. For more details, see

   https://incidentdatabase.ai/

   https://ai-incidents.mitre.org/

   https://oecd.ai/en/incidents-methodology

Appendix 38: AI System Post-Implementation Review Questionnaire

1. For techniques to carry out a Post-Implementation Review, see

   https://www.projectmanager.com/blog/post-implementation-review

   https://www.migso-pcubed.com/blog/project-management-delivery/post-implementation-review-best-practices/

   Also, see "Post Implementation Review Guide" at

   https://policy.federation.edu.au/forms/18.1%20Post%20Implementation%20Review%20Guide.pdf

Appendix 39: AI Audit Findings Report Example

1. For additional examples of Audit Reports, see

   https://www.isaca.org/resources/isaca-journal/issues/2020/volume-1/is-audit-basics-the-components-of-the-it-audit-report

   https://onlinelibrary.wiley.com/doi/pdf/10.1002/0471784788.app2

   https://templatelab.com/audit-report/

https://www.auditboard.com/blog/4-key-resources-effective-audit-reporting/

https://www.theiia.org/globalassets/site/auditing-report-writing-toolkit.pdf

https://www.wallstreetmojo.com/audit-report-examples/

Epilogue

1. As quoted on page 55, in book *12 Bytes*, published by Vintage Books, UK, 2022.

2. For more details, see

   https://www.slalom.com/us/en/insights/slalom-ai-free-research-report-2024?=d

3. For more details, see

   https://www.slalom.com/us/en/insights/six-critical-success-factors-to-realize-ai-potential

4. For more details, see Critical Success Factors for Artificial Intelligence Projects, Victoria Uren (v.uren@aston.ac.uk), Aston Business School, Aston University, Birmingham, B4 7ET, UK.

   https://publications.aston.ac.uk/id/eprint/41673/1/euroma2020_full_paper_CSF_AI_1.5.pdf

5. For more details, see Critical Success Factors Influencing Artificial Intelligence Adoption in the Food Supply Chains.

   https://bura.brunel.ac.uk/bitstream/2438/22997/3/FullText.pdf

Additional Resources

AI-Related Books

Amosov, N. M. (1967): Modelling of Thinking and the Mind. New York: Spartan Books.

Armer, P. (1962): Attitudes Toward Intelligent Machines. Santa Monica, Cal., USA, Rand Corporation.

Bartlett, Sir Frederic (1958): Thinking. New York. Basic Books.

Blanchard, B. (1939): The nature of thought. London: Allen and Unwin.

Caron, A. J. (1965): "Impact on motivational variables on knowledge seeking behaviour" in Aschner M. J. and Bish C. E. (Editors): Productive thinking in education. Washington, D.C.: The National Education Association.

Cottrell, Stella (2023): Critical thinking skills. Bloomsbury Academic.

Dewey, J. (1933): How we think. New York: D. C. Health and Co.

Dimnet, E. (1944): The art of thinking. New York: Simon and Schuster.

Drever, J. (1971): A dictionary of psychology. London: Penguin Books.

Green, A. K. (1931): Aristotle's psychology of conduct. London: Williams and Norgate.

Hullfish, H. G., Smith, P. G. (1967): Reflective thinking: The method of education. New York: Dodd, Mead and Co.

Jonassen, D. (2000): "Toward a design theory of problem solving." Educational Technology: Research & Development, 48 (4), 63-85.

Kahneman, Daniel (2012): Thinking, fast and slow. Penguin.

Kyriazoglou (a): "Understanding Digital Age Effects"
https://bookboon.com/en/understanding-digital-age-effects-ebook

Kyriazoglou (b): "Data Protection and Privacy Management System – Vol. 1"
https://bookboon.com/en/data-protection-and-privacy-management-system-ebook

Kyriazoglou (c): "IT Management Controls"
https://bookboon.com/en/it-management-controls-ebook

McCullogh, W. C., Pfeiffer, J. (1949): "Of digital computers called brains," Scientific Monthly 69: 368-376.

© John Kyriazoglou 2025
J. Kyriazoglou, *AI Management Framework*, https://doi.org/10.1007/979-8-8688-1536-2

Newell A., Simon, H. A. (1961). "Computer simulation of human thinking," Science 134: 2011-2017.

Rutherford, Albert (2018): Models for critical thinking. Kindle Direct Publishing. USA.

Sagan, C. (1975): "Alien beings may share human understanding." Varsity 96:25, Nov. 7, 1975.

Schuster, Steven (2023): The Critical Thinker. Available at `www.stevens chusterbooks.com`.

Suller, John R. (2010): Psychology of the digital age. Cambridge University Press.

Taube, M. (1961): Computers and common sense. McGraw Hill.

Thompson, R. (1966): The psychology of thinking. London: Penguin Books.

Turing, A. M. (1950): "Computing machinery and intelligence." Mind, Oct. 1950, 59: 433-460.

Von Neumann, J. (1964): The Computer and the Brain. Yale University Press.

Published Works of John Kyriazoglou

Books: IT Controls

Book 1. "IT-Business Alignment" (Part 1)
`http://bookboon.com/en/it-business-alignment-part-i-ebook`
Book 2. "IT-Business Alignment" (Part 2)
`http://bookboon.com/en/it-business-alignment-part-ii-ebook`
Book 3. "IT Management Controls"
`https://bookboon.com/en/it-management-controls-ebook`
Book 4. IT Glossary
`https://www.morebooks.de/shop-ui/shop/product/9786205523520`
Book 5. "IT Management Controls"
`https://bookboon.com/en/it-management-controls-ebook`
Book 6. ISO 27001: 2022 Implementation Handbook
`https://www.amazon.com/dp/9606582663?ref_=pe_93986420_774957520`
Book 7. Information Security Incident and Data Breach Management
`https://link.springer.com/book/10.1007/979-8-8688-0870-8`
Books: IT Auditing
Book 1. IT Audit Guides
`https://bookboon.com/en/it-audit-guide-part-1-ebook`

Book 2. IT Governance Controls – Book 2
https://bookboon.com/en/it-governance-controls-book-2-ebook
Book 3. IT Audit Execution Tools – Book 3
https://bookboon.com/en/it-audit-execution-tools-book-3-ebook
Book 4. IT Audit Support Tools 1 – Book 4
https://bookboon.com/en/it-audit-support-tools-1-book-4-ebook
Book 5. IT Audit Support Tools 2 – Book 5
https://bookboon.com/en/it-audit-support-tools-2-book-5-ebook

Books: Digital Age Management

Book 1. Understanding Digital Age Effects
https://bookboon.com/en/understanding-digital-age-effects-ebook
Book 2. Preparing Digital Management Actions
https://bookboon.com/en/preparing-digital-management-actions-ebook
Book 3. Implementing Corporate Digital Management Actions
https://bookboon.com/en/implementing-corporate-digital-management-actions-ebook
Book 4. Implementing Personal Digital Management Actions
https://bookboon.com/en/implementing-personal-digital-management-actions-ebook
Book 5. Digital Age Management Support Tools
https://bookboon.com/en/digital-age-management-support-tools-ebook

Books: Data Protection and Privacy System

Book 1. Data Protection and Privacy Management System – Vol. 1
https://bookboon.com/en/data-protection-and-privacy-management-system-ebook
Book 2. DP&P Strategies, Policies and Plans – Vol. 2
http://bookboon.com/en/dpp-strategies-policies-and-plans-ebook
Book 3. Data Protection Impact Assessment – Vol. 3
http://bookboon.com/en/data-protection-impact-assessment-ebook
Book 4. Data Protection Specialized Controls – Vol. 4
http://bookboon.com/en/data-protection-specialized-controls-ebook
Book 5. Security and Data Privacy Audit Questionnaires – Vol. 5
http://bookboon.com/en/security-and-data-privacy-audit-questionnaires-ebook

Books: Data Protection (GDPR) Audit Guide

Book 1. Data Protection Audit Process

https://bookboon.com/en/data-protection-audit-process-i-ebook

Book 2. DP Audit Questionnaires

https://bookboon.com/en/dp-audit-questionnaires-ii-ebook

Book 3. DP Audit Report

https://bookboon.com/en/dp-audit-report-ebook

Book 4. DP Audit Support Tools 1

https://bookboon.com/en/dp-audit-support-tools-1-ebook

Book 5. DP Audit Support Tools 2

https://bookboon.com/en/dp-audit-support-tools-2-ebook

Books: Business Management

Book 1. "How to improve your company's performance"

http://bookboon.com/en/how-to-improve-your-companys-performance-ebook

Book 2. "Improving Corporate Performance with BSC"

http://bookboon.com/en/improving-performance-with-balanced-scorecard-ebook

Book 3. "Auditing and Improving Business Performance"

https://www.amazon.com/dp/B008818IVY

Book 4. Case Studies in Internal Controls

https://bookboon.com/en/case-studies-in-internal-controls-ebook

Book 5. "How to Improve Your Production" (Part 1)

http://bookboon.com/en/how-to-improve-your-production-part-i-ebook

Book 6. "How to Improve Your Production" (Part 2)

http://bookboon.com/en/how-to-improve-your-production-part-ii-ebook

Book 7. SME GDPR Guide

https://bookboon.com/en/sme-gdpr-guide-ebook

Book 8. SME GDPR Daily Operations Manual

https://bookboon.com/en/sme-gdpr-daily-operations-manual-ebook

Book 9. SME GDPR Support Tools

https://bookboon.com/en/sme-gdpr-support-tools-ebook

Books: Duty of Care

Books 1–8. **"Duty of Care" small ebooks, accessible at**

http://bookboon.com/en/governance-aspects-of-duty-of-care-ebook

http://bookboon.com/en/operations-aspects-of-duty-of-care-ebook

http://bookboon.com/en/principles-and-methods-of-duty-of-care-ebook

http://bookboon.com/en/plans-of-duty-of-care-ebook

http://bookboon.com/en/policies-of-duty-of-care-ebook

http://bookboon.com/en/hr-management-controls-of-duty-of-care-ebook

http://bookboon.com/en/the-duty-of-care-management-approach-part-1-ebook

http://bookboon.com/en/implementing-duty-of-care-duties-part-2-ebook

Books: Workplace Wellness

Book 1. Approaching Workplace Wellness

https://bookboon.com/en/approaching-workplace-wellness-ebook

Book 2. Workplace Wellness – Governance and Spirituality

https://bookboon.com/en/workplace-wellness-governance-and-spirituality-ebook

Book 3. Workplace Wellness: Relationships and Resilience

https://bookboon.com/en/workplace-wellness-relationships-and-resilience-ebook

Book 4. "How to Improve Your Workplace Wellness: Volume II"

https://bookboon.com/en/how-to-improve-your-workplace-wellness-volume-ii-ebook

Book 5. "How to Improve Your Workplace Wellness: Volume III"

https://bookboon.com/en/how-to-improve-your-workplace-wellness-volume-iii-ebook

Book 6. "Corporate Wellness: Management and Evaluation Toolkit"

http://bookboon.com/en/corporate-wellness-ebook

Index

A, B

AI, *see* Artificial intelligence (AI)
Ancient Greek Wisdom Principles, 23, 338
    courage, 25, 35–37
    criterion, 23
    faith, 24, 27–29
    friendship, 24, 31–33
    harmony, 24, 30, 31
    justice, 24, 28, 29
    Kalokagathia, 24, 33–35
    outcome, result, and output, 37
    recommendations (REC), 37
    temperance, 24–26
ANPD, *see* Autoridade Nacional de
    Proteção de Dados (ANPD)
Artificial intelligence (AI)
    algorithmic assessment, 354
    Ancient Greek Wisdom Principles, 23–39
    audit reports, 360
    concepts/terms, 351
    data governance jobs, 352
    error correction, 357
    incident reporting policy, 359
    incident response procedure, 360
    management system, 3–20
    model development procedures, 354
    post-implementation review, 360
    risk management, 352
    third-party controls, 352
    trustworthiness, 353
    user support procedure, 358
    verification, 357

Assess corporate governance
    assessment actions, 255
    audit process, 257
    corporate strategy, 257
    ethical issues, 256
    goal/objectives, 254
    guidelines, 258
    implementation approach, 253
    infrastructure/systems, 254
    IP protection policy, 259
    knowledge retention management, 259
    management (*see* HR
        management issues)
    requirements/standards/rules, 255
    rules and values, 258
Audit process, 228–230
    challenges, 225
    compliance documentation, 242–245
    controls and documentation, 248
    corporate governance,
        245–247, 253–267
    data privacy and protection
        controls, 248–250
    execution stage, 234–237
        compliance testing, 236
        evaluation/document finding, 237
        substantive, 236
        testing process, 235
        weakness testing, 235
    explainable AI techniques (XAI), 226
    follow-up process, 239
    goals/objectives, 224

369

J. Kyriazoglou, *AI Management Framework*, https://doi.org/10.1007/979-8-8688-1536-2

H

I

GPSR Compliance

The European Union's (EU) General Product Safety Regulation (GPSR) is a set of rules that requires consumer products to be safe and our obligations to ensure this.

If you have any concerns about our products, you can contact us on

ProductSafety@springernature.com

In case Publisher is established outside the EU, the EU authorized representative is:

Springer Nature Customer Service Center GmbH
Europaplatz 3
69115 Heidelberg, Germany